CICERO'S BRUTUS,

OR

HISTORY OF FAMOUS ORATORS:

ALSO,

HIS ORATOR,

OR

ACCOMPLISHED SPEAKER.

Now first translated into English by E. Jones

PREFACE.

As the following Rhetorical Pieces have never appeared before in the English language, I thought a Translation of them would be no unacceptable offering to the Public. The character of the Author (Marcus Tullius Cicero) is so universally celebrated, that it would be needless, and indeed impertinent, to say any thing to recommend them.

The first of them was the fruit of his retirement, during the remains of the *Civil War* in Africa; and was composed in the form of a Dialogue. It contains a few short, but very masterly sketches of all the Speakers who had flourished either in Greece or Rome, with any reputation of Eloquence, down to his own time; and as he generally touches the principal incidents of their lives, it will be considered, by an attentive reader, as a *concealed epitome of the Roman history*. The conference is supposed to have been held with Atticus, and their common friend Brutus, in Cicero's garden at Rome, under the statue of Plato, whom he always admired, and usually imitated in his dialogues: and he seems in this to have copied even his *double titles*, calling it *Brutus, or the History of famous Orators*. It was intended as a *supplement*, or *fourth book*, to three former ones, on the qualifications of an Orator.

The second, which is intitled *The Orator*, was composed a very short time afterwards (both of them in the 61st year of his age) and at the request of Brutus. It contains a plan, or critical delineation, of what he himself esteemed the most finished Eloquence, or style of Speaking. He calls it *The Fifth Part, or Book*, designed to complete his *Brutus*, and *the former three* on the same subject. It was received with great approbation; and in a letter to Lepta, who had complimented him upon it, he declares, that whatever judgment he had in Speaking, he had thrown it all into that work, and was content to risk his reputation on the merit of it. But it is particularly recommended to our curiosity, by a more exact account of the rhetorical *composition*, or *prosaic harmony* of the ancients, than is to be met with in any other part of his works.

As to the present Translation, I must leave the merit of it to be decided by the Public; and have only to observe, that though I have not, to my knowledge, omitted a single sentence of the original, I was obliged, in some places, to paraphrase my author, to render his meaning intelligible to a modern reader. My chief aim was to be clear and perspicuous: if I have succeeded in *that*, it is all I pretend to. I must leave it to abler pens to copy the *Eloquence* of Cicero. *Mine* is unequal to the task.

BRUTUS, OR THE HISTORY OF ELOQUENCE.

When I had left Cilicia, and arrived at Rhodes, word was brought me of the death of Hortensius. I was more affected with it than, I believe, was generally expected. For, by the loss of my friend, I saw myself for ever deprived of the pleasure of his acquaintance, and of our mutual intercourse of good offices. I likewise reflected, with Concern, that the dignity of our College must suffer greatly by the decease of such an eminent augur. This reminded me, that *he* was the person who first introduced me to the College, where he attested my qualification upon oath; and that it was *he* also who installed me as a member; so that I was bound by the constitution of the Order to respect and honour him as a parent. My affliction was increased, that, in such a deplorable dearth of wife and virtuous citizens, this excellent man, my faithful associate in the service of the Public, expired at the very time when the Commonwealth could least spare him, and when we had the greatest reason to regret the want of his prudence and authority. I can add, very sincerely, that in *him* I lamented the loss, not (as most people imagined) of a dangerous rival and competitor, but of a generous partner and companion in the pursuit of same. For if we have instances in history, though in studies of less public consequence, that some of the poets have been greatly afflicted at the death of their contemporary bards; with what tender concern should I honour the memory of a man, with whom it is more glorious to have disputed the prize of eloquence, than never to have met with an antagonist! especially, as he was always so far from obstructing *my* endeavours, or I *his*, that, on the contrary, we mutually assisted each other, with our credit and advice.

But as *he*, who had a perpetual run of felicity, left the world at a happy moment for himself, though a most unfortunate one for his fellow- citizens; and died when it would have been much easier for him to lament the miseries of his country, than to assist it, after living in it as long as he *could* have lived with honour and reputation;—we may, indeed, deplore his death as a heavy loss to *us* who survive him. If, however, we consider it merely as a personal event, we ought rather to congratulate his fate, than to pity it; that, as often as we revive the memory of this illustrious and truly happy man, we may appear at least to have as much affection for him as for ourselves. For if we only lament that we are no longer permitted to enjoy him, it must, indeed, be acknowledged that this is a heavy misfortune to *us*; which it, however, becomes us to support with moderation, less our sorrow should be suspected to arise from motives of interest, and not from friendship. But if we afflict ourselves, on the supposition that *he* was the sufferer;—we misconstrue an event, which to *him* was certainly a very happy one.

If Hortensius was now living, he would probably regret many other advantages in common with his worthy fellow-citizens. But when he beheld the Forum, the great theatre in which he used to exercise his genius, no longer accessible to that accomplished eloquence, which could charm the ears of a Roman, or a Grecian audience; he must have felt a pang of which none, or at least but few, besides himself, could be susceptible. Even *I* am unable to restrain my tears, when I behold my country no longer defensible by the genius, the prudence, and the authority of a legal magistrate,—the only weapons which I have learned to weild, and to which I have long been accustomed, and which are most suitable to the character of an illustrious citizen, and of a virtuous and well-regulated state.

But if there ever was a time, when the authority and eloquence of an honest individual could have wrested their arms from the hands of his distracted fellow-citizens; it was then when the proposal of a compromise of our mutual differences was rejected, by the hasty imprudence of some, and the timorous mistrust of others. Thus it happened, among other misfortunes of a more deplorable nature, that when my declining age, after a life spent in the service of the Public, should have reposed in the peaceful harbour, not of an indolent, and a total inactivity, but of a moderate and becoming retirement; and when my eloquence was properly mellowed, and had acquired its full maturity;—thus it happened, I say, that recourse was then had to those fatal arms, which the persons who had learned the use of them in honourable conquest, could no longer employ to any salutary purpose. Those, therefore, appear to me to have enjoyed a fortunate and a happy life, (of whatever State they were members, but especially in *our's*) who held their authority and reputation, either for their military or political services, without interruption: and the sole remembrance of them, in our present melancholy situation, was a pleasing relief to me, when we lately happened to mention them in the course of conversation.

For, not long ago, when I was walking for my amusement, in a private avenue at home, I was agreeably interrupted by my friend Brutus, and T. Pomponius, who came, as indeed they frequently did, to visit me;—two worthy citizens who were united to each other in the closest friendship, and were so dear and so agreeable to me, that, on the first sight of them, all my anxiety for the Commonwealth subsided. After the usual salutations, —"Well, gentlemen," said I, "how go the times? What news have you brought?" "None," replied Brutus, "that you would wish to hear, or that I can venture to tell you for truth."—"No," said Atticus; "we are come with an intention that all matters of state should be dropped; and rather to hear something from you, than to say any thing which might serve to distress you." "Indeed," said I, "your company is a present remedy for my sorrow; and your letters, when absent, were so encouraging, that they first revived my attention to my studies."—"I remember," replied Atticus, "that Brutus sent you a letter from Asia, which I read with infinite pleasure: for he advised you in it like a man of sense, and gave you every consolation which the warmest friendship could suggest."— "True," said I, "for it was the receipt of that letter which recovered me from a growing indisposition, to behold once more the cheerful face of day; and as the Roman State, after the dreadful defeat near Cannae, first raised its drooping head by the victory of Marcellus at Nola, which was succeeded by many other victories; so, after the dismal wreck of our affairs, both public and private, nothing occurred to me before the letter of my friend Brutus, which I thought to be worth my attention, or which contributed, in any degree, to the anxiety of my heart."—"That was certainly my intention," answered Brutus; "and if I had the happiness to succeed, I was sufficiently rewarded for my trouble. But I could wish to be informed, what you received from Atticus which gave you such uncommon pleasure."—"That," said I, "which not only entertained me; but, I hope, has restored me entirely to myself."—"Indeed!" replied he; "and what miraculous composition could that be?"—"Nothing," answered I; "could have been a more acceptable, or a more seasonable present, than that excellent Treatise of his which roused me from a state of languor and despondency." —"You mean," said he, "his short, and, I think, very accurate abridgment of Universal History."—"The very same," said I; "for that little Treatise has absolutely saved me."—"I am heartily glad of it," said Atticus; "but what could you discover in it which was either new to you, or so wonderfully beneficial as you pretend?"—"It certainly furnished many hints," said I, "which were entirely new to me: and the exact order of time which you observed through the whole, gave me the opportunity I had long wished for, of beholding the history of all nations in one regular and comprehensive view. The attentive perusal of it proved an excellent remedy for my sorrows, and led me to think of attempting something on your own plan, partly to amuse myself, and partly to return your favour, by a grateful, though not an equal acknowledgment. We are commanded, it is true, in that precept of Hesiod, so much admired by the learned, to return with the same measure we have received; or, if possible, with a larger. As to a friendly inclination, I shall certainly return you a full proportion of it; but as to a recompence in kind, I confess it to be out of my power, and therefore hope you will excuse me: for I have no first-fruits (like a prosperous husbandman) to acknowledge the obligation I have received; my whole harvest having sickened and died, for want of the usual manure: and as little am I able to present you with any thing from those hidden stores which are now consigned to perpetual darkness, and to which I am denied all access; though, formerly, I was almost the only person who was able to command them at pleasure. I must therefore, try my skill in a long- neglected and uncultivated soil; which I will endeavour to improve with so much care, that I may be able to repay your liberality with interest; provided my genius should be so happy as to resemble a fertile field, which, after being suffered to lie fallow a considerable time, produces a heavier crop than usual."—"Very well," replied Atticus, "I shall expect the fulfilment of your promise; but I shall not insist upon it till it suits your convenience; though, after all, I shall certainly be better pleased if you discharge the obligation."—"And I also," said Brutus, "shall expect that you perform your promise to my friend Atticus: nay, though I am only his voluntary solicitor, I shall, perhaps, be very pressing for the discharge of a debt, which the creditor himself is willing to submit to your own choice."—"But I shall refuse to pay you," said I, "unless the original creditor takes no farther part in the suit." —"This is more than I can promise," replied he, "for I can easily foresee, that this easy man, who disclaims all severity, will urge his demand upon you, not indeed to distress you, but yet very closely and seriously."—"To speak ingenuously," said Atticus, "my friend Brutus, I believe, is not much mistaken: for as I now find you in good spirits, for the first time, after a tedious interval of despondency, I shall soon make bold to apply to you; and as this gentleman has promised his assistance, to recover what you owe me, the least I can do is to solicit, in my turn, for what is due to him."

"Explain your meaning," said I.—"I mean," replied he, "that you must write something to amuse us; for your pen has been totally silent this long time; and since your Treatise on Politics, we have had nothing from you of any kind; though it was the perusal of that which fired me with the ambition to write an Abridgment of Universal History. But we shall, however, leave you to answer this demand, when, and in what manner you shall think most convenient. At present, if you are not otherwise engaged, you must give us your sentiments on a subject on which we both desire to be better informed."—"And what is that?" said I.—"What you gave me a hasty sketch of," replied he, "when I saw you last at Tusculanum,—the History of Famous Orators;—*when* they made their appearance, and *who* and *what* they were; which, furnished such an agreeable train of conversation, that when I related the substance of it to *your*, or I ought rather to have said our *common* friend, Brutus, he expressed a violent desire to hear the whole of it from your own mouth. Knowing you, therefore, to be at leisure, we have taken the present opportunity to wait upon you; so that, if it is really convenient, you will oblige us both by resuming the subject."—"Well, gentlemen," said I, "as you are so pressing, I will endeavour to satisfy you in the best manner I am able."— "You are *able* enough," replied he; "only unbend yourself a little, or, if you can set your mind at full liberty."—"If I remember right," said I, "Atticus, what gave rise to the conversation, was my observing, that the cause of Deiotarus, a most excellent Sovereign, and a faithful ally, was pleaded by our friend Brutus, in my hearing, with the greatest elegance and dignity."—"True," replied he, "and you took occasion from the ill success of Brutus, to lament the loss of a fair administration of justice in the Forum."—"I did so," answered I, "as indeed I frequently do: and whenever I see you, my Brutus, I am concerned to think where your wonderful genius, your finished erudition, and unparalleled industry will find a theatre to display themselves. For after you had thoroughly improved your abilities, by pleading a variety of important causes; and when my declining vigour was just giving way, and lowering the ensigns of dignity to your more active talents; the liberty of the State received a fatal overthrow, and that Eloquence, of which we are now to give the History, was condemned to perpetual silence."—"Our other misfortunes," replied Brutus, "I lament sincerely; and I think I ought to lament them:— but as to Eloquence, I am not so fond of the influence and the glory it bestows, as of the study and the practice of it, which nothing can deprive me of, while you are so well disposed to assist me: for no man can be an eloquent speaker, who has not a clear and ready conception. Whoever, therefore, applies himself to the study of Eloquence, is at the same time improving his judgment, which is a talent equally necessary in all military operations."

"Your remark," said I, "is very just; and I have a higher opinion of the merit of eloquence, because, though there is scarcely any person so diffident as not to persuade himself, that he either has, or may acquire every other accomplishment which, formerly, could have given him consequence in the State; I can find no person who has been made an orator by the success of his military prowess.—But that we may carry on the conversation with greater ease, let us seat ourselves."—As my visitors had no objection to this, we accordingly took our seats in a private lawn, near a statue of Plato.

Then resuming the conversation,—"to recommend the study of eloquence," said I, "and describe its force, and the great dignity it confers upon those who have acquired it, is neither our present design, nor has any necessary connection with it. But I will not hesitate to affirm, that whether it is acquired by art or practice, or the mere powers of nature, it is the most difficult of all attainments; for each of the five branches of which it is said to consist, is of itself a very important art; from whence it may easily be conjectured, how great and arduous must be the profession which unites and comprehends them all.

"Greece alone is a sufficient witness of this:—for though she was fired with a wonderful love of Eloquence, and has long since excelled every other nation in the practice of it, yet she had all the rest of the arts much earlier; and had not only invented, but even compleated them, a considerable time before she was mistress of the full powers of elocution. But when I direct my eyes to Greece, your beloved Athens, my Atticus, first strikes my sight, and is the brightest object in my view: for in that illustrious city the *orator* first made his appearance, and it is there we shall find the earliest records of eloquence, and the first specimens of a discourse conducted by rules of art. But even in Athens there is not a single production now extant which discovers any taste for ornament, or seems to have been the effort of a real orator, before the time of Pericles (whose name is prefixed to some orations which still remain) and his cotemporary Thucydides; who flourished,—not in the infancy of the State, but when it was arrived at its full maturity of power.

"It is, however, supposed, that Pisistratus (who lived many years before) together with Solon, who was something older, and Clisthenes, who survived them both, were very able speakers for the age they lived in. But some years after these, as may be collected from the Attic Annals, came the above-mentioned Themistocles, who is said to have been as much distinguished by his eloquence as by his political abilities;—and after him the celebrated Pericles, who, though adorned with every kind of excellence, was most admired for his talent of speaking. Cleon also (their cotemporary) though a turbulent citizen, was allowed to be a tolerable orator.

"These were immediately succeeded by Alcibiades, Critias, and Theramenes, whose manner of speaking may be easily inferred from the writings of Thucydides, who lived at the same time: their discourses were nervous and stately, full of sententious remarks, and so excessively concise as to be sometimes obscure. But as soon as the force of a regular and a well-adjusted speech was understood, a sudden crowd of rhetoricians appeared, — such as Gorgias the Leontine, Thrasymachus the Chalcedonian, Protagoras the Abderite, and Hippias the Elean, who were all held in great esteem,— with many others of the same age, who professed (it must be owned, rather too arrogantly) to teach their scholars,—*how the worse might be made, by the force of eloquence, to appear the better cause*. But these were openly opposed by the famous Socrates, who, by an adroit method of arguing which was peculiar to himself, took every opportunity to refute the principles of their art. His instructive conferences produced a number of intelligent men, and *Philosophy* is said to have derived her birth from him; —not the doctrine of *Physics*, which was of an earlier date, but that Philosophy which treats of men, and manners, and of the nature of good and evil. But as this is foreign to our present subject, we must defer the Philosophers to another opportunity, and return to the Orators, from whom I have ventured to make a sort digression.

"When the professors therefore, abovementioned were in the decline of life, Isocrates made his appearance, whos house stood open to all Greece as the *School of Eloquence*. He was an accomplished orator, and an excellent teacher; though he did not display his talents in the Forum, but cherished and improved that glory within the walls of his academy, which, in my opinion, no poet has ever yet acquired. He composed many valuable specimens of his art, and taught the principles of it to others; and not only excelled his predecessors in every part of it, but first discovered that a certain *metre* should be observed in prose, though totally different from the measured rhyme of the poets. Before *him*, the artificial structure and harmony of language was unknown;—or if there are any traces of it to be discovered, they appear to have been made without design; which, perhaps, will be thought a beauty:—but whatever it may be deemed, it was, in the present case, the effect rather of native genius, or of accident, than of art and observation. For mere nature itself will measure and limit our sentences by a convenient compass of words; and when they are thus confined to a moderate flow of expression, they will frequently have a *numerous* cadence:—for the ear alone can decide what is full and complete, and what is deficient; and the course of our language will necessarily be regulated by our breath, in which it is excessively disagreeable, not only to fail, but even to labour.

"After Isocrates came Lysias, who, though not personally engaged in forensic causes, was a very artful and an elegant composer, and such a one as you might almost venture to pronounce a complete orator: for Demosthenes is the man who approaches the character so nearly, that you may apply it to him without hesitation. No keen, no artful turns could have been contrived for the pleadings he has left behind him, which he did not readily discover;—nothing could have been expressed with greater nicety, or more clearly and poignantly, than it has been already expressed by him;—and nothing greater, nothing more rapid and forcible, nothing adorned with a nobler elevation either of language, or sentiment, can be conceived than what is to be found in his orations. He was soon rivalled by his cotemporaries Hyperides, Aeschines, Lycurgus, Dinarchus, and Demades (none of whose writings are extant) with many others that might be mentioned: for this age was adorned with a profusion of good orators; and the genuine strength and vigour of Eloquence appears to me to have subsisted to the end of this period, which was distinguished by a natural beauty of composition without disguise or affectation.

"When these orators were in the decline of life, they were succeeded by Phalereus; who was then in the prime of youth. He was indeed a man of greater learning than any of them, but was fitter to appear on the parade, than in the field; and, accordingly, he rather pleased and entertained the Athenians, than inflamed their passions; and marched forth into the dust and heat of the Forum, not from a weather-beaten tent, but from the shady recesses of Theophrastus, a man of consummate erudition. He was the first who relaxed the force of Eloquence, and gave her a soft and tender air: and he rather chose to be agreeable, as indeed he was, than great and striking; but agreeable in such a manner as rather charmed, than warmed the mind of the hearer. His greatest ambition was to impress his audience with a high opinion of his elegance, and not, as Eupolis relates of Pericles, to *sting* as well as to *please*.

"You see, then, in the very city in which Eloquence was born and nurtured, how late it was before she grew to maturity; for before the time of Solon and Pisistratus, we meet with no one who is so much as mentioned for his talent of speaking. These, indeed, if we compute by the Roman date, may be reckoned very ancient; but if by that of the Athenians, we shall find them to be moderns. For though they flourished in the reign of Servius Tullius, Athens had then subsisted much longer than Rome has at present. I have not, however, the least doubt that the power of Eloquence has been always more or less conspicuous. For Homer, we may suppose, would not have ascribed such superior talents of elocution to Ulysses, and Nestor (one of whom he celebrates for his force, and the other for his sweetness) unless the art of Speaking had then been held in some esteem; nor could the Poet himself have been master of such an ornamental style, and so excellent a vein of Oratory as we actually find in him.—The time indeed in which he lived is undetermined: but we are certain that he flourished many years before Romulus: for he was at least of as early a date as the elder Lycurgus, the legislator of the Spartans.

"But a particular attention to the art, and a greater ability in the practice of it, may be observed in Pisistratus. He was succeeded in the following century by Themistocles, who, according to the Roman date, was a person of the remotest antiquity; but, according to that of the Athenians, he was almost a modern. For he lived when Greece was in the height of her power, but when the city of Rome had but lately freed herself from the shackles of regal tyranny;—for the dangerous war with the Volsci, who were headed by Coriolanus (then a voluntary exile) happened nearly at the same time as the Persian war; and we may add, that the fate of both commanders was remarkably similar. Each of them, after distinguishing himself as an excellent citizen, being driven from his country by the wrongs of an ungrateful people, went over to the enemy: and each of them repressed the efforts of his resentment by a voluntary death. For though you, my Atticus, have represented the exit of Coriolanus in a different manner, you must give me leave to dispatch him in the way I have mentioned."—"You may use your pleasure," replied Atticus with a smile: "for it is the privilege of rhetoricians to exceed the truth of history, that they may have an opportunity of embellishing the fate of their heroes: and accordingly, Clitarchus and Stratocles have entertained us with the same pretty fiction about the death of Themistocles, which you have invented for Coriolanus. Thucydides, indeed, who was himself an Athenian of the highest rank and merit, and lived nearly at the same time, has only informed us that he died, and was privately buried in Attica, adding, that it was suspected by some that he had poisoned himself. But these ingenious writers have assured us, that, having slain a bull at the altar, he caught the blood in a large bowl, and, drinking it off, fell suddenly dead upon the ground. For this species of death had a tragical air, and might be described with all the pomp of rhetoric; whereas the ordinary way of dying afforded no opportunity for ornament. As it will, therefore, suit your purpose, that Coriolanus should resemble Themistocles in every thing, I give you leave to introduce the fatal bowl; and you may still farther heighten the catastrophe by a solemn sacrifice, that Coriolanus may appear in all respects to have been a second Themistocles."

"I am much obliged to you," said I, "for your courtesy: but, for the future, I shall be more cautious in meddling with History when you are present; whom I may justly commend as a most exact and scrupulous relator of the Roman History; but nearly at the time we are speaking of (though somewhat later) lived the above-mentioned Pericles, the illustrious son of Xantippus, who first improved his eloquence by the friendly aids of literature;—not that kind of literature which treats professedly of the art of Speaking, of which there was then no regular system; but after he had studied under Anaxagoras the Naturalist, he easily transferred his capacity from abstruse and intricate speculations to forensic and popular debates.

"All Athens was charmed with the sweetness of his language; and not only admired him for his fluency, but was awed by the superior force and the *terrors* of his eloquence. This age, therefore, which may be considered as the infancy of the Art, furnished Athens with an Orator who almost reached the summit of his profession: for an emulation to shine in the Forum is not usually found among a people who are either employed in settling the form of their government, or engaged in war, or struggling with difficulties, or subjected to the arbitrary power of Kings. Eloquence is the attendant of peace, the companion of ease and prosperity, and the tender offspring of a free and a well established constitution. Aristotle, therefore, informs us, that when the Tyrants were expelled from Sicily, and private property (after a long interval of servitude) was determined by public trials, the Sicilians Corax and Tisias (for this people, in general, were very quick and acute, and had a natural turn for controversy) first attempted to write precepts on the art of Speaking. Before them, he says, there was no one who spoke by method, and rules of art, though there were many who discoursed very sensibly, and generally from written notes: but Protagoras took the pains to compose a number of dissertations, on such leading and general topics as are now called common places. Gorgias, he adds, did the same, and wrote panegyrics and invectives on every subject: for he thought it was the province of an Orator to be able either to exaggerate, or extenuate, as occasion might require. Antiphon the Rhamnusian composed several essays of the same species; and (according to Thucydides, a very respectable writer, who was present to hear him) pleaded a capital cause in his own defence, with as much eloquence as had ever yet been displayed by any man. But Lysias was the first who openly professed the *Art*; and, after him, Theodorus, being better versed in the theory than the practice of it, begun to compose orations for others to pronounce; but reserved the method of doing it to himself. In the same manner, Isocrates at first disclaimed the Art, but wrote speeches for other people to deliver; on which account, being often prosecuted for assisting, contrary to law, to circumvent one or another of the parties in judgment, he left off composing orations for other people, and wholly applied himself to writing rules and systems.

"Thus then we have traced the birth and origin of the Orators of Greece, who were, indeed, very ancient, as I have before observed, if we compute by the Roman Annals; but of a much later date, if we reckon by their own: for the Athenian State had signalized itself by a variety of great exploits, both at home and abroad, a considerable time before she was ravished with the charms of Eloquence. But this noble Art was not common to Greece in general, but almost peculiar to Athens. For who has ever heard of an Argive, a Corinthian, or a Theban Orator at the times we are speaking of? unless, perhaps, some merit of the kind may be allowed to Epaminondas, who was a man of uncommon erudition. But I have never read of a

Lacedemonian Orator, from the earliest period of time to the present. For Menelaus himself, though said by Homer to have possessed a sweet elocution, is likewise described as a man of few words. Brevity, indeed, upon some occasions, is a real excellence; but it is very far from being compatible with the general character of Eloquence.

"The Art of Speaking was likewise studied, and admired, beyond the limits of Greece; and the extraordinary honours which were paid to Oratory have perpetuated the names of many foreigners who had the happiness to excel in it. For no sooner had Eloquence ventured to sail from the Pireaeus, but she traversed all the isles, and visited every part of Asia; till at last she infected herself with their manners, and lost all the purity and the healthy complexion of the Attic style, and indeed had almost forgot her native language. The Asiatic Orators, therefore, though not to be undervalued for the rapidity and the copious variety of their elocution, were certainly too loose and luxuriant. But the Rhodians were of a sounder constitution, and more resembled the Athenians. So much, then, for the Greeks; for, perhaps, what I have already said of them, is more than was necessary."

"As to the necessity of it," answered Brutus, "there is no occasion to speak of it: but what you have said of them has entertained me so agreeably, that instead of being longer, it has been much shorter than I could have wished."—"A very handsome compliment," said I;—"but it is time to begin with our own countrymen, of whom it is difficult to give any further account than what we are able to conjecture from our Annals.—For who can question the address, and the capacity of Brutus, the illustrious founder of your family? That Brutus, who so readily discovered the meaning of the Oracle, which promised the supremacy to him who should first salute his mother? That Brutus, who concealed the most consummate abilities under the appearance of a natural defect of understanding? Who dethroned and banished a powerful monarch, the son of an illustrious sovereign? Who settled the State, which he had rescued from arbitrary power, by the appointment of an annual magistracy, a regular system of laws, and a free and open course of justice? And who abrogated the authority of his colleague, that he might rid the city of the smallest vestige of the *regal* name?—Events, which could never have been produced without exerting the powers of Persuasion!—We are likewise informed that a few years after the expulsion of the Kings, when the Plebeians retired to the banks of the Anio, about three miles from the city, and had possessed themselves of what is called The *sacred* Mount, M. Valerius the dictator appeased their fury by a public harangue; for which he was afterwards rewarded with the highest posts of honour, and was the first Roman who was distinguished by the surname of *Maximus*. Nor can L. Valerius Potitus be supposed to have been destitute of the powers of utterance, who, after the odium which had been excited against the Patricians by the tyrannical government of the *Decemviri*, reconciled the people to the Senate, by his prudent laws and conciliatory speeches. We may likewise suppose, that Appius Claudius was a man of some eloquence; since he dissuaded the Senate from consenting to a peace with King Pyrrhus, though they were much inclined to it. The same might be said of Caius Fabricius, who was dispatched to Pyrrhus to treat for the ransom of his captive fellow- citizens; and of Titus Coruncanius, who appears by the memoirs of the pontifical college, to have been a person of no contemptible genius: and likewise of M. Curius (then a tribune of the people) who, when the Interrex Appius *the Blind*, an artful Speaker, held the *Comitia* contrary to law, by refusing to admit any consuls of plebeian rank, prevailed upon the Senate to protest against the conduct: of his antagonist; which, if we consider that the Moenian law was not then in being, was a very bold attempt. We may also conjecture, that M. Popilius was a man of abilities, who, in the time of his consulship, when he was solemnizing a public sacrifice in the proper habit of his office, (for he was also a Flamen Carmentalis) hearing of the mutiny and insurrection of the people against the Senate, rushed immediately into the midst of the assembly, covered as he was with his sacerdotal robes, and quelled the sedition by his authority and the force of his elocution. I do not pretend to have read that the persons I have mentioned were then reckoned Orators, or that any fort of reward or encouragement was given to Eloquence: I only conjecture what appears very probable. It is also recorded, that C. Flaminius, who, when tribune of the people proposed the law for dividing the conquered territories of the Gauls and Piceni among the citizens, and who, after his promotion to the consulship, was slain near the lake Thrasimenus, became very popular by the mere force of his address, Quintus Maximus Verrucosus was likewise reckoned a good Speaker by his cotemporaries; as was also Quintus Metellus, who, in the second Punic war, was joint consul with L. Veturius Philo. But the first person we have any certain account of, who was publicly distinguished as an *Orator*, and who really appears to have been such, was M. Cornelius Cethegus; whose eloquence is attested by Q. Ennius, a voucher of the highest credibility; since he actually heard him speak, and gave him this character after his death; so that there is no reason to suspect that he was prompted by the warmth of his friendship to exceed the bounds of truth. In his ninth book of Annals, he has mentioned him in the following terms:

"*Additur Orator Corneliu' suaviloquenti*
Ore Cethegus Marcu', Tuditano collega,
Marci Filius."

"*Add the* Orator *M. Cornelius Cethegus, so much admired for his mellifluent tongue; who was the colleague of Tuditanus, and the son of Marcus.*"

"He expressly calls him an *Orator*, you see, and attributes to him a remarkable sweetness of elocution; which, even now a-days, is an excellence of which few are possessed: for some of our modern Orators are so insufferably harsh, that they may rather be said to bark than to speak. But what the Poet so much admires in his friend, may certainly be considered as one of the principal ornaments of Eloquence. He adds;

" *——is dictus, ollis popularibus olim,*
Qui tum vivebant homines, atque aevum agitabant,
Flos delibatus populi."

"*He was called by his cotemporaries, the choicest Flower of the State*."

"A very elegant compliment! for as the glory of a man is the strength of his mental capacity, so the brightest ornament of that is Eloquence; in which, whoever had the happiness to excel, was beautifully styled, by the Ancients, the *Flower* of the State; and, as the Poet immediately subjoins,

"'—_Suadaeque medulla:'

"the very marrow and quintessence of Persuasion_."

"That which the Greeks call [Greek: Peitho], *(i.e. Persuasion)* and which it is the chief business of an Orator to effect, is here called *Suada* by Ennius; and of this he commends Cethegus as the *quintessence*; so that he makes the Roman Orator to be himself the very substance of that amiable Goddess, who is said by Eupolis to have dwelt on the lips of Pericles. This Cethegus was joint-consul with P. Tuditanus in the second Punic war; at which time also M. Cato was Quaestor, about one hundred and forty years before I myself was promoted to the consulship; which circumstance would have been absolutely lost, if it had not been recorded by Ennius; and the memory of that illustrious citizen, as has probably been the case of many others, would have been obliterated by the rust of antiquity. The manner of speaking which was then in vogue, may easily be collected from the writings of *Naevius*: for Naevius died, as we learn from the memoirs of the times, when the persons above-mentioned were consuls; though Varro, a most accurate investigator of historical truth, thinks there is a mistake in this, and fixes the death of Naevius something later. For Plautus died in the consulship of P. Claudius and L. Porcius, twenty years after the consulship of the persons we have been speaking of, and when Cato was Censor. Cato, therefore, must have been younger than Cethegus, for he was consul nine years after him: but we always consider him as a person of the remotest antiquity, though he died in the consulship of Lucius Marcius and M. Manilius, and but eighty-three years before my own promotion to the same office. He is certainly, however, the most ancient Orator we have, whose writings may claim our attention; unless any one is pleased with the above-mentioned speech of Appius, on the peace with Pyrrhus, or with a set of panegyrics on the dead, which, I own, are still extant. For it was customary in most families of note to preserve their images, their trophies of honour, and their memoirs, either to adorn a funeral when any of the family deceased, or to perpetuate the fame of their ancestors, or prove their own nobility. But the truth of History has been much corrupted by these laudatory essays; for many circumstances were recorded in them which never existed; such as false triumphs, a pretended succession of consulships, and false alliances and elevations, when men of inferior rank were confounded with a noble family of the same name: as if I myself should pretend that I am descended from M. Tullius, who was a Patrician, and shared the consulship with Servius Sulpicius, about ten years after the expulsion of the kings.

"But the real speeches of Cato are almost as numerous as those of Lysias the Athenian; a great number of whose are still extant. For Lysias was certainly an Athenian; because he not only died but received his birth at Athens, and served all the offices of the city; though Timaesus, as if he acted by the Licinian or the Mucian law, remands him back to Syracuse.

There is, however, a manifest resemblance between *his* character and that of *Cato*: for they are both of them distinguished by their acuteness, their elegance, their agreeable humour, and their brevity. But the Greek has the happiness to be most admired: for there are some who are so extravagantly fond of him, as to prefer a graceful air to a vigorous constitution, and who are perfectly satisfied with a slender and an easy shape, if it is only attended with a moderate share of health. It must, however, be acknowledged, that even Lysias often displays a strength of arm, than which nothing can be more strenuous and forcible; though he is certainly, in all respects, of a more thin and feeble habit than Cato, notwithstanding he has so many admirers, who are charmed with his very slenderness. But as to Cato, where will you find a modern Orator who condescends to read him?—nay, I might have said, who has the least knowledge of him?—And yet, good Gods! what a wonderful man! I say nothing of his merit as a Citizen, a Senator, and a General; we must confine our attention to the Orator. Who, then, has displayed more dignity as a panegyrist?—more severity as an accuser?—more ingenuity in the turn of his sentiments?—or more neatness and address in his narratives and explanations? Though he composed above a hundred and fifty orations, (which I have seen and read) they are crowded with all the beauties of language and sentiment. Let us select from these what deserves our notice and applause: they will supply us with all the graces of Oratory. Not to omit his *Antiquities*, who will deny that these also are adorned with every flower, and with all the lustre of Eloquence? and yet he has scarcely any admirers; which some ages ago was the case of Philistus the Syracusan, and even of Thucydides himself. For as the lofty and elevated style of Theopompus soon diminished the reputation of their pithy and laconic harangues, which were sometimes scarcely intelligible through their excessive brevity and quaintness; and as Demosthenes eclipsed the glory of Lysias, so the pompous and stately elocution of the moderns has obscured the lustre of Cato. But many of us are shamefully ignorant and inattentive; for we admire the Greeks for their antiquity, and what is called their Attic neatness, and yet have never noticed the same quality in Cato. It was the distinguishing character, say they, of Lysias and Hyperides. I own it, and I admire them for it: but why not allow a share of it to Cato? They are fond, they tell us, of the *Attic* style of Eloquence: and their choice is certainly judicious, provided they borrow the blood and the healthy juices, as well as the bones and membranes. What they recommend, however, is, to do it justice, an agreeable quality. But why must Lysias and Hyperides be so fondly courted, while Cato is entirely overlooked? His language indeed has an antiquated air, and some of his expressions are rather too harsh and crabbed. But let us remember that this was the language of the time: only change and modernize it, which it was not in his power to do;—add the improvements of number and cadence, give an easier turn to his sentences, and regulate the structure and connection of his words, (which was as little practised even by the older Greeks as by him) and you will discover no one who can claim the preference to Cato. The Greeks themselves acknowledge that the chief beauty of composition results from the frequent use of those *translatitious* forms of expression which they call *Tropes*, and of those various attitudes of language and sentiment which they call *Figures*: but it is almost incredible in what numbers, and with what amazing variety, they are all employed by Cato. I know, indeed, that he is not sufficiently polished, and that recourse must be had to a more perfect model for imitation: for he is an author of such antiquity, that he is the oldest now extant, whose writings can be read with patience; and the ancients in general acquired a much greater reputation in every other art, than in that of Speaking. But who that has seen the statues of the moderns, will not perceive in a moment, that the figures of Canachus are too stiff and formal, to resemble life? Those of Calamis, though evidently harsh, are somewhat softer. Even the statues of Myron are not sufficiently alive; and yet you would not hesitate to pronounce them beautiful. But those of Polycletes are much finer, and, in my mind, completely finished. The case is the same in Painting; for in the works of Zeuxis, Polygnotus, Timanthes, and several other masters who confined themselves to the use of four colours, we commend the air and the symmetry of their figures; but in Aetion, Nicomachus, Protogenes, and Apelles, every thing is finished to perfection. This, I believe, will hold equally true in all the other arts; for there is not one of them which was invented and completed at the same time. I cannot doubt, for instance, that there were many Poets before Homer: we may infer it from those very songs which he himself informs us were sung at the feasts of the Phaeacians, and of the profligate suitors of Penelope. Nay, to go no farther, what is become of the ancient poems of our own countrymen?"

"Such as the Fauns and rustic Bards compos'd,
When none the rocks of poetry had cross'd,
Nor wish'd to form his style by rules of art,
Before this vent'rous man: &c.

"Old Ennius here speaks of himself; nor does he carry his boast beyond the bounds of truth: the case being really as he describes it. For we had only an Odyssey in Latin, which resembled one of the rough and unfinished statues of Daedalus; and some dramatic pieces of Livius, which will scarcely bear a second reading. This Livius exhibited his first performance at Rome in the Consulship of M. Tuditanus, and C. Clodius the son of Caecus, the year before Ennius was born, and, according to the account of my friend Atticus, (whom I choose to follow) the five hundred and fourteenth from the building of the city. But historians are not agreed about the date of the year. Attius informs us that Livius was taken prisoner at Tarentum by Quintus Maximus in his fifth Consulship, about thirty years after he is said by Atticus, and our ancient annals, to have introduced the drama. He adds that he exhibited his first dramatic piece about eleven years after, in the Consulship of C. Cornelius and Q. Minucius, at the public games which Salinator had vowed to the Goddess of Youth for his victory over the Senones. But in this, Attius was so far mistaken, that Ennius, when the persons above-mentioned were Consuls, was forty years old: so that if Livius was of the same age, as in this case he would have been, the first dramatic author we had must have been younger than Plautus and Naevius, who had exhibited a great number of plays before the time he specifies. If these remarks, my Brutus, appear unsuitable to the subject before us, you must throw the whole blame upon Atticus, who has inspired me with a strange curiosity to enquire into the age of illustrious men, and the respective times of their appearance."—"On the contrary," said Brutus, "I am highly pleased that you have carried your attention so far; and I think your remarks well adapted to the curious task you have undertaken, the giving us a history of the different classes of Orators in their proper order."—"You understand me right," said I; "and I heartily wish those venerable Odes were still extant, which Cato informs us in his Antiquities, used to be sung by every guest in his turn at the homely feasts of our ancestors, many ages before, to commemorate the feats of their heroes. But the *Punic war* of that antiquated Poet, whom Ennius so proudly ranks among the *Fauns and rustic Bards*, affords me as exquisite a pleasure as the finest statue that was ever formed by Myron. Ennius, I allow, was a more finished writer: but if he had really undervalued the other, as he pretends to do, he would scarcely have omitted such a bloody war as the first *Punic*, when he attempted professedly to describe all the wars of the Republic. Nay he himself assigns the reason.

"Others" (said he) "that cruel war have sung:"

Very true, and they have sung it with great order and precision, though not, indeed, in such elegant strains as yourself. This you ought to have acknowledged, as you must certainly be conscious that you have borrowed many ornaments from Naevius; or if you refuse to own it, I shall tell you plainly that you have *pilfered* them.

"Cotemporary with the Cato above-mentioned (though somewhat older) were C. Flaminius, C. Varro, Q. Maximus, Q. Metellus, P. Lentulus, and P. Crassus who was joint Consul with the elder Africanus. This Scipio, we are told, was not destitute of the powers of Elocution: but his son, who adopted the younger Scipio (the son of Paulus Aemilius) would have stood foremost in the list of Orators, if he had possessed a firmer constitution. This is evident from a few Speeches, and a Greek History of his, which are very agreeably written. In the same class we may place Sextus Aelius, who was the best lawyer of his time, and a ready speaker. A little after these, was C. Sulpicius Gallus, who was better acquainted with the Grecian literature than all the rest of the nobility, and was reckoned a graceful Orator, being equally distinguished, in every other respect, by the superior elegance of his taste; for a more copious and splendid way of speaking began now to prevail. When this Sulpicius, in quality of Praetor, was celebrating the public shews in honour of Apollo, died the Poet Ennius, in the Consulship of Q. Marcius and Cn. Servilius, after exhibiting his Tragedy of *Thyestes*. At the same time lived Tiberius Gracchus, the son of Publius, who was twice Consul and Censor: a Greek Oration of his to the Rhodians is still extant, and he bore the character of a worthy citizen, and an eloquent Speaker. We are likewise told that P. Scipio Nasica, surnamed The Darling of the People, and who also had the honor to be twice chosen Consul and Censor, was esteemed an able Orator: To him we may add L. Lentulus, who was joint Consul with C. Figulus;—Q. Nobilior, the son of Marcus, who was inclined to the study of literature by his father's example, and presented Ennius (who had served under his father in Aetolia) with the freedom of the City, when he founded a colony in quality of Triumvir: and his colleague, T. Annius Luscus, who is said to have been tolerably eloquent. We are likewise informed that L. Paulus, the father of Africanus, defended the character of an eminent citizen in a public speech; and that Cato, who died in the 83d year of his age, was then living, and actually pleaded, that very year, against the defendant Servius Galba, in the open Forum, with great energy and spirit:—he has left a copy of this Oration behind him. But when Cato was in the decline of life, a crowd of Orators, all younger than himself, made their appearance at the same time: For A. Albinus, who wrote a History in Greek, and shared the Consulship with L. Lucullus, was greatly admired for his learning and Elocution: and almost equal to him were Servius Fulvius, and Servius Fabius Pictor, the latter of whom was well acquainted with the laws of his country, the Belles Lettres, and the History of Antiquity. Quintus Fabius Labeo was likewise adorned with the same accomplishments. But Q. Metellus whose four sons attained the consular dignity, was admired for his Eloquence beyond the rest;—he undertook the defence of L. Cotta, when he was accused by Africanus,—and composed many other Speeches, particularly that against Tiberius Gracchus, which we have a full account of in the Annals of C. Fannius. L. Cotta himself was likewise reckoned a *veteran*; but C. Laelius, and P. Africanus were allowed by all to be more finished Speakers: their Orations are still extant, and may serve as specimens of their respective abilities. But Servius Galba, who was something older than any of them, was indisputably the best speaker of the age. He was the first among the Romans who displayed the proper and distinguishing talents of an Orator, such as, digressing from his subject to embellish and diversify it,—soothing or alarming the passions, exhibiting every circumstance in the strongest light,—imploring the compassion of his audience, and artfully enlarging on those topics, or general principles of Prudence or Morality, on which the stress of his argument depended: and yet, I know not how, though he is allowed to have been the greatest Orator of his time, the Orations he has left are more lifeless, and have a more antiquated air, than those of Laelius, or Scipio, or even of Cato himself: in short, the strength and substance of them has so far evaporated, that we have scarcely any thing of them remaining but the bare skeletons. In the same manner, though both Laelius and Scipio are greatly extolled for their abilities; the preference was given to Laelius as a speaker; and yet his Oration, in defence of the privileges of the Sacerdotal College, has no greater merit than any one you may please to fix upon of the numerous speeches of Scipio. Nothing, indeed, can be sweeter and milder than that of Laelius, nor could any thing have been urged with greater dignity to support the honour of religion: but, of the two, Laelius appears to me to be rougher, and more old-fashioned than Scipio; and, as different Speakers have different tastes, he had in my mind too strong a relish for antiquity, and was too fond of using obsolete expressions. But such is the jealousy of mankind, that they will not allow the same person to be possessed of too many perfections. For as in military prowess they thought it impossible that any man could vie with Scipio, though Laelius had not a little distinguished himself in the war with Viriathus; so for learning, Eloquence, and wisdom, though each was allowed to be above the reach of any other competitor, they adjudged the preference to Laelius. Nor was this only the opinion of the world, but it seems to have been allowed by mutual consent between themselves: for it was then a general custom, as candid in this respect as it was fair and just in every other, to give his due to each. I accordingly remember that P. Rutilius Rufus once told me at Smyrna, that when he was a young man, the two Consuls P. Scipio and D. Brutus, by order of the Senate, tried a capital cause of great consequence. For several persons of note having been murdered in the Silan Forest, and the domestics, and some of the sons, of a company of gentlemen who farmed the taxes of the pitch-manufactory, being charged with the fact, the Consuls were ordered to try the cause in person. Laelius, he said, spoke very sensibly and elegantly, as indeed he always did, on the side of the farmers of the customs. But the Consuls, after hearing both sides, judging it necessary to refer the matter to a second trial, the same Laelius, a few days after, pleaded their cause again with more accuracy, and much better than at first. The affair, however, was once more put off for a further hearing. Upon this, when his clients attended Laelius to his own house, and, after thanking him for what he had already done, earnestly begged him not to be disheartened by the fatigue he had suffered;—he assured them he had exerted his utmost to defend their reputation; but frankly added, that he thought their cause would be more effectually supported by Servius Galba, whose manner of speaking was more embellished and more spirited than his own. They, accordingly, by the advice of Laelius, requested Galba to undertake it. To this he consented; but with the greatest modesty and reluctance, out of respect to the illustrious advocate he was going to succeed:—and as he had only the next day to prepare himself, he spent the whole of it in considering and digesting his cause. When the day of trial was come, Rutilius himself, at the request of the defendants, went early in the morning to Galba, to give him notice of it, and conduct him to the court in proper time. But till word was brought that the Consuls were going to the bench, he confined himself in his study, where he suffered no one to be admitted; and continued very busy in dictating to his Amanuenses, several of whom (as indeed he often used to do) he kept fully employed at once. While he was thus engaged, being informed that it was high time for him to appear in court, he left his house with so much life in his eyes, and such an ardent glow upon his countenance, that you would have thought he had not only *prepared* his cause, but actually *carried* it. Rutilius added, as another circumstance worth noticing, that his scribes, who attended him to the bar, appeared excessively fatigued: from whence he thought it probable that he was equally warm and vigorous in the composition, as in the delivery of his speeches. But to conclude the story, Galba pleaded his cause before Laelius himself, and a very numerous and attentive audience, with such uncommon force and dignity, that every part of his Oration received the applause of his hearers: and so powerfully did he move the feelings, and affect the pity of the judges, that his clients were immediately acquitted of the charge, to the satisfaction of the whole court.

"As, therefore, the two principal qualities required in an Orator, are to be neat and clear in stating the nature of his subject, and warm and forcible in moving the passions; and as he who fires and inflames his audience, will always effect more than he who can barely inform and amuse them; we may conjecture from the above narrative, which I was favoured with by Rutilius, that Laelius was most admired for his elegance, and Galba for his pathetic force. But this force of his was most remarkably exerted, when, having in his Praetorship put to death some Lusitanians, contrary (it was believed) to his previous and express engagement;—T. Libo the Tribune exasperated the people against him, and preferred a bill which was to operate against his conduct as a subsequent law. M. Cato (as I have before mentioned) though extremely old, spoke in support of the bill with great vehemence; which Speech he inserted in his Book of *Antiquities,* a few days, or at most only a month or two, before his death. On this occasion, Galba refusing to plead to the charge, and submitting his fate to the generosity of the people, recommended his children to their protection, with tears in his eyes; and particularly his young ward the son of C. Gallus Sulpicius his deceased friend, whose orphan state and piercing cries, which were the more regarded for the sake of his illustrious father, excited their pity in a wonderful manner;—and thus (as Cato informs us in his History) he escaped the flames which would otherwise have consumed him, by employing the children to move the compassion of the people. I likewise find (what may be easily judged from his Orations still extant) that his prosecutor Libo was a man of some Eloquence."

As I concluded these remarks with a short pause;—"What can be the reason," said Brutus, "if there was so much merit in the Oratory of Galba, that there is no trace of it to be seen in his Orations;—a circumstance which

I have no opportunity to be surprized at in others, who have left nothing behind them in writing."—"The reasons," said I, "why some have not wrote any thing, and others not so well as they spoke, are very different. Some of our Orators have writ nothing through mere indolence, and because they were loath to add a private fatigue to a public one: for most of the Orations we are now possessed of were written not before they were spoken, but some time afterwards. Others did not choose the trouble of improving themselves; to which nothing more contributes than frequent writing; and as to perpetuating the fame of their Eloquence, they thought it unnecessary; supposing that their eminence in that respect was sufficiently established already, and that it would be rather diminished than increased by submitting any written specimen of it to the arbitrary test of criticism. Some also were sensible that they spoke much better than they were able to write; which is generally the case of those who have a great genius, but little learning, such as Servius Galba. When he spoke, he was perhaps so much animated by the force of his abilities, and the natural warmth and impetuosity of his temper, that his language was rapid, bold, and striking; but afterwards, when he took up the pen in his leisure hours, and his passion had sunk into a calm, his Elocution became dull and languid. This indeed can never happen to those whose only aim is to be neat and polished; because an Orator may always be master of that discretion which will enable him both to speak and write in the same agreeable manner: but no man can revive at pleasure the ardour of his passions; and when that has once subsided, the fire and pathos of his language will be extinguished. This is the reason why the calm and easy spirit of Laelius seems still to breathe in his writings, whereas the force of Galba is entirely withered and lost.

"We may also reckon in the number of middling Orators, the two brothers L. and Sp. Mummius, both whose Orations are still in being:—the style of Lucius is plain and antiquated; but that of Spurius, though equally unembellished, is more close, and compact; for he was well versed in the doctrine of the Stoics. The Orations of Sp. Alpinus, their cotemporary, are very numerous: and we have several by L. and C. Aurelius Oresta, who were esteemed indifferent Speakers. P. Popilius also was a worthy citizen, and had a tolerable share of utterance: but his son Caius was really eloquent. To *these* we may add C. Tuditanus, who was not only very polished, and genteel, in his manners and appearance, but had an elegant turn of expression; and of the same class was M. Octavius, a man of inflexible constancy in every just and laudable measure; and who, after being affronted and disgraced in the most public manner, defeated his rival Tiberius Gracchus by the mere dint of his perseverance. But M. Aemilius Lepidus, who was surnamed Porcina, and flourished at the same time as Galba, though he was indeed something younger, was esteemed an Orator of the first eminence; and really appears, from his Orations which are still extant, to have been a masterly writer. For he was the first Speaker, among the Romans, who gave us a specimen of the easy gracefulness of the Greeks; and who was distinguished by the measured flow of his language, and a style regularly polished and improved by art. His manner was carefully studied by C. Carbo and Tib. Gracchus, two accomplished youths who were nearly of an age: but we must defer their character as public Speakers, till we have finished our account of their elders. For Q. Pompeius, according to the style of the time, was no contemptible Orator; and actually raised himself to the highest honours of the State by his own personal merit, and without being recommended, as usual, by the quality of his ancestors. Lucius Cassius too derived his influence, which was very considerable, not indeed from his *Eloquence*, but from his manly way of speaking: for it is remarkable that he made himself popular, not, as others did, by his complaisance and liberality, but by the gloomy rigour and severity of his manners. His law for collecting the votes of the people by way of ballot, was strongly opposed by the Tribune M. Antius Briso, who was supported by M. Lepidus one of the Consuls: and it was afterwards objected to Africanus, that Briso dropped the opposition by his advice. At this time the two Scipios were very serviceable to a number of clients by their superior judgment, and Eloquence; but still more so by their extensive interest and popularity. But the written speeches of Pompeius (though it must be owned they have rather an antiquated air) discover an amazing sagacity, and are very far from being dry and spiritless. To these we must add P. Crassus, an orator of uncommon merit, who was qualified for the profession by the united efforts of art and nature, and enjoyed some other advantages which were almost peculiar to his family. For he had contracted an affinity with that accomplished Speaker Servius Galba above-mentioned, by giving his daughter in marriage to Galba's son; and being likewise himself the son of Mucius, and the brother of P. Scaevola, he had a fine opportunity at home (which he made the best use of) to gain a thorough knowledge of the Civil Law. He was a man of unusual application, and was much beloved by his fellow-citizens; being constantly employed either in giving his advice, or pleading causes in the Forum. Cotemporary with the Speakers I have mentioned were the two C. Fannii, the sons of C. and M. one of whom, (the son of C.) who was joint Consul with Domitius, has left us an excellent speech against Gracchus, who proposed the admission of the Latin and Italian allies to the freedom of Rome."—"Do you really think, then," said Atticus, "that Fannius was the author of that Oration? For when we were young, there were different opinions about it. Some asserted it was wrote by C. Persius, a man of letters, and the same who is so much extolled for his learning by Lucilius: and others believed it was the joint production of a number of noblemen, each of whom contributed his best to complete it."—"This I remember," said I; "but I could never persuade myself to coincide with either of them. Their suspicion, I believe, was entirely founded on the character of Fannius, who was only reckoned among the *middling* Orators; whereas the speech in question is esteemed the best which the time afforded. But, on the other hand, it is too much of a piece to have been the mingled composition of many: for the flow of the periods, and the turn of the language, are perfectly similar, throughout the whole of it.—and as to *Persius*, if *he* had composed it for Fannius to pronounce, Gracchus would certainly have taken some notice of it in his reply; because Fannius rallies Gracchus pretty severely, in one part of it, for employing Menelaus of Marathon, and several others, to manufacture his speeches. We may add that Fannius himself was no contemptible Orator: for he pleaded a number of causes, and his Tribuneship, which was chiefly conducted under the management and direction of P. Africanus, was very far from being an idle one. But the other C. Fannius, (the son of M.) and son- in-law of C. Laelius, was of a rougher cast, both in his temper, and manner of speaking. By the advice of his father-in-law, (of whom, by the bye, he was not remarkably fond, because he had not voted for his admission into the college of augurs, but gave the preference to his younger son-in-law Q. Scaevola; though Laelius genteely excused himself, by saying that the preference was not given to the youngest son, but to his wife the eldest daughter,) by his advice, I say, he attended the lectures of Panaetius. His abilities as a Speaker may be easily conjectured from his History, which is neither destitute of elegance, nor a perfect model of composition. As to his brother Mucius the augur, whenever he was called upon to defend himself, he always pleaded his own cause; as, for instance, in the action which was brought against him for bribery by T. Albucius. But he was never ranked among the Orators; his chief merit being a critical knowledge of the Civil Law, and an uncommon accuracy of judgment. L. Caelius Antipater likewise (as you may see by his works) was an elegant and a handsome writer for the time he lived in; he was also an excellent Lawyer, and taught the principles of jurisprudence to many others, particularly to L. Crassus. As to Caius Carbo and T. Gracchus, I wish they had been as well inclined to maintain peace and good order in the State, as they were qualified to support it by their Eloquence: their glory would then have been out-rivaled by no one. But the latter, for his turbulent Tribuneship, which he entered upon with a heart full of resentment against the great and good, on account of the odium he had brought upon himself by the treaty of Numantia, was slain by the hands of the Republic: and the other, being impeached of a seditious affectation of popularity, rescued himself from the severity of the judges by a voluntary death. That both of them were excellent Speakers, is very plain from the general testimony of their cotemporaries: for as to their Speeches now extant, though I allow them to be very artful and judicious, they are certainly defective in Elocution. Gracchus had the advantage of being carefully instructed by his mother Cornelia from his very childhood, and his mind was enriched with all the stores of Grecian literature: for he was constantly attended by the ablest masters from Greece, and particularly, in his youth, by Diophanes of Mitylene, who was the most eloquent Grecian of his age: but though he was a man of uncommon genius, he had but a short time to improve and display it. As to Carbo, his whole life was spent in trials, and forensic debates. He is said by very sensible men who heard him, and, among others, by our friend L. Gellius who lived in his family in the time of his Consulship, to have been a sonorous, a fluent, and a spirited Speaker, and likewise, upon occasion, very pathetic, very engaging, and excessively humorous: Gellius used to add, that he applied himself very closely to his studies, and bestowed much of his time in writing and private declamation. He was, therefore, esteemed the best pleader of his time; for no sooner had he began to distinguish himself in the Forum, but the depravity of the age gave birth to a number of law-suits; and it was first found necessary, in the time of his youth, to settle the form of public trials, which had never been done before. We accordingly find that L. Piso, then a Tribune of the people, was the first who proposed a law against bribery; which he did when Censorinus and Manilius were Consuls. This Piso too was a professed pleader, and the proposer and opposer of a great number of laws: he left some Orations behind him, which are now lost, and a Book of

Annals very indifferently written. But in the public trials, in which Carbo was concerned, the assistance of an able advocate had become more necessary than ever, in consequence of the law for voting by ballots, which was proposed and carried by L. Cassius, in the Consulship of Lepidus and Mancinus.

"I have likewise been often assured by the poet Attius, (an intimate friend of his) that your ancestor D. Brutus, the son of M. was no inelegant Speaker; and that for the time he lived in, he was well versed both in the Greek and Roman literature. He ascribed the same accomplishments to Q. Maximus, the grandson of L. Paulus: and added that, a little prior to Maximus, the Scipio, by whose instigation (though only in a private capacity) T. Gracchus was assassinated, was not only a man of great ardour in all other respects, but very warm and spirited in his manner of speaking. P. Lentulus too, the Father of the Senate, had a sufficient share of eloquence for an honest and useful magistrate. About the same time L. Furius Philus was thought to speak our language as elegantly, and more correctly than any other man; P. Scaevola to be very artful and judicious, and rather more fluent than Philus; M. Manilius to possess almost an equal share of judgment with the latter; and Appius Claudius to be equally fluent, but more warm and pathetic. M. Fulvius Flaccus, and C. Cato the nephew of Africanus, were likewise tolerable Orators: some of the writings of Flaccus are still in being, in which nothing, however, is to be seen but the mere scholar. P. Decius was a professed rival of Flaccus; he too was not destitute of Eloquence; but his style, as well as his temper, was too violent. M. Drusus the son of C. who, in his Tribuneship, baffled [Footnote: *Laffiea*. In the original it runs, "*Caium Gracchum collegam, iterum Tribinum fecit.*" but this was undoubtedly a mistake of the transcriber, as being contrary not only to the truth of History, but to Cicero's own account of the matter in lib. IV.

"I find," said Brutus, "that the case is much the same among us, as with the Greeks; and that the Stoics, in general, are very judicious at an argument, which they conduct by certain rules of art, and are likewise very neat and exact in their language; but if we take them from this, to speak in Public, they make a poor appearance. Cato, however, must be excepted; in whom, though as rigid a Stoic as ever existed, I could not wish for a more consummate degree of Eloquence: I can likewise discover a moderate share of it in Fannius,—not so much in Rutilius;—but none at all in Tubero."—"True," said I; "and we may easily account for it: Their whole attention was so closely confined to the study of Logic, that they never troubled themselves to acquire the free, diffusive, and variegated style which is so necessary for a public Speaker. But your uncle, you doubtless know, was wise enough to borrow only that from the Stoics, which they were able to furnish for his purpose (the art of reasoning:) but for the art of Speaking, he had recourse to the masters of Rhetoric, and exercised himself in the manner they directed. If, however, we must be indebted for everything to the Philosophers, the Peripatetic discipline is, in my mind, much the properest to form our language. For which reason, my Brutus, I the more approve your choice, in attaching yourself to a sect, (I mean the Philosophers of the Old Academy,) in whose system, a just and accurate way of reasoning is enlivened by a perpetual sweetness and fluency of expression: but even the delicate and flowing style of the Peripatetics, and Academics, is not sufficient to complete an Orator; nor yet can he be complete without it. For as the language of the Stoics is too close, and contracted, to suit the ears of common people; so that of the latter is too diffusive and luxuriant for a spirited contest in the Forum, or a pleading at the bar. Who had a richer style than Plato? The Philosophers tell us, that if Jupiter himself was to converse in Greek, he would speak like *him*. Who also was more nervous than Aristotle? Who sweeter than Theophrastus? We are told that even Demosthenes attended the lectures of Plato, and was fond of reading what he published; which, indeed, is sufficiently evident from the turn, and the majesty of his language and he himself has expressly mentioned it in one of his Letters. But the style of this excellent Orator is, notwithstanding, much too fierce for the Academy; as that of the Philosophers is too mild and placid for the Forum. I shall now, with your leave, proceed to the age and merits of the rest of the Roman Orators."—"Nothing," said Atticus, "(for I can safely answer for my friend Brutus) would please us better."—"Curio, then," said I, "was nearly of the age I have just mentioned,—a celebrated Speaker, whose genius may be easily decided from his Orations. For, among several others, we have a noble Speech of his for Ser. Fulvius, in a prosecution for incest. When we were children, it was esteemed the best then extant; but now it is almost overlooked among the numerous performances of the same kind which have been lately published."—"I am very sensible," replied Brutus, "to whom we are obliged for the numerous performances you speak of."—"And I am equally sensible," said I, "who is the person you intend: for I have at least done a service to my young countrymen, by introducing a loftier, and more embellished way of speaking, than was used before: and, perhaps, I have also done some harm, because after *mine* appeared, the Speeches of our ancestors and predecessors began to be neglected by most people; though never by *me*, for I can assure you, I always prefer them to my own."—"But you must reckon me," said Brutus, "among the *most people*; though I now see, from your recommendation, that I have a great many books to read, of which before I had very little opinion."—"But this celebrated Oration," said I, "in the prosecution for incest, is in some places excessively puerile; and what is said in it of the passion of love, the inefficacy of questioning by tortures, and the danger of trusting to common hear-say, is indeed pretty enough, but would be insufferable to the tutored ears of the moderns, and to a people who are justly distinguished for the solidity of their knowledge. He likewise wrote several other pieces, spoke a number of good Orations, and was certainly an eminent pleader; so that I much wonder, considering how long he lived, and the character he bore, that he was never preferred to the Consulship. But I have a man here, [Footnote: He refers, perhaps, to the Works of Gracchus, which he might then have in his hand; or, more probably, to a statue of him, which stood near the place where he and his friends were sitting.] (C. Gracchus) who had an amazing genius, and the warmest application; and was a Scholar from his very childhood: For you must not imagine, my Brutus, that we have ever yet had a Speaker, whose language was richer and more copious than his."—"I really think so," answered Brutus; "and he is almost the only author we have, among the ancients, that I take the trouble to read." "And he well *deserves* it," said I; "for the Roman name and literature were great losers by his untimely fate. I wish he had transferred his affection for his brother to his country! How easily, if he had thus prolonged his life, would he have rivalled the glory of his father, and grandfather! In Eloquence, I scarcely know whether we should yet have had his equal. His language was noble; his sentiments manly and judicious; and his whole manner great and striking. He wanted nothing but the finishing touch: for though his first attempts were as excellent as they were numerous, he did not live to complete them. In short, my Brutus, *he,* if any one, should be carefully studied by the Roman youth: for he is able, not only to edge, but to feed and ripen their talents. After *him* appeared C. Galba, the son of the eloquent Servius, and the son-in-law of P. Crassus, who was both an eminent Speaker, and a skilful Civilian. He was much commended by our fathers, who respected him for the sake of *his*: but he had the misfortune to be stopped in his career. For being tried by the Mamilian law, as a party concerned in the conspiracy to support Jugurtha, though he exerted all his abilities to defend himself, he was unhappily cast. His peroration, or, as it is often called, his epilogue, is still extant; and was so much in repute, when we were school-boys, that we used to learn it by heart: he was the first member of the Sacerdotal College, since the building of Rome, who was publicly tried and condemned. As to P. Scipio, who died in his Consulship, he neither spoke much, nor often: but he was inferior to no one in the purity of his language, and superior to all in wit and pleasantry. His colleague L. Bestia, who begun his Tribuneship very successfully, (for, by a law which he preferred for the purpose, he procured the recall of Popillius, who had been exiled by the influence of Caius Gracchus) was a man of spirit, and a tolerable Speaker: but he did not finish his Consulship so happily. For, in consequence of the invidious law of Mamilius above-mentioned, C. Galba one of the Priests, and the four Consular gentlemen L. Bestia, C. Cato, Sp. Albinus, and that excellent citizen L. Opimius, who killed Gracchus; of which he was acquitted by the people, though he had constantly sided against them,—were all condemned by their judges, who were of the Gracchan party. Very unlike him in his Tribuneship, and indeed in every other part of his life, was that infamous citizen C. Licinius Nerva; but he was not destitute of Eloquence. Nearly at the same time, (though, indeed, he was somewhat older) flourished C. Fimbria, who was rather rough and abusive, and much too warm and hasty: but his application, and his great integrity and firmness made him a serviceable Speaker in the Senate. He was likewise a tolerable Pleader, and Civilian, and distinguished by the same rigid freedom in the turn of his language, as in that of his virtues. When we were boys, we used to think his Orations worth reading; though they are now scarcely to be met with. But C. Sextius Calvinus was equally elegant both in his taste, and his language, though, unhappily, of a very infirm constitution:—when the pain in his feet intermitted, he did not decline the trouble of pleading, but he did not attempt it very often. His fellow-citizens, therefore, made use of his advice, whenever they had occasion for it; but of his patronage, only when his health permitted. Cotemporary with these, my good friend, was your namesake M. Brutus, the disgrace of your noble family; who, though he bore that honourable name, and had the best of men, and an eminent Civilian, for his father, confined his practice to accusations, as Lycurgus is said to have done at Athens. He never sued for any of our magistracies; but was a severe, and a troublesome prosecutor: so that we easily see that, in *him*, the natural goodness of the flock was corrupted by the vicious inclinations of the man. At the same time lived L. Caesulenus, a man of Plebeian rank, and a professed accuser, like the former: I myself heard him in his old age, when he endeavoured, by the Aquilian law, to subject L. Sabellius to a fine, for a breach of justice. But I should not have taken any notice of such a low-born wretch, if I had not thought that no person I ever heard, could give a more suspicious turn to the cause of the defendant, or exaggerate it to a higher degree of criminality. T. Albucius, who lived in the same age, was well versed in the Grecian literature, or, rather, was almost a Greek himself. I speak of him, as I think; but any person, who pleases, may judge what he was by his Orations. In his youth, he studied at Athens, and returned from thence a thorough proficient in the doctrine of Epicurus; which, of all others, is the least adapted to form an orator. His cotemporary, Q. Catulus, was an accomplished Speaker, not in the ancient taste, but (unless any thing more perfect can be exhibited) in the finished style of the moderns. He had a plentiful stock of learning; an easy, winning elegance, not only in his manners and disposition, but in his very language; and an unblemished purity and correctness of style. This may be easily seen by his Orations; and particularly, by the History of his Consulship, and of his subsequent transactions, which he composed in the soft and agreeable manner of Xenophon, and made a present of to the poet, A. Furius, an intimate acquaintance of his: but this performance is as little known, as the three books of Scaurus before-mentioned."—"Indeed, I must confess," said Brutus, "that both the one and the other, are perfectly unknown to me: but that is entirely my *own* fault. I shall now, therefore, request a sight of them from *you*; and am resolved, in future, to be more careful in collecting such valuable curiosities."—"This Catulus," said I, "as I have just observed, was distinguished by the purity of his language; which, though a material accomplishment, is too much neglected by most of the Roman orators; for as to the elegant tone of his voice, and the sweetness of his accent, as you knew his son, it will be needless to take any notice of them. His son, indeed, was not in the list of Orators: but whenever he had occasion to deliver his sentiments in public, he neither wanted judgment, nor a neat and liberal turn of expression. Nay, even the father himself was not reckoned the foremost in the list of Orators: but still he had that kind of merit, that notwithstanding, after you had heard two or three speakers, who were particularly eminent in their profession, you might judge him inferior; yet, whenever you heard him *alone*, and without an immediate opportunity of making a comparison, you would not only be satisfied with him, but scarcely wish for a better advocate. As to Q. Metellus Numidicus, and his Colleague M. Silanus, they spoke, on matters of government, with as much eloquence as was really necessary for men of their illustrious character, and of consular dignity. But M. Aurelius Scaurus, though he spoke in public but seldom, always spoke very neatly, and he had a more elegant command of the Roman language than most men. A. Albinus was a speaker of the same kind; but Albinus, the Flamen, was esteemed an *orator*. Q. Capio too had a great deal of spirit, and was a brave citizen: but the unlucky chance of war was imputed to him as a crime, and the general odium of the people proved his ruin. C. and L. Memmius were likewise indifferent orators, and distinguished by the bitterness and asperity of their accusations: for they prosecuted many, but seldom spoke for the defendant. Sp. Torius, on the other hand, was distinguished by his *popular* way of speaking; the very same man, who, by his corrupt and frivolous law, diminished [Footnote: By dividing great part of them among the people.] the taxes which were levied on the public lands. M. Marcellus, the father of Aeserninus, though not reckoned a professed pleader, was a prompt, and, in some degree, a practised speaker; as was also his son P. Lentulus. L. Cotta likewise, a man of Praetorian rank, was esteemed a tolerable orator; but he never made any great progress; on the contrary, he purposely endeavoured, both in the choice of his words, and the rusticity of his pronunciation, to imitate the manner of the ancients. I am indeed sensible that in this instance of Cotta, and in many others, I have, and shall again insert in the list of Orators, those who, in reality, had but little claim to the character. For it was, professedly, my design, to collect an account of all the Romans, without exception, who made it their business to excel in the profession of *Eloquence*: and it may be easily seen from this account, by what slow gradations they advanced, and how excessively difficult it is, in every thing, to rise to the summit of perfection. As a proof of this, how many orators have been already recounted, and how much time have we bestowed upon them, before we could force our way, after infinite fatigue and drudgery, as, among the Greek's, to *Demosthenes* and *Hyperides*, so now, among our own countrymen, to *Antonius* and *Crassus*! For, in my mind, these were consummate Orators, and the first among the Romans whose diffusive Eloquence rivalled the glory of the Greeks. Antonius discovered every thing which could be of service to his cause, and that in the very order in which it would be most so: and as a skilful General posts the cavalry, the infantry, and the light troops, where each of them can act to most advantage; so Antonius drew up his arguments in those parts of his discourse, where they were likely to have the best effect. He had a quick and retentive memory, and a frankness of manner which precluded any suspicion of artifice. All his speeches were, in appearance, the unpremeditated effusions of an honest heart; and yet, in reality, they were preconcerted with so much skill, that the judges were, sometimes, not so well prepared, as they should have been, to withstand the force of them. His language, indeed, was not so refined as to pass for the standard of elegance; for which reason he was thought to be rather a careless speaker; and yet, on the other hand, it was neither vulgar nor incorrect, but of that solid and judicious turn, which constitutes the real merit of an Orator, as to the choice of his words. For, as to a purity of style, though this is certainly (as before observed) a very commendable quality, it is not so much so for its intrinsic consequence, as because it is too generally neglected. In short, it is not so meritorious to speak our native tongue correctly, as it is scandalous to speak it otherwise; nor is it so much the property of a good Orator, as of a well-bred Citizen. But in the choice of his words (in which he had more regard to their weight than their brilliance) and likewise in the structure of his language, and the compass of his periods, Antonius conformed himself to the dictates of reason, and, in a great measure, to the nicer rules of art: though his chief excellence was a judicious management of the figures and decorations of sentiment. This was likewise the distinguishing excellence of Demosthenes; in which he was so far superior to all others, as to be allowed, in the opinion of the best judges, to be the Prince of Orators. For the *figures* (as they are called by the Greeks) are the principal ornaments of an able speaker, I mean those which contribute not so much to paint and embellish our language, as to give a lustre to our sentiments. But besides these, of which Antonius had a great command, he had a peculiar excellence in his manner of delivery, both as to his voice and gesture; for the latter was such as to correspond to the meaning of every sentence, without beating time to the words. His hands, his shoulders, the turn of his body, the stamp of his foot, his posture, his air, and, in short, his every motion, was adapted to his language and sentiments: and his voice was strong and firm, though naturally hoarse;—a defect which he alone was capable of improving to his advantage; for in capital causes, it had a mournful dignity of accent, which was exceedingly proper, both to win the assent of the judges, and excite their compassion for a suffering client: so that in *him* the observation of Demosthenes was eminently verified, who being asked what was the *first* quality of a good

Orator, what the *second*, and what the *third*, constantly replied, A good enunciation.

"But many thought that he was equalled, and others that he was even excelled by Lucius Crassus. All, however, were agreed in this, that whoever had either of them for his advocate, had no cause to wish for a better. For my own part, notwithstanding the uncommon merit I have ascribed to Antonius, I must also acknowlege, that there cannot be a more finished character than that of Crassus. He possessed a wonderful dignity of elocution, with an agreeable mixture of wit and pleasantry, which was perfectly genteel, and without the smallest tincture of scurrility. His style was correct and elegant without stiffness or affectation: his method of reasoning was remarkably clear and distinct: and when his cause turned upon any point of law, or equity, he had an inexhaustible fund of arguments, and comparative illustrations. For as Antonius had an admirable turn for suggesting apposite hints, and either suppressing or exciting the suspicions of the hearer; so no man could explain and define, or discuss a point of equity, with a more copious facility than Crassus; as sufficiently appeared upon many other occasions, but particularly in the cause of M. Curius, which was tried before the Centum Viri. For he urged a great variety of arguments in the defence of right and equity, against the literal *jubeat* of the law; and supported them by such a numerous series of precedents, that he overpowered Q. Scaevola (a man of uncommon penetration, and the ablest Civilian of his time) though the case before them was only a matter of legal right. But the cause was so ably managed by the two advocates, who were nearly of an age, and both of consular rank, that while each endeavoured to interpret the law in favour of his client, Crassus was universally allowed to be the best Lawyer among the Orators, and Scaevola to be the most eloquent Civilian of the age: for the latter could not only discover with the nicest precision what was agreeable to law and equity; but had likewise a conciseness and propriety of expression, which was admirably adapted to his purpose. In short, he had such a wonderful vein of oratory in commenting, explaining, and discussing, that I never beheld his equal; though in amplifying, embellishing, and refuting, he was rather to be dreaded as a formidable critic, than admired as an eloquent speaker."—"Indeed," said Brutus, "though I always thought I sufficiently understood the character of Scaevola, by the account I had heard of him from C. Rutilius, whose company I frequented for the sake of his acquaintance with him, I had not the least idea of his merit as an orator. I am now, therefore, not a little pleased to be informed, that our Republic has had the honour of producing so accomplished a man, and such an excellent genius."—"Really, my Brutus," said I, "you may take it from me, that the Roman State had never been adorned with two finer characters than these. For, as I have before observed, that the one was the best Lawyer among the Orators, and the other the best Speaker among the Civilians of his time; so the difference between them, in all other respects, was of such a nature, that it would almost be impossible for you to determine which of the two you would rather choose to resemble. For, as Crassus was the closest of all our elegant speakers, so Scaevola was the most elegant among those who were distinguished by the frugal accuracy of their language: and as Crassus tempered his affability with a proper share of severity, so the rigid air of Scaevola was not destitute of the milder graces of an affable condescension. Though this was really their character, it is very possible that I may be thought to have embellished it beyond the bounds of truth, to give an agreeable air to my narrative: but as your favourite sect, my Brutus, the Old Academy, has defined all Virtue to be a just Mediocrity, it was the constant endeavour of these two eminent men to pursue this Golden Mean; and yet it so happened, that while each of them shared a part of the other's excellence, he preserved his own entire."—"To speak what I think," replied Brutus, "I have not only acquired a proper acquaintance with their characters from your account of them, but I can likewise discover, that the same comparison might be drawn between *you* and Serv. Sulpicius, which you have just been making between Crassus and Scaevola." —"In what manner?" said I. —"Because *you*," replied Brutus, "have taken the pains to acquire as extensive a knowledge of the law as is necessary for an Orator; and Sulpicius, on the other hand, took care to furnish himself with sufficient eloquence to support the character of an able Civilian. Besides, your age corresponded as nearly to his, as the age of Crassus did to that of Scaevola."—"As to my own abilities," said I, "the rules of decency forbid me to speak of them: but your character of Servius is a very just one, and I may freely tell you what I think of him. There are few, I believe, who have applied themselves more assiduously to the art of Speaking than he did, or indeed to the study of every useful science. In our youth, we both of us followed the same liberal exercises; and he afterwards accompanied me to Rhodes, to pursue those studies which might equally improve him as a Man and a Scholar; but when he returned from thence, he appears to me to have been rather ambitious to be the foremost man in a secondary profession, than the second in that which claims the highest dignity. I will not pretend to say that he could not have ranked himself among the foremost in the latter profession; but he rather chose to be, what he actually made himself, the first Lawyer of his time."—"Indeed!" said Brutus: "and do you really prefer Servius to Q. Scaevola?"—"My opinion," said I, "Brutus, is, that Q. Scaevola, and many others, had a thorough practical knowledge of the law; but that Servius alone understood it as *science*: which he could never have done by the mere study of the law, and without a previous acquaintance with the art which teaches us to divide a whole into its subordinate parts, to, decide an indeterminate idea by an accurate definition: to explain what is obscure, by a clear interpretation; and first to discover what things are of a *doubtful* nature, then to distinguish them by their different degrees of probability; and lastly, to be provided with a certain rule or measure by which we may judge what is true, and what false, and what inferences fairly may, or may not be deduced from any given premises. This important art he applied to those subjects which, for want of it, were necessarily managed by others without due order and precision."—"You mean, I suppose," said Brutus, "the Art of Logic."—"You suppose very right," answered I: "but he added to it an extensive acquaintance with polite literature, and an elegant manner of expressing himself; as is sufficiently evident from the incomparable writings he has left behind him. And as he attached himself, for the improvement of his eloquence, to L. Lucilius Balbus, and C. Aquilius Gallus, two very able speakers; he effectually thwarted the prompt celerity of the latter (though a keen, experienced man) both in supporting and refuting a charge, by his accuracy and precision, and overpowered the deliberate formality of Balbus (a man of great learning and erudition) by his adroit and dextrous method of arguing: so that he equally possessed the good qualities of both, without their defects. As Crassus, therefore, in my mind, acted more prudently than Scaevola; (for the latter was very fond of pleading causes, in which he was certainly inferior to Crassus; whereas the former never engaged himself in an unequal competition with Scaevola, by assuming the character of a Civilian;) so Servius pursued a plan which sufficiently discovered his wisdom; for as the profession of a Pleader, and a Lawyer, are both of them held in great esteem, and give those who are masters of them the most extensive influence among their fellow-citizens; he acquired an undisputed superiority in the one, and improved himself as much in the other as was necessary to support the authority of the Civil Law, and promote him to the dignity of a Consul."—"This is precisely the opinion I had formed of him," said Brutus. "For, a few years ago I heard him often and very attentively at Samos, when I wanted to be instructed by him in the Pontifical Law, as far as it is connected with the Civil; and I am now greatly confirmed in my opinion of him, by finding that it coincides so exactly with yours. I am likewise not a little pleased to observe, that the equality of your ages, your sharing the same honours and preferments, and the vicinity of your respective studies and professions, has been so far from precipitating either of you into that envious detraction of the other's merit, which most people are tormented with, that, instead of wounding your mutual friendship, it has only served to increase and strengthen it; for, to my own knowlege, he had the same affection for, and the same favourable sentiments of *you*, which I now discover in you towards *him*. I cannot, therefore, help regretting very sincerely, that the Roman State has so long been deprived of the benefit of his advice, and of your Eloquence;—a circumstance which is indeed calamitous enough in itself; but must appear much more so to him who considers into what hands that once respectable authority has been of late, I will not say transferred, but forcibly wrested."—"You certainly forget," said Atticus, "that I proposed, when we began the conversation, to drop all matters of State; by all means, therefore, let us keep to our plan: for if we once begin to repeat our grievances, there will be no end, I need not say to our inquiries, but to our sighs and lamentations."—"Let us proceed, then," said I, "without any farther digression, and pursue the plan we set out upon. Crassus (for he is the Orator we were just speaking of) always came into the Forum ready prepared for the combat. He was expected with impatience, and heard with pleasure. When he first began his Oration (which he always did in a very accurate style) he seemed worthy of the great expectations he had raised. He was very moderate in the sway of his body, had no remarkable variation of voice, never advanced from the ground he stood upon, and seldom stamped his foot: his language was forcible, and sometimes warm and pathetic; he had many strokes of humour, which were always tempered with a becoming dignity; and, what is a difficult character to hit, he was at once very florid, and very concise. In a close contest, he never met with his equal; and there was scarcely any kind of causes, in which he had not signalized his abilities; so that he enrolled himself very early among the first Orators of the time. He accused C. Carbo, though a man of great

Eloquence, when he was but a youth;—and displayed his talents in such a manner, that they were not only applauded, but admired by every body. He afterwards defended the Virgin Licinia, when he was only twenty-seven years of age; on which occasion he discovered an uncommon share of Eloquence, as is evident from those parts of his Oration which he left behind him in writing. As he was then desirous to have the honour of settling the colony of Narbonne (as he afterwards did) he thought it adviseable to recommend himself, by undertaking the management of some popular cause. His Oration, in support of the act which was proposed for that purpose, is still extant; and discovers a greater maturity of genius than might have been expected at that time of life. He afterwards pleaded many other causes: but his tribuneship was such a remarkably silent one, that if he had not supped with Granius the beadle when he enjoyed that office (a circumstance which has been twice mentioned by Lucilius) we should scarcely have known that a tribune of that name had existed."—"I believe so," replied Brutus: "but I have heard as little of the tribuneship of Scaevola, though I must naturally suppose that he was the colleague of Crassus."—"He was so," said I, "in all his other preferments; but he was not tribune till the year after him; and when he sat in the Rostrum in that capacity, Crassus spoke in support of the Servilian law. I must observe, however, that Crassus had not Scaevola for his colleague in the censorship; for none of the Scaevolas ever sued for that office. But when the last-mentioned Oration of Crassus was published (which I dare say you have frequently read) he was thirty-four years of age, which was exactly the difference between his age and mine. For he supported the law I have just been speaking of, in the very consulship under which I was born; whereas he himself was born in the consulship of Q. Caepio, and C. Laelius, about three years later than Antonius. I have particularly noticed this circumstance, to specify the time when the Roman Eloquence attained its first *maturity*; and was actually carried to such a degree of perfection, as to leave no room for any one to carry it higher, unless by the assistance of a more complete and extensive knowledge of philosophy, jurisprudence, and history."—"But does there," said Brutus, "or will there ever exist a man, who is furnished with all the united accomplishments you require?"—"I really don't know," said I; "but we have a speech made by Crassus in his consulship, in praise of Q. Caepio, intermingled with a defence of his conduct, which, though a short one if we consider it as an Oration, is not so as a Panegyric;—and another, which was his last, and which he spoke in the 48th year of his age, at the time he was censor. In these we have the genuine complexion of Eloquence, without any painting or disguise: but his periods (I mean Crassus's) were generally short and concise; and he was fond of expressing himself in those minuter sentences, or members, which the Greeks call Colons."—"As you have spoken so largely," said Brutus, "in praise of the two last-mentioned Orators, I heartily wish that Antonius had left us some other specimen of his abilities, than his trifling Essay on the Art of Speaking, and Crassus more than he has: by so doing, they would have transmitted their fame to *posterity*; and to us a valuable system of Eloquence. For as to the elegant language of Scaevola, we have sufficient proofs of it in the Orations he has left behind him."—"For my part," said I, "the Oration I was speaking of, on Caepio's case, has been my pattern, and my tutoress, from my very childhood. It supports the dignity of the Senate, which was deeply interested in the debate; and excites the jealousy of the audience against the party of the judges and accusers, whose power it was necessary to expose in the most popular terms. Many parts of it are very strong and nervous, many others very cool and composed; and some are distinguished by the asperity of their language, and not a few by their wit and pleasantry: but much more was said than was committed to writing, as is sufficiently evident from several heads of the Oration, which are merely proposed without any enlargement or explanation. But the oration in his censorship against his colleague Cn. Domitius, is not so much an Oration, as an analysis of the subject, or a general sketch of what he had said, with here and there a few ornamental touches, by way of specimen: for no contest was ever conducted with greater spirit than this. Crassus, however, was eminently distinguished by the popular turn of his language: but that of Antonius was better adapted to judicial trials, than to a public debate. As we have had occasion to mention him, Domitius himself must not be left unnoticed: for though he is not enrolled in the list of Orators, he had a sufficient share both of utterance and genius, to support his character as a magistrate and his dignity as a consul. I might likewise observe of C. Caelius, that he was a man of great application, and many eminent qualities, and had eloquence enough to support the private interests of his friends, and his own dignity in the State. At the same time lived M. Herennius, who was reckoned among the middling Orators, whose principal merit was the purity and correctness of their language; and yet, in a suit for the consulship, he got the better of L. Philippus, a man of the first rank and family, and of the most extensive connections, and who was likewise a member of the College, and a very eloquent speaker. *Then* also lived C. Clodius, who, besides his consequence as a nobleman of the first distinction, and a man of the most powerful influence, was likewise possessed of a moderate share of Eloquence. Nearly of the same age was C. Titius, a Roman knight, who, in my judgment, arrived at as high a degree of perfection as a Roman orator was able to do, without the assistance of the Grecian literature, and a good share of practice. His Orations have so many delicate turns, such a number of well-chosen examples, and such an agreeable vein of politeness, that they almost seem to have been composed in the true Attic style. He likewise transferred his delicacies into his very Tragedies, with ingenuity enough, I confess, but not in the tragic taste. But the poet L. Afranius, whom he studiously imitated, was a very smart writer, and, as you well know, a man of great expression in the dramatic way. Q. Rubrius Varro, who with C. Marius, was declared an enemy by the Senate, was likewise a warm, and a very spirited prosecutor. My relation, M. Gratidius, was a plausible speaker of the same kind, well versed in the Grecian literature, formed by nature for the profession of Eloquence, and an intimate acquaintance of M. Antonius: he commanded under him in Cilicia, where he lost his life: and he once commenced a prosecution against C. Fimbria, the father of M. Marius Gratidianus. There have likewise been several among the Allies, and the Latins, who were esteemed good Orators; as, for instance, Q. Vettius of Vettium, one of the Marsi, whom I myself was acquainted with, a man of sense, and a concise speaker; —the Q. and D. Valerii of Sora, my neighbours and acquaintances, who were not so remarkable for their talent of speaking, as for their skill both in the Greek and Roman literature; and C. Rusticellus of Bononia, an experienced Orator, and a man of great natural volubility. But the most eloquent of all those who were not citizens of Rome, was T. Betucius Barrus of Asculum, some of whose Orations, which were spoken in that city, are still extant: that which he made at Rome against Caepio, is really an excellent one: the speech which Caepio delivered in answer to it, was made by Aelius, who composed a number of Orations, but pronounced none himself. But among those of a remoter date, L. Papirius of Fregellae in Latium, who was almost cotemporary with Ti. Gracchus, was universally esteemed the most eloquent: we have a speech of his in vindication of the Fregellani, and the Latin Colonies, which was delivered before the Senate."—"And what then is the merit," said Brutus, "which you mean to ascribe to these provincial Orators?"—"What else," replied I, "but the very same which I have ascribed to the city-orators; excepting that their language is not tinctured with the same fashionable delicacy?"—"What fashionable delicacy do you mean?" said he.—"I cannot," said I, "pretend to define it: I only know that there is such a quality existing. When you go to your province in Gaul, you will be convinced of it. You will there find many expressions which are not current in Rome; but these may be easily changed, and corrected. But, what is of greater importance, our Orators have a particular accent in their manner of pronouncing, which is more elegant, and has a more agreeable effect than any other. This, however, is not peculiar to the Orators, but is equally common to every well-bred citizen. I myself remember that T. Tineas, of Placentia, who was a very facetious man, once engaged in a repartee skirmish with my old friend Q. Granius, the public crier."—"Do you mean that Granius," said Brutus, "of whom Lucilius has related such a number of stories?"—"The very same," said I: "but though Tineas said as many smart things as the other, Granius at last overpowered him by a certain vernacular *goût*, which gave an additional relish to his humour: so that I am no longer surprised at what is said to have happened to Theophrastus, when he enquired of an old woman who kept a stall, what was the price of something which he wanted to purchase. After telling him the value of it,—"Honest *stranger*," said she, "I cannot afford it for less": "an answer which nettled him not a little, to think that *he* who had resided almost all his life at Athens, and spoke the language very correctly, should be taken at last for a foreigner. In the same manner, there is, in my opinion, a certain accent as peculiar to the native citizens of Rome, as the other was to those of Athens. But it is time for us to return home; I mean to the Orators of our own growth. Next, therefore, to the two capital Speakers above-mentioned, (that is Crassus and Antonius) came L. Philippus,—not indeed till a considerable time afterwards; but still he must be reckoned the next. I do not mean, however, though nobody appeared in the interim who could dispute the prize with him, that he was entitled to the second, or even the third post of honour. For, as in a Chariot-race I cannot properly consider *him* as either the second, or third winner, who has scarcely got clear of the starting-post, before the first has reached the goal; so, among Orators, I can scarcely honour him with the name of a competitor, who has been so far distanced by the foremost as hardly to appear on the same ground with him. But yet there were certainly some talents to be observed in Philippus, which any person who considers them, without subjecting them to a comparison with the superior merits of the two before-mentioned, must allow to have been respectable. He had an uncommon freedom of address, a large fund of humour, great facility in the invention of his sentiments, and a ready and easy manner of expressing them. He was likewise, for the time he lived in, a great adept in the literature of the Greeks; and, in the heat of a debate, he could sting, and gash, as well as ridicule his opponents. Almost cotemporary with these was L. Gellius, who was not so much to be valued for his positive, as for his negative merits: for he was neither destitute of learning, nor invention, nor unacquainted with the history and the laws of his country; besides which, he had a tolerable freedom of expression. But he happened to live at a time when many excellent Orators made their appearance; and yet he served his friends upon many occasions to good purpose: in short, his life was so long, that he was successively cotemporary with a variety of Orators of different dates, and had an extensive series of practice in judicial causes. Nearly at the same time lived D. Brutus, who was fellow-consul with Mamercus;— and was equally skilled both in the Grecian and Roman literature. L. Scipio likewise was not an unskilful Speaker; and Cnaeus Pompeius, the son of Sextus, had some reputation as an Orator; for his brother Sextus applied the excellent genius he was possessed of, to acquire a thorough knowledge of the Civil Law, and a complete acquaintance with geometry and the doctrine of the Stoics. A little before these, M. Brutus, and very soon after him, C. Bilienus, who was a man of great natural capacity, made themselves, by nearly the same application, equally eminent in the profession of the law;—the latter would have been chosen Consul, if he had not been thwarted by the repeated promotion of Marius, and some other collateral embarrassments which attended his suit. But the eloquence of Cn. Octavius, which was wholly unknown before his elevation to the Consulship, was effectually displayed, after his preferment to that office, in a great variety of speeches. It is, however, time for us to drop those who were only classed in the number of good *speakers*, and turn our attention to such as were really *Orators*."—"I think so too," replied Atticus; "for I understood that you meant to give us an account, not of those who took great pains to be eloquent, but of those who were so in reality."—"C. Julius then," said I, (the son of Lucius) was certainly superior, not only to his predecessors, but to all his cotemporaries, in wit and humour: he was not, indeed, a nervous and striking Orator, but, in the elegance, the pleasantry, and the agreeableness of his manner, he has not been excelled by any man. There are some Orations of his still extant, in which, as well as in his Tragedies, we may discover a pleasing tranquillity of expression with very little energy. P. Cethegus, his cotemporary, had always enough to say on matters of civil regulation; for he had studied and comprehended them with the minutest accuracy; by which means he acquired an equal authority in the Senate with those who had served the office of consul, and though he made no figure in a public debate, he was a serviceable veteran in any suit of a private nature. Q. Lucretius Vispillo was an acute Speaker, and a good Civilian in the same kind of causes: but Osella was better qualified for a public harangue, than to conduct a judicial process. T. Annius Velina was likewise a man of sense, and a tolerable pleader; and T. Juventius had a great deal of practice in the same way:—the latter indeed was rather too heavy and unanimated, but at the same time he was keen and artful, and knew how to seize every advantage which was offered by his antagonist; to which we may add, that he was far from being a man of no literature, and had an extensive knowledge of the Civil Law. His scholar, P. Orbius, who was almost cotemporary with me, had no great practice as a pleader; but his skill in the Civil Law was nothing inferior to his master's. As to Titus Aufidius, who lived to a great age, he was a professed imitator of both; and was indeed a worthy inoffensive man, but seldom spoke at the bar. His brother, M. Virgilius, who when he was a tribune of the people, commenced a prosecution against L. Sylla, then advanced to the rank of General, had as little practice as Aufidius. Virgilius's colleague, P. Magius, was more copious and diffusive. But of all the Orators, or rather *Ranters*, I ever knew, who were totally illiterate and unpolished, and (I might have added) absolutely coarse and rustic, the readiest and keenest, were Q. Sertorius, and C. Gorgonius, the one of consular, and the other of equestrian rank. T. Junius (the son of L.) who had served the office of tribune, and prosecuted and convicted P. Sextius of bribery, when he was praetor elect, was a prompt and an easy speaker: he lived in great splendor, and had a very promising genius; and, if he had not been of a weak, and indeed a sickly constitution, he would have advanced much farther than he did in the road to preferment. I am sensible, however, that in the account I have been giving, I have included many who were neither real, nor reputed Orators; and that I have omitted others, among those of a remoter date, who well deserved not only to have been mentioned, but to be recorded with honour. But this I was forced to do, for want of better information: for what could I say concerning men of a distant age, none of whose productions are now remaining, and of whom no mention is made in the writings of other people? But I have omitted none of those who have fallen within the compass of my own knowledge, or that I myself remember to have heard. For I wish to make it appear, that in such a powerful and ancient republic as ours, in which the greatest rewards have been proposed to Eloquence, though all have desired to be good speakers, not many have attempted the talk, and but very few have succeeded. But I shall give my opinion of every one in such explicit terms, that it may be easily understood whom I consider as a mere Declaimer, and whom as an Orator."

"About the same time, or rather something later than the above-mentioned Julius, but almost cotemporary with each other, were C. Cotta, P. Sulpicius, Q. Varius, Cn. Pomponius, C. Curio, L. Fufius, M. Drusus, and P. Antistius; for no age whatsoever has been distingushed by a more numerous progeny of Orators. Of these, Cotta and Sulpicius, both in my opinion, and in that of the Public at large, had an evident claim to the preference."—"But wherefore," interrupted Atticus, "do you say, *in your own opinion, and in that of the Public at large?* In deciding the merits of an Orator, does the opinion of the vulgar, think you, always coincide with that of the learned? Or rather does not one receive the approbation of the populace, while another of a quite opposite character is preferred by those who are better qualified to give their judgment?"—"You have started a very pertinent question," said I; "but, perhaps, *the Public at large* will not approve my answer to it."—"And what concern need *that* give you," replied Atticus, "if it meets the approbation of Brutus?"— "Very true," said I; "for I had rather my *sentiments* on the qualifications of an Orator would please you and Brutus, than all the world besides: but as to my *Eloquence*, I should wish *this* to please every one. For he who speaks in such a manner as to please the people, must inevitably receive the approbation of the learned. As to the truth and propriety of what I hear, I am indeed to judge of this for myself, as well as I am able: but the general merit of an Orator must and will be decided by the effects which his eloquence produces. For (in my opinion at least) there are three things which an Orator should be able to effect; *viz.* to *inform* his hearers, to *please* them, and to *move their passions*. By what qualities in the Speaker each of these, effects may be produced, or by what deficiencies they are either lost, or but imperfectly performed, is an enquiry which none but an artist can resolve: but whether an audience is really so affected by an Orator as shall best answer his purpose, must be left to their own feelings, and the decision of the Public. The learned, therefore, and the people at large, have never disagreed about who was a good Orator, and who was otherwise. For do you suppose, that while the Speakers above-mentioned were in being, they had not the same degree of reputation among the learned as among the populace? If you had enquired of one of the latter, *who was the most eloquent man in the city*, he might have hesitated whether to say *Antonius* or *Crassus*; or this man, perhaps, would have mentioned the one, and that the other. But would any one have given the preference to *Philippus*, though otherwise a smooth, a sensible, and a facetious Speaker? —that *Philippus* whom we, who form our judgment upon these matters by rules of art, have decided to have been the next in merit? Nobody would, I am certain. For it is the invariable, property of an accomplished Orator, to be reckoned such in the opinion of the people. Though Antigenidas, therefore, the musician, might say to his scholar, who was but coldly received by the Public, Play on, to please me and the Muses;—I shall say to my friend Brutus, when he mounts the Rostra, as he frequently does,— Play to me and the people;—that those who hear him may be sensible of the effect of his Eloquence, while I can likewise amuse myself with remarking the causes which produce it. When a Citizen hears an able Orator, he readily credits what is said;—he imagines every thing to be true, he believes and relishes the force of it; and, in short, the persuasive language of the Speaker wins his absolute, his hearty assent. You, who are possessed of a critical knowledge of the art, what more will you require? The listening multitude is charmed and captivated by the force of his Eloquence, and feels a pleasure which is not to be resisted. What here can you find to censure? The whole audience is either flushed with joy, or overwhelmed with grief;—it smiles, or weeps,—it loves, or hates,—it scorns or envies,—and, in short, is alternately seized with the various emotions of pity, shame, remorse, resentment, wonder, hope, and fear, according as it is influenced by the language, the sentiments, and the action of the speaker. In this case, what necessity is there to await the sanction of a critic? For here, whatever is approved by the feelings of the people, must be equally so by men of taste and erudition: and, in this instance of public decision, there can be no disagreement between the opinion of the vulgar, and that of the learned. For though many good Speakers have appeared in every species of Oratory, which of them who was thought to excel the rest in the judgment of the populace, was not approved as such by every man of learning? or which of our ancestors, when the choice of a pleader was left to his own option, did not immediately fix it either upon Crassus or Antonius? There were certainly many others to be had: but though any person might have hesitated to which of the above two he should give the preference, there was nobody, I believe, who would have made choice of a third. And in the time of my youth, when Cotta and Hortensius were in such high reputation, who, that had liberty to choose for himself, would have employed any other?"—"But what occasion is there," said Brutus, "to quote the example of other speakers to support your assertion? have we not seen what has always been the wish of the defendant, and what the judgment of Hortensius, concerning yourself? for whenever the latter shared a cause with you, (and I was often present on those occasions) the peroration, which requires the greatest exertion of the powers of Eloquence, was constantly left to *you*."—"It was," said I; "and Hortensius (induced, I suppose, by the warmth of his friendship) always resigned the post of honour to me. But, as to myself, what rank I hold in the opinion of the people I am unable to determine: as to others, however, I may safely assert, that such of them as were reckoned most eloquent in the judgment of the vulgar, were equally high in the estimation of the learned. For even Demosthenes himself could not have said what is related of Antimachus, a poet of Claros, who, when he was rehearsing to an audience assembled for the purpose, that voluminous piece of his which you are well acquainted with, and was deserted by all his hearers except Plato, in the midst of his performance, cried out, "I shall proceed notwithstanding_; for Plato alone is of *more consequence to me than many thousands*." "The remark was very just. For an abstruse poem, such as his, only requires the approbation of the judicious few; but a discourse intended for the people should be perfectly suited to their taste. If Demosthenes, therefore, after being deserted by the rest of his audience, had even Plato left to hear him, and no one else, I will answer for it, he could not have uttered another syllable. 'Nay, or could you yourself, my Brutus, if the whole assembly was to leave you, as it once did Curio?"—"To open my whole mind to you," replied he, "I must confess that even in such causes as fall under the cognizance of a few select judges, and not of the people at large, if I was to be deserted by the casual crowd who came to hear the trial, I should not be able to proceed."—"The case, then, is plainly this," said I: "as a flute, which will not return its proper sound when it is applied to the lips, would be laid aside by the musician as useless; so, the ears of the people are the instrument upon which an Orator is to play: and if these refuse to admit the breath he bestows upon them, or if the hearer, like a restive horse, will not obey the spur, the speaker must cease to exert himself any farther. There is, however, the exception to be made; the people sometimes give their approbation to an orator who does not deserve it. But even here they approve what they have had no opportunity of comparing with something better: as, for instance, when they are pleased with an indifferent, or, perhaps, a bad speaker. His abilities satisfy their expectation: they have seen nothing preferable: and, therefore, the merit of the day, whatever it may happen to be, meets their full applause. For even a middling Orator, if he is possessed of any degree of Eloquence, will always captivate the ear; and the order and beauty of a good discourse has an astonishing effect upon the human mind. Accordingly, what common hearer who was present when Q. Scaevola pleaded for M. Coponius, in the cause above- mentioned, would have wished for, or indeed thought it possible to find any thing which was more correct, more elegant, or more complete? When he attempted to prove, that, as M. Curius was left heir to the estate only in case of the death of his future ward before he came of age, he could not possibly be a legal heir, when the expected ward was never born;—what did he leave unsaid of the scrupulous regard which should be paid to the literal meaning of every testament? what of the accuracy and preciseness of the old and established forms; of law? and how carefully did he specify the manner in which the will would have been expressed, if it had intended that Curius should be the heir in case of a total default of issue? in what a masterly manner did he represent the ill consequences to the Public, if the letter of a will should be disregarded, its intention decided by arbitrary conjectures, and the written bequests of plain illiterate men, left to the artful interpretation of a pleader? how often did he urge the authority of his father, who had always been an advocate for a strict adherence to the letter of a testament? and with what emphasis did he enlarge upon the necessity of supporting the common forms of law? All which particulars he discussed not only very artfully, and skilfully; but in such a neat,—such a close,—and, I may add, in so florid, and so elegant a style, that there was not a single person among the common part of the audience, who could expect any thing more complete, or even think it possible to exist. But when Crassus, who spoke on the opposite side, began with the story of a notable youth, who having found a cock-boat as he was rambling along the shore, took it into his head immediately that he would build a ship to it;—and when he applied the tale to Scaevola, who, from the cock-boat of an argument [which he had deduced from certain imaginary ill consequences to the Public] represented the decision of a private will to be a matter of such importance as to deserve he attention of the *Centum-viri*;—when Crassus, I say, in the beginning of his discourse, had thus taken off the edge of the strongest plea of his antagonist, he entertained his hearers with many other turns of a similar kind; and, in a short time, changed the serious apprehensions of all who were present into open mirth and good-humour; which is one of those three effects which I have just observed an Orator should be able to produce. He then proceeded to remark that it was evidently the intention and the will of the testator, that in cafe, either by death, or default of issue, there should happen to be no son to fall to his charge, the inheritance should devolve to Curius:—'that most people in a similar case would express themselves in the same manner, and that it would certainly stand good in law, and always had. By these, and many other observations of the same kind, he gained the assent of his hearers; which is another of the three duties of an Orator. Lastly, he supported, at all events, the true meaning and spirit of a will, against the literal construction: justly observing, that there would be an endless cavilling about words, not only in wills, but in all other legal deeds, if the real intention of the party was to be disregarded: and hinting very smartly, that his friend Scaevola had assumed a most unwarrantable degree of importance, if no person must afterwards presume to indite a legacy, but in the musty form which he himself might please to prescribe. As he enlarged on each of these arguments with great force and propriety, supported them by a number of precedents, exhibited them in a variety of views, and enlivened them with many occasional turns of wit and pleasantry, he gained so much applause, and gave such general satisfaction, that it was scarcely remembered that any thing had been said on the contrary side of the question. This was the third, and the most important duty we assigned to an Orator.

"Here, if one of the people was to be judge, the same person who had heard the first Speaker with a degree of admiration, would, on hearing the second, despise himself for his former want of judgment:—whereas a man of taste and erudition, on hearing Scaevola, would have observed that he was really master of a rich and ornamental style; but if, on comparing the manner in which each of them concluded his cause, it was to be enquired which of the two was the best Orator, the decision of the man of learning would not have differed from that of the vulgar. What advantage, then, it will be said, has the skilful critic over the illiterate hearer? A great and very important advantage; if it is indeed a matter of any consequence, to be able to discover by what means that which is the true and real end of speaking, is either obtained or lost. He has likewise this additional superiority, that when two or more Orators, as has frequently happened, have shared the applauses of the Public, he can judge, on a careful observation of the principal merits of each, what is the most perfect character of Eloquence: since whatever does not meet the approbation of the people, must be equally condemned by a more intelligent hearer. For as it is easily understood by the sound of a harp, whether the strings are skilfully touched; so it may likewise be discovered from the manner in which the passions of an audience are affected, how far the Speaker is able to command them. A man, therefore, who is a real connoisseur in the art, can sometimes by a single glance as he passes through the Forum, and without stopping to listen attentively to what is said, form a tolerable judgment of the ability of the Speaker. When he observes any of the Bench either yawning, or speaking to the person who is next to him, or looking carelessly about him, or sending to enquire the time of day, or teazing the Quaestor to dismiss the court; he concludes very naturally that the cause upon trial is not pleaded by an Orator who understands how to apply the powers of language to the passions of the judges, as a skilful musician applies his fingers to the harp. On the other hand, if, as he passes by, he beholds the judges looking attentively before them, as if they were either receiving some material information, or visibly approved what they had already heard—if he sees them listening to the voice of the Pleader with a kind of extasy like a fond bird to some melodious tune;— and, above all, if he discovers in their looks any strong indications of pity, abhorrence, or any other emotion of the mind;—though he should not be near enough to hear a single word, he immediately discovers that the cause is managed by a real Orator, who is either performing, or has already played his part to good purpose."

After I had concluded these digressive remarks, my two friends were kind enough to signify their approbation, and I resumed my subject.—"As this digression," said I, "took its rise from Cotta and Sulpicius, whom I mentioned as the two most approved Orators of the age they lived in, I shall first return to *them,* and afterwards notice the rest in their proper order, according to the plan we began upon. I have already observed that there are two classes of *good* Orators (for we have no concern with any others) of which the former are distinguished by the simple neatness and brevity of their language, and the latter by their copious dignity and elevation: but although the preference must always be given to that which is great and striking; yet, in speakers of real merit, whatever is most perfect of the kind, is justly entitled to our commendation. It must, however, be observed, that the close and simple Orator should be careful not to sink into a driness and poverty of expression; while, on the other hand, the copious and more stately Speaker should be equally on his guard against a swelling and empty parade of words.

"To begin with Cotta, he had a ready, quick Invention, and spoke correctly and freely; and as he very prudently avoided every forcible exertion of his voice on account of the weakness of his lungs, so his language was equally adapted to the delicacy of his constitution. There was nothing in his style but what was neat, compact, and healthy; and (what may justly be considered as his greatest excellence) though he was scarcely able, and therefore never attempted to force the passions of the judges by a strong and spirited elocution, yet he managed them so artfully, that the gentle emotions he raised in them, answered exactly the same purpose, and produced the same effect, as the violent ones which were excited by Sulpicius. For Sulpicius was really the most striking, and, if I may be allowed the expression, the most tragical Orator I ever heard:—his voice was strong and sonorous, and yet sweet, and flowing:—his gesture, and the sway of his body, was graceful and ornamental, but in such a style as to appear to have been formed for the Forum, and not for the stage:—and his language, though rapid and voluble, was neither loose nor exuberant. He was a professed imitator of Crassus, while Cotta chose Antonius for his model: but the latter wanted the force of Antonius, and the former the agreeable humour of Crassus."—"How extremely difficult, then," said Brutus, "must be the art of speaking, when such consummate Orators as these were each of them destitute of one of its principal beauties!"—"We may likewise observe," said I, "in the present instance, that two Orators may have the highest degree of merit, who are totally unlike each other: for none could be more so than Cotta and Sulpicius, and yet both of them were far superior to any of their cotemporaries. It is therefore the business of every intelligent matter to take notice what is the natural bent of his pupil's capacity; and, taking that for his guide, to imitate the conduct of Socrates with his two scholars Theopompus and Ephorus, who, after remarking the lively genius of the former, and the mild and timid bashfulness of the latter, is reported to have said that he applied a spur to the one, and a curb to the other. The Orations now extant, which bear the name of Sulpicius, are supposed to have been written after his decease by my cotemporary P. Canutius, a man indeed of inferior rank, but who, in my mind, had a great command of language. But we have not a single speech of Sulpicius that was really his own: for I have often heard him say, that he neither had, nor ever could commit any thing of the kind to writing. And as to Cotta's speech in defence of himself, called a vindication of the *Varian Law*, it was composed, at his own request, by L. Aelius. This Aelius was a man of merit, and a very worthy Roman knight, who was thoroughly versed in the Greek and Roman literature. He had likewise a critical knowledge of the antiquities of his country, both as to the date and particulars of every new improvement, and every memorable transaction, and was perfectly well read in the ancient writers;—a branch of learning in which he was succeeded by our friend Varro, a man of genius, and of the most extensive erudition, who afterwards enlarged the plan by many valuable collections of his own, and gave a much fuller and more elegant system of it to the Public. For Aelius himself chose to assume the character of a Stoic, and neither aimed to be, nor ever was an Orator: but he composed several Orations for other people to pronounce; as for Q. Metellus, F. Q. Caepio, and Q. Pompeius Rufus; though the latter composed those speeches himself which he spoke in his own defence, but not without the assistance of Aelius. For I myself was present at the writing of them, in the younger part of my life, when I used to attend Aelius for the benefit of his instructions. But I am surprised, that Cotta, who was really an excellent Orator, and a man of good learning, should be willing that the trifling Speeches of Aelius mould be published to the world as *his*.

"To the two above-mentioned, no third person of the same age was esteemed an equal: Pomponius, however, was a Speaker much to my taste; or, at least, I have very little fault to find with him. But there was no employment for any in capital causes, excepting for those I have already mentioned; because Antonius, who was always courted on these occasions, was very ready to give his service; and Crassus, though not so compliable, generally consented, on any pressing sollicitation, to give *his*. Those who had not interest enough to engage either of these, commonly applied to Philip, or Caesar; but when Cotta and Sulpicius were at liberty, they generally had the preference: so that all the causes in which any honour was to be acquired, were pleaded by these six Orators. We may add, that trials were not so frequent then as they are at present; neither did people employ, as they do now, several pleaders on the same side of the question,—a practice which is attended with many disadvantages. For hereby we are often obliged to speak in reply to those whom we had not an opportunity of hearing; in which case, what has been alledged on the opposite side, is often represented to us either falsely or imperfectly; and besides, it is a very material circumstance, that I myself should be present to see with what countenance my antagonist supports his allegations, and, still more so, to observe the effect of every part of his discourse upon the audience. And as every defence should be conducted upon one uniform plan, nothing can be more improperly contrived, than to re-commence it by assigning the peroration, or pathetical part of it, to a second advocate. For every cause can have but one natural introduction and conclusion; and all the other parts of it, like the members of an animal body, will best retain their proper strength and beauty, when they are regularly disposed and connected. We may add, that as it is very difficult in a single Oration of any length, to avoid saying something which does not comport with the rest of it so well as it ought to do, how much more difficult must it be to contrive that nothing shall be said, which does not tally exactly with the speech of another person who has spoken before you? But as it certainly requires more labour to plead a whole cause, than only a part of it, and as many advantageous connections are formed by assisting in a suit in which several persons are interested, the custom, however preposterous in itself, has been readily adopted.

"There were some, however, who esteemed Curio the third best Orator of the age; perhaps, because his language was brilliant and pompous, and because he had a habit (for which I suppose he was indebted to his domestic education) of expressing himself with tolerable correctness: for he was a man of very little learning. But it is a circumstance of great importance, what sort of people we are used to converse with at home, especially in the more early part of life; and what sort of language we have been accustomed to hear from our tutors and parents, not excepting the mother. We have all read the Letters of Cornelia, the mother of the Gracchi; and are satisfied, that her sons were not so much nurtured in their mother's lap, as in the elegance and purity of her language. I have often too enjoyed the agreeable conversation of Laelia, the daughter of Caius, and observed in her a strong tincture of her father's elegance. I have likewise conversed with his two daughters, the Muciae, and his granddaughters, the two Liciniae, with one of whom (the wife of Scipio) you, my Brutus, I believe, have sometimes been in company."—"I have," replied he, "and was much pleased with her conversation; and the more so, because she was the daughter of Crassus."—"And what think you," said I, "of Crassus, the son of that Licinia, who was adopted by Crassus in his will?"—"He is said," replied he, "to have been a man of great genius: and the Scipio you have mentioned, who was my colleague, likewise appears to me to have been a good Speaker, and an elegant companion."—"Your opinion, my Brutus," said I, "is very just. For this family, if I may be allowed the expression, seems to have been the offspring of Wisdom. As to their two grandfathers, Scipio and Crassus, we have taken notice of them already: as we also have of their great grandfathers, Q. Metellus, who had four sons,—P. Scipio, who, when a private citizen, freed the Republic from the arbitrary influence of T. Gracchus,—and Q. Scaevola, the augur, who was the ablest and most affable Civilian of his time. And lastly, how illustrious are the names of their next immediate progenitors, P. Scipio, who was twice Consul, and was called the Darling of the People,—and C. Laelius, who was esteemed the wisest of men?"—"A generous stock indeed!" cries Brutus, "into which the wisdom of many has been successively ingrafted, like a number of scions on the same tree!"—"I have likewise a suspicion," replied I, "(if we may compare small things with great) that Curio's family, though he himself was left an orphan, was indebted to his father's instruction, and good example, for the habitual purity of their language: and so much the more, because, of all those who were held in any estimation for their Eloquence, I never knew one who was so totally rude and unskilled in every branch of liberal science. He had not read a single poet, or studied a single orator; and he knew little or nothing either of Public, Civil, or Common law. We might say almost the same, indeed, of several others, and some of them very able Orators, who (we know) were but little acquainted with these useful parts of knowledge; as, for instance, of Sulpicius and Antonius. But this deficiency was supplied in them by an elaborate knowledge of the art of Speaking; and there was not one of them who was totally unqualified in any of the five [Footnote: Invention, Disposition, Elocution, Memory, and Pronunciation.] principal parts of which it is composed; for whenever this is the case, (and it matters not in which of those parts it happens) it intirely incapacitates a man to shine as an Orator. Some, however, excelled in one part, and some in another. Thus Antonius could readily invent such arguments as were most in point, and afterwards digest and methodize them to the best advantage; and he could likewise retain the plan he had formed with great exactness: but his chief merit was the goodness of his delivery, in which he was justly allowed to excel. In some of these qualifications he was upon an equal footing with Crassus, and in others he was superior: but then the language of Crassus was indisputably preferable to *his*. In the same manner, it cannot be said that either Sulpicius or Cotta, or any other Speaker of repute, was absolutely deficient in any one of the five parts of Oratory. But we may justly infer from the example of Curio, that nothing will more recommend an Orator, than a brilliant and ready flow of expression; for he was remarkably dull in the invention, and very loose and unconnected in the disposition of his arguments. The two remaining parts are Pronunciation and Memory; in each of which he was so poorly qualified, as to excite the laughter and the ridicule of his hearers. His gesture was really such as C. Julius represented it, in a severe sarcasm, that will never be forgotten; for as he was swaying and reeling his whole body from side to side, Julius enquired very merrily, *who it was that was speaking from a boat*. To the same purpose was the jest of Cn. Sicinius, a very vulgar sort of man, but exceedingly humourous, which was the only qualification he had to recommend him as an Orator. When this man, as Tribune of the people, had summoned Curio and Octavius, who were then Consuls, into the Forum, and Curio had delivered a tedious harangue, while Octavius sat silently by him, wrapt up in flannels, and besmeared with ointments, to ease the pain of the gout;"—"*Octavius," said he, "you are infinitely obliged to your colleague; for if he had not tossed and flung himself about to-day, in the manner he did, you would have certainly have been devoured by the flies.*"—"As to his memory, it was so extremely treacherous, that after he had divided his subject into three general heads, he would sometimes, in the course of speaking, either add a fourth, or omit the third. In a capital trial, in which I had pleaded for Titinia, the daughter of Cotta, when he attempted to reply to me in defence of Serv. Naevius, he suddenly forgot every thing he had intended to say, and attributed it to the pretended witchcraft, and magic artifices of Titinia. These were undoubted proofs of the weakness of his memory. But, what is still more inexcusable, he sometimes forgot, even in his written treatises, what he had mentioned but a little before. Thus, in a book of his, in which he introduces himself as entering into conversation with our friend Pansa, and his son Curio, when he was walking home from the Senate- house; the Senate is supposed to have been summoned by Caesar in his first Consulship; and the whole conversation arises from the son's enquiry what the House had resolved upon. Curio launches out into a long invective against the conduct of Caesar, and, as is generally the custom in dialogues, the parties are engaged in a close dispute on the subject: but very unhappily, though the conversation commences at the breaking up of the Senate which Caesar held when he was first Consul, the author censures those very actions of the same Caesar, which did not happen till the next, and several other succeeding years of his government in Gaul."—"Is it possible then," said Brutus, with an air of surprize, "that any man, (and especially in a written performance) could be so forgetful as not to discover, upon a subsequent perusal of his own work, what an egregious blunder he had committed?"—"Very true," said I; "for if he wrote with a design to discredit the measures which he represents in such an odious light, nothing could be more stupid than not to commence his dialogue at a period which was subsequent to those measures. But he so entirely forgets himself, as to tell us, that he did not choose to attend a Senate which was held in one of Caesar's future consulships, in the very same dialogue in which he introduces himself as returning home from a Senate which was held in his first consulship. It cannot, therefore, be wondered at, that he who was so remarkably defective in a faculty which is the steward of our other intellectual powers, as to forget, even in a written treatise, a material circumstance which he had mentioned but a little before, should find his memory fail him, as it generally did, in a sudden and unpremeditated harangue. It accordingly happened, though he had many connections, and was fond of speaking in public, that few causes were intrusted to his management. But, among his cotemporaries, he was esteemed next in merit to the first Orators of the age; and that merely, as I said before, for his good choice of words, and his uncommon readiness, and great fluency of expression. His Orations, therefore, may deserve a cursory perusal. It is true, indeed, they are much too languid and spiritless; but they may yet be of service to enlarge and improve an accomplishment, of which he certainly had a moderate share; and which has so much force and efficacy, that it gave Curio the appearance and reputation of an Orator, without the assistance of any other good quality.

"But to return to our subject,—C. Carbo, of the same age, was likewise reckoned an Orator of the second class: he was the son, indeed, of the truly eloquent man before-mentioned, but was far from being an acute Speaker himself: he was, however, esteemed an Orator. His language was tolerably nervous, he spoke with ease,—and there was an air of authority in his address that was perfectly natural. But Q. Varius was a man of quicker invention, and, at the same time, had an equal freedom of expression: besides which, he had a bold and spirited delivery, and a vein of elocution which was neither poor, nor coarse and vulgar;—in short, you need not hesitate to pronounce him an *Orator*. Cn. Pomponius was a vehement, a rousing, and a fierce and eager Speaker, and more inclined to act the part of a prosecutor, than of an advocate. But far inferior to these was L. Fufius; though his application was, in some measure, rewarded by the success of his prosecution against M. Aquilius. For as to M. Drusus, your great uncle, who spoke like an Orator only upon matters of government;—L. Lucullus, who was indeed an artful Speaker, and your father, my Brutus, who was well acquainted with the Common and Civil Law; —M. Lucullus, and M. Octavius, the son of Cnaeus, who was a man of so much authority and address, as to procure the repeal of Sempronius's corn-act, by the suffrages of a full assembly of the people;—Cn. Octavius, the son of Marcus,—and M. Cato, the father, and Q. Catulus, the son;—we must excuse these (if I may so express myself) from the fatigues and dangers of the field,—that is, from the management of judicial causes, and place them in garison over the general interests of the Republic, a duty to which they seem to have been sufficiently adequate. I should have assigned the same post to Q. Caepio, if he had not been so violently attached to the Equestrian Order, as to set himself at variance with the Senate. I have also remarked, that Cn. Carbo, M. Marius, and several others of the same stamp, who would not have merited the attention of an audience that had any taste for elegance, were extremely well suited to address a tumultuous crowd. In the same class, (if I may be allowed to interrupt the series of my narrative) L. Quintius lately made his appearance: though Palicanus, it must be owned, was still better adapted to please the ears of the populace. But, as I have mentioned this inferior kind of Speakers, I must be so just to L. Apuleius Saturninus, as to observe that, of all the factious declaimers since the time of the Gracchi, he was generally esteemed the ablest: and yet he caught the attention of the Public, more by his appearance, his gesture, and his dress, than by any real fluency of expression, or even a tolerable share of good sense. But C. Servilius Glaucia, though the most abandoned wretch that ever existed, was very keen and artful, and excessively humourous; and notwithstanding the meanness of his birth, and the depravity of his life, he would have been advanced to the dignity of a Consul in his Praetorship, if it had been judged lawful to admit his suit: for the populace were entirely at his devotion, and he had secured the interest of the Knights, by an act he had procured in their favour. He was slain in the open Forum, while he was Praetor, on the same day as the tribune Saturninus, in the Consulship of Marius and Flaccus; and bore a near resemblance to Hyperbolus, the Athenian, whose profligacy was so severely stigmatized in the old Attic Comedies. These were succeeded by Sext. Titius, who was indeed a voluble Speaker, and possessed a ready comprehension, but he was so loose and effeminate in his gesture, as to furnish room for the invention of a dance, which was called the *Titian jigg*: so careful should we be to avoid every oddity in our manner of speaking, which may afterwards be exposed to ridicule by a ludicrous imitation.

"But we have rambled back insensibly to a period which has been already examined: let us, therefore, return to that which we were reviewing a little before. Cotemporary with Sulpicius was P. Antistius,—a plausible declaimer, who, after being silent for several years, and exposed, (as he often was) not only to the contempt, but the derision of his hearers, first spoke with applause in his tribuneship, in a real and very interesting protest against the illegal application of C. Julius for the consulship; and that so much the more, because though Sulpicius himself, who then happened to be his colleague, spoke on the same side of the debate, Antistius argued more copiously, and to better purpose. This raised his reputation so high, that many, and (soon afterwards) every cause of importance, was eagerly recommended to his patronage. To speak the truth, he had a quick conception, a methodical judgment, and a retentive memory; and though his language was not much embellished, it was very far from being low. In short, his style was easy, and flowing, and his appearance rather genteel than otherwise: but his action was a little defective, partly through the disagreeable tone of his voice, and partly by a few ridiculous gestures, of which he could not entirely break himself. He flourished in the time between the flight and the return of Sylla, when the Republic was deprived of a regular administration of justice, and of its former dignity and splendor. But the very favourable reception he met with was, in some measure, owing to the great scarcity of good Orators which then prevailed in the Forum. For Sulpicius was dead; Cotta and Curio were abroad; and no pleaders of any eminence were left but Carbo and Pomponius, from each of whom he easily carried off the palm. His nearest successor in the following age was L. Sisenna, who was a man of learning, had a taste for the liberal Sciences, spoke the Roman language with accuracy, was well acquainted with the laws and constitution of his country, and had a tolerable share of wit; but he was not a Speaker of any great application, or extensive practice; and as he happened to live in the intermediate time between the appearance of

Sulpicius and Hortensius, he was unable to equal the former, and forced to yield to the superior talents of the latter. We may easily form a judgment of his abilities from the historical Works he has left behind him; which, though evidently preferable to any thing of the kind which had appeared before, may serve as a proof that he was far below the standard of perfection, and that this species of composition had not then been improved to any great degree of excellence among the Romans. But the genius of Q. Hortensius, even in his early youth, like one of Phidias's statues, was no sooner beheld than it was universally admired! He spoke his first Oration in the Forum in the consulship of L. Crassus and Q. Scaevola, to whom it was personally adressed; and though he was then only nineteen years old, he descended from the Rostra with the hearty approbation not only of the audience in general, but of the two Consuls themselves, who were the most intelligent judges in the whole city. He died in the consulship of L. Paulus and C. Marcellus; from which it appears that he was four-and-forty years a Pleader. We shall review his character more at large in the sequel: but in this part of my history, I chose to include him in the number of Orators who were rather of an earlier date. This indeed must necessarily happen to all whose lives are of any considerable length: for they are equally liable to a comparison with their Elders and their Juniors; as in the case of the poet Attius, who says that both he and Pacuvius applied themselves to the cultivation of the drama under the fame Aediles; though, at the time, the one was eighty, and the other only thirty years old. Thus Hortensius may be paralleled not only with those who were properly his contemporaries, but with me, and you, my Brutus, and with others of a prior date. For he began to speak in public while Crassus was living but his fame increased when he appeared as a joint advocate with Antonius and Philip (at that time in the decline of life) in defence of Cn. Pompeius,— a cause in which (though a mere youth) he distinguished himself above the rest. He may therefore be included in the lift of those whom I have placed in the time of Sulpicius; but among his proper coëvals, such as M. Piso, M. Crassus, Cn. Lentulus, and P. Lentulus Sura, he excelled beyond the reach of competition; and after these he happened upon me, in the early part of my life (for I was eight years younger than himself) and spent a number of years with me in pursuit of the same forensic glory: and at last, (a little before his death) he once pleaded with *you*, in defence of Appius Claudius, as I have frequently done for others. Thus you see, my Brutus, I am come insensibly to *yourself*, though there was undoubtedly a great variety of Orators between my first appearance in the Forum, and yours. But as I determined, when we began the conversation, to make no mention of those among them who are still living, to prevent your enquiring too minutely what is my opinion concerning each; I shall confine myself to such as are now no more."—"That is not the true reason," said Brutus, "why you choose to be silent about the living."—"What then do you suppose it to be," said I? —"You are only fearful," replied he, "that your remarks should afterwards be mentioned by us in other company, and that, by this means, you should expose yourself to the resentment of those, whom you may not think it worth your while to notice."—"Indeed," answered I, "I have not the least doubt of your secresy."—"Neither have you any reason," said he; "but after all, I suppose, you had rather be silent *yourself*, than rely upon our taciturnity."—"To confess the truth," replied I, "when I first entered upon the subject, I never imagined that I should have extended it to the age now before us; whereas I have been drawn by a continued series of history among the moderns of latest date." —"Introduce, then," said he, "those intermediate Orators you may think worthy of our notice: and afterwards let us return to yourself, and Hortensius."—"To Hortensius," replied I, "with all my heart; but as to my *own* character, I shall leave it to other people to examine, if they choose to take the trouble."—"I can by no means agree to *that*," said he: "for though every part of the account you have favoured us with, has entertained me very agreeably, it now begins to seem tedious, because I am impatient to hear something of *yourself*: I do not mean the wonderful qualities, but the *progressive steps*, and advances of your Eloquence; for the former are sufficiently known already both to me, and the whole world."—"As you do not require me," said I, "to sound the praises of my own genius, but only to describe my labour and application to improve it, your request shall be complied with. But to preserve the order of my narrative, I shall first introduce such other Speakers as I think ought to be previously noticed: and I shall begin with M. Crassus, who was contemporary with Hortensius. With a tolerable share of learning, and a very moderate capacity, his application, assiduity, and interest, procured him a place among the ablest Pleaders of the time for several years. His language was pure, his expression neither low nor ungenteel, and his ideas well digested: but he had nothing in him that was florid, and ornamental; and the real ardor of his mind was not supported by any vigorous exertion of his voice, so that he pronounced almost every thing in the same uniform tone. His equal, and professed antagonist C. Fimbria was not able to maintain his character so long; and though he always spoke with a strong and elevated voice, and poured forth a rapid torrent of well-chosen expressions, he was so immoderately vehement that you might justly be surprised that the people should have been so absent and inattentive as to admit a *madman*, like him, into the lift of Orators. As to Cn. Lentulus, his action acquired him a reputation for his Eloquence very far beyond his real abilities: for though he was not a man of any great penetration (notwithstanding he carried the appearance of it in his countenance) nor possessed any real fluency of expression (though he was equally specious in this respect as in the former)—yet by his sudden breaks, and exclamations, he affected such an ironical air of surprize, with a sweet and sonorous turn of voice, and his whole action was so warm and lively, that his defects were scarcely noticed. For as Curio acquired the reputation of an Orator with no other quality than a tolerable freedom of Elocution; so Cn. Lentulus concealed the mediocrity of his other accomplishments by his *action*, which was really excellent. Much the same might be said of P. Lentulus, whose poverty of invention and expression was secured from notice by the mere dignity of his presence, his correct and graceful gesture, and the strength and sweetness of his voice: and his merit depended so entirely upon his action, that he was more deficient in every other quality than his namesake. But M. Piso derived all his talents from his erudition; for he was much better versed in the Grecian literature than any of his predecessors. He had, however, a natural keenness of discernment, which he greatly improved by art, and exerted with great address and dexterity, though in very indifferent language: but he was frequently warm and choleric, sometimes cold and insipid, and now and then rather smart and humourous. He did not long support the fatigue, and emulous contention of the Forum; partly, on account of the weakness of his constitution; and partly, because he could not submit to the follies and impertinencies of the common people (which we Orators are forced to swallow) either, as it was generally supposed, from a peculiar moroseness of temper, or from a liberal and ingenuous pride of heart. After acquiring, therefore, in his youth, a tolerable degree of reputation, his character began to sink: but in the trial of the Vestals, he again recovered it with some additional lustre, and being thus recalled to the theatre of Eloquence, he kept his rank, as long as he was able to support the fatigue of it; after which his credit declined, in proportion as he remitted his application.—P. Murena had a moderate genius, but was passionately fond of the study of Antiquity; he applied himself with equal diligence to the Belles Lettres, in which he was tolerably versed; in short, he was a man of great industry, and took the utmost pains to distinguish himself.—C. Censorinus had a good stock of Grecian literature, explained whatever he advanced with great neatness and perspicuity, and had a graceful action, but was too cold and unanimated for the Forum.—L. Turius with a very indifferent genius, but the most indefatigable application, spoke in public very often, in the best manner he was able; and, accordingly, he only wanted the votes of a few Centuries to promote him to the Consulship.—C. Macer was never a man of much interest or authority, but was one of the most active Pleaders of his time; and if his life, his manners, and his very looks, had not ruined the credit of his genius, he would have ranked higher in the lift of Orators. He was neither copious, nor dry and barren; neither eat and embellished, nor wholly inelegant; and his voice, his gesture, and every part of his action, was without any grace: but in inventing and digesting his ideas, he had a wonderful accuracy, such as no man I ever saw either possessed or exerted in a more eminent degree; and yet, some how, he displayed it rather with the air of a Quibbler, than of an Orator. Though he had acquired some reputation in public causes, he appeared to most advantage and was most courted and employed in private ones.—C. Piso, who comes next in order, had scarcely any exertion, but he was a Speaker of a very convertible style; and though, in fact, he was far from being slow of invention, he had more penetration in his look and appearance than he really possessed.—His cotemporary M. Glabrio, though carefully instructed by his grandfather Scaevola, was prevented from distinguishing himself by his natural indolence and want of attention.—L. Torquatus, on the contrary, had an elegant turn of expression, and a clear comprehension, and was perfectly genteel and well-bred in his whole manner.—But Cn. Pompeius, my coeval, a man who was born to excel in every thing, would have acquired a more distinguished reputation for his Eloquence, if he had not been diverted from the pursuit of it by the more dazzling charms of military fame. His language was naturally bold and elevated, and he was always master of his subject; and as to his powers of enunciation, his voice was sonorous and manly, and his gesture noble, and full of dignity. —D. Silanus, another of my cotemporaries, and your father-in-law, was not a man of much application, but he had a very competent share of discernment, and elocution.—Q. Pompeius, the son of Aulus, who had the title of *Bithynicus*, and was about two years older than myself, was, to my own knowledge, remarkably fond of the study of Eloquence, had an uncommon stock of learning, and was a man of indefatigable industry and perseverance: for he was connected with me and M. Piso, not only as an intimate acquaintance, but as an associate in our studies, and private exercises. His elocution was but poorly recommended by his action: for though the former was sufficiently copious and diffusive, there was nothing graceful in the latter.—His contemporary, P. Autronius, had a very clear, and strong voice; but he was distinguished by no other accomplishment.—L. Octavius Reatinus died in his youth, while he was in full practice: but he ascended the rostra with more assurance, than ability.—C. Staienus, who changed his name into Aelius by a kind of self- adoption, was a warm, an abusive, and indeed a furious speaker; which was so agreeable to the taste of many, that he would have risen to some rank in the State, if it had not been for a crime of which he was clearly convicted, and for which he afterwards suffered.—At the same time were the two brothers C. and L. Caepasius, who, though men of an obscure family, and little previous consequence, were yet, by mere dint of application, suddenly promoted to the Quaestorship, with no other recommendation than a provincial and unpolished kind of Oratory.—That I may not seem to have put a wilful slight on any of the vociferous tribe, I must also notice C. Cosconius Calidianus, who, without any discernment, amused the people with a rapidity of language (if such it might be called) which he attended with a perpetual hurry of action, and a most violent exertion of his voice.—Of much the same cast was Q. Arrius, who may be considered as a second-hand M. Crassus. He is a striking proof of what consequence it is in such a city as ours to devote one's-self to the occasions of *the many*, and to be as active as possible in promoting their safety, or their honour. For by these means, though of the lowest parentage, having raised himself to offices of rank, and to considerable wealth and influence, he likewise acquired the reputation of a tolerable patron, without either learning or abilities. But as inexperienced champions, who, from a passionate desire to distinguish themselves in the Circus, can bear the blows of their opponents without shrinking, are often overpowered by the heat of the sun, when it is increased by the reflection of the sand; so *he*, who had hitherto supported even the sharpest encounters with good success, could not stand the severity of that year of judicial contest, which blazed upon him like a summer's sun."

"Upon my word," cried Atticus, "you are now treating us with the very *dregs* of Oratory, and you have entertained us in this manner for some time: but I did not offer to interrupt you, because I never dreamed you would have descended so low as to mention the *Staieni* and *Autronii*!"— "As I have been speaking of the dead, you will not imagine, I suppose," said I, "that I have done it to court their favour: but in pursuing the order of history, I was necessarily led by degrees to a period of time which falls within the compass of our own knowledge. But I wish it to be noticed, that after recounting all who ever ventured to speak in public, we find but few, (very few indeed!) whose names are worth recording; and not many who had even the repute of being Orators. Let us, however, return to our subject. T. Torquatus, then, the son of Titus, was a man of learning, (which he first acquired in the school of Molo in Rhodes,) and of a free and easy elocution which he received from Nature. If he had lived to a proper age, he would have been chosen Consul, without any canvassing; but he had more ability for speaking than inclination; *so* that, in fact, he did not do justice to the art he professed; and yet he was never wanting to his duty, either in the private causes of his friends and dependents, or in his senatorial capacity.—My townsman too, P. Pontidius, pleaded a number of private causes. He had a rapidity of expression, and a tolerable quickness of comprehension: but he was very warm, and indeed rather too choleric and irascible; so that he often wrangled not only with his antagonist, but (what appears very strange) with the judge himself, whom it was rather his business to sooth and gratify.

—M. Messala, who was something younger than myself, was far from being a poor and an abject Pleader, and yet he was not a very embellished one. He was judicious, penetrating, and wary, very exact in digesting and methodizing his subject, and a man of uncommon diligence and application, and of very extensive practice.—As to the two Metelli (Celer and Nepos) these also had a moderate share of employment at the bar; but being destitute neither of learning nor abilities, they chiefly applied themselves (and with some success) to debates of a more popular kind.—But Caius Lentulus Marcellinus, who was never reckoned a bad Speaker, was esteemed a very eloquent one in his Consulship. He wanted neither sentiment, nor expression; his voice was sweet and sonorous; and he had a sufficient stock of humour.—C. Memmius, the son of Lucius, was a perfect adept in the *belles lettres* of the Greeks; for he had an insuperable disgust to the literature of the Romans. He was a neat and polished Speaker, and had a sweet and harmonious turn of expression; but as he was equally averse to every laborious effort either of the mind or the tongue, his Eloquence declined in proportion as he lessened his application."— "But I heartily wish," said Brutus, "that you would give us your opinion of those Orators who are still living; or, if you are determined to say nothing of the rest, there are two at least, (that is Caesar and Marcellus, whom I have often heard you speak of with the highest approbation) whose characters would give me as much entertainment as any of those you have already specified."—"But why," answered I, "would you expect that I would give you my opinion of men who are as well known to yourself as to me?"—"Marcellus, indeed," replied he, "I am very well acquainted with; but as to Caesar, I know little of *him*. For I have *heard* the former very often: but, by the time I was able to judge for myself, the latter had set out for his province."—"Mighty well," said I; "and what think you of him you have heard so often?"—"What else can I think," replied he, "but that you will soon have an Orator, who will very nearly resemble yourself?"—"If that is the case," answered I, "pray think of him as favourably as you can." "I do," said he; "for he pleases me very highly; and not without reason. He is absolutely master of his trade, and, neglecting every other profession, has applied himself solely to *this*; and, for that purpose, has persevered in the rigorous task of composing a daily Essay in writing. His words are well chosen; his language is full and copious; and every thing he says receives an additional ornament from the graceful tone of his voice, and the dignity of his action. In short, he is so compleat an Orator, that there is no quality I know of, in which I can think him deficient. But he is still more to be admired, for being able, in these unhappy times, (which are marked with a distress that, by some cruel fatality, has overwhelmed us all) to console himself, as opportunity offers, with the consciousness of his own integrity, and by the frequent renewal of his literary pursuits. I saw him lately at Mitylene; and then (as I have already hinted) I saw him a thorough man. For though I had before discovered in him a strong resemblance of yourself, the likeness was much improved, after he was enriched by the instructions of your learned, and very intimate friend Cratippus."— "Though I acknowledge," said I, "that I have listened with pleasure to your Elogies on a very worthy man, for whom I have the warmest esteem, they have led me insensibly to the recollection of our common miseries, which our present conversation was intended to suspend. But I would willingly hear what is Atticus's opinion of Caesar."—"Upon my word," replied Atticus, "you are wonderfully consistent with your plan, to say nothing *yourself* of the living: and indeed, if you was to deal with *them*, as you already have with the *dead*, and say something of every paltry fellow that occurs to your memory, you would plague us with *Autronii* and *Steiani* without end. But though you might possibly have it in view not to incumber yourself with such a numerous crowd of insignificant wretches; or perhaps, to avoid giving any one room to complain that he was either unnoticed, or not extolled according to his imaginary merit; yet, certainly, you might have said something of Caesar; especially, as your opinion of *his* abilities is well known to every body, and his concerning *your's* is very far from being a secret. But, however," said he, (addressing himself to Brutus) "I really think of Caesar, and every body else says the same of this accurate connoisseur in the Art of Speaking, that he has the purest and the most elegant command of the Roman language of all the Orators that have yet appeared: and that not merely by domestic habit, as we have lately heard it observed of the families of the Laelii and the Mucii, (though even here, I believe, this might partly have been the case) but he chiefly acquired and brought it to its present perfection, by a studious application to the most intricate and refined branches of literature, and by a careful and constant attention to the purity of his style. But that *he*, who, involved as he was in a perpetual hurry of business, could dedicate to *you*, my Cicero, a laboured Treatise on the Art of Speaking correctly; that *he*, who, in the first book of it, laid it down as an axiom, that an accurate choice of words is the foundation of Eloquence; and who has bestowed," said he, (addressing himself again to Brutus) "the highest encomiums on this friend of ours, who yet chooses to leave Caesar's character to *me*;—that *he* should be a perfect master of the language of polite conservation, is a circumstance which is almost too obvious to be mentioned." "I said, *the highest encomiums*," pursued Atticus, "because he says in so many words, when he addresses himself to Cicero—*if others have bestowed all their time and attention to acquire a habit of expressing themselves with ease and correctness, how much is the name and dignity of the Roman people indebted to you, who are the highest pattern, and indeed the first inventor of that rich fertility of language which distinguishes your performances?*"—Indeed," said Brutus, "I think he has extolled your merit in a very friendly, and a very magnificent style: for you are not only the *highest pattern*, and even the *first inventor* of all our *fertility* of language, which alone is praise enough to content any reasonable man, but you have added fresh honours to the name and dignity of the

Roman people; for the very excellence in which we had hitherto been conquered by the vanquished Greeks, has now been either wrested from their hands, or equally shared, at least, between us and them. So that I prefer this honourable testimony of Caesar, I will not say to the public thanksgiving, which was decreed for your *own* military services, but to the triumphs of many heroes."—"Very true," replied I, "provided this honourable testimony was really the voice of Caesar's judgment, and not of his friendship: for *he* certainly has added more to the dignity of the Roman people, whoever he may be (if indeed any such man has yet existed) who has not only exemplified and enlarged, but first produced this rich fertility of expression, than the doughty warrior who has stormed a few paltry castles of the Ligurians, which have furnished us, you know, with many repeated triumphs. In reality, if we can submit to hear the truth, it may be asserted (to say nothing of those god-like plans, which, supported by the wisdom of our Generals, has frequently saved the sinking State both abroad and at home) that an Orator is justly entitled to the preference to any Commander in a petty war. But the General, you will say, is the more serviceable man to the public. Nobody denies it: and yet (for I am not afraid of provoking your censure, in a conversation which leaves each of us at liberty to say what he thinks) I had rather be the author of the single Oration of Crassus, in defence of Curius, than be honoured with two Ligurian triumphs. You will, perhaps, reply, that the storming a castle of the Ligurians was a thing of more consequence to the State, than that the claim of Curius should be ably supported. This I own to be true. But it was also of more consequence to the Athenians, that their houses should be securely roofed, than to have their city graced with a most beautiful statue of Minerva: and yet, notwithstanding this, I would much rather have been a Phidias, than the most skilful joiner in Athens. In the present case, therefore, we are not to consider a man's usefulness, but the strength of his abilities; especially as the number of painters and statuaries, who have excelled in their profession, is very small; whereas, there can never be any want of joiners and mechanic labourers. But proceed, my Atticus, with Caesar; and oblige us with the remainder of his character."—"We see then," said he, "from what has just been mentioned, that a pure and correct style is the groundwork, and the very basis and foundation, upon which an Orator must build his other accomplishments: though, it is true, that those who had hitherto possessed it, derived it more from early habit, than from any principles of art. It is needless to refer you to the instances of Laelius and Scipio; for a purity of language, as well as of manners, was the characteristic of the age they lived in. It could not, indeed, be applied to every one; for their two cotemporaries, Caecilius and Pacuvius, spoke very incorrectly: but yet people in general, who had not resided out of the city, nor been corrupted by any domestic barbarisms, spoke the Roman language with purity. Time, however, as well at Rome as in Greece, soon altered matters for the worse: for this city, (as had formerly been the case at Athens) was resorted to by a crowd of adventurers from different parts, who spoke very corruptly; which shews the necessity of reforming our language, and reducing it to a certain standard, which shall not be liable to vary like the capricious laws of custom. Though we were then very young, we can easily remember T. Flaminius, who was joint-consul with Q. Metellus: he was supposed to speak his native language with correctness, but was a man of no Literature. As to Catulus, he was far indeed from being destitute of learning, as you have already observed: but his reputed purity of diction was chiefly owing to the sweetness of his voice, and the delicacy of his accent. Cotta, who, by his broad pronunciation, threw off all resemblance of the elegant tone of the Greeks, and affected a harsh and rustic utterance, quite opposite to that of Catulus, acquired the same reputation of correctness by pursuing a wild and unfrequented path. But Sisenna, who had the ambition to think of reforming our phraseology, could not be lashed out of his whimsical and new-fangled turns of expression, by all the raillery of C. Rufius."—"What do you refer to?" said Brutus; "and who was the Caius Rufius you are speaking of?"—"He was a noted prosecutor," replied he, "some years ago. When this man had supported an indictment against one Christilius, Sisenna, who was counsel for the defendant, told him, that several parts of his accusation were absolutely *spitatical*. [Footnote: In the original *sputatilica*, worthy to be spit upon. It appears, from the connection, to have been a very unclassical word, whimsically derived by the author of it from *sputa*, spittle.] *My Lords*, cried Rufius to the judges, *I shall be cruelly over-reached, unless you give me your assistance. His charge overpowers my comprehension; and I am afraid he has some unfair design upon me. What, in the name of Heaven, can be intend by* SPITATICAL? *I know the meaning of* SPIT, *or* SPITTLE; *but this horrid* ATICAL, *at the end of it, absolutely puzzles me.* The whole Bench laughed very heartily at the singular oddity of the expression: my old friend, however, was still of opinion, that to speak correctly, was to speak differently from other people. But Caesar, who was guided by the principles of art, has corrected the imperfections of a vicious custom, by adopting the rules and improvements of a good one, as he found them occasionally displayed in the course of polite conversation. Accordingly, to the purest elegance of expression, (which is equally necessary to every well-bred Citizen, as to an Orator) he has added all the various ornaments of Elocution; so that he seems to exhibit the finest painting in the most advantageous point of view. As he has such extraordinary merit even in the common run of his language, I must confess that there is no person I know of, to whom he should yield the preference. Besides, his manner of speaking, both as to his voice and gesture, is splendid and noble, without the least appearance of artifice or affectation: and there is a dignity in his very presence, which bespeaks a great and elevated mind."—"Indeed," said Brutus, "his Orations please me highly; for I have had the satisfaction to read several of them. He has likewise wrote some commentaries, or short memoirs, of his own transactions;"—"and such," said I, "as merit the highest approbation: for they are plain, correct, and graceful, and divested of all the ornaments of language, so as to appear (if I may be allowed the expression) in a kind of undress. But while he pretended only to furnish the loose materials, for such as might be inclined to compose a regular history, he may, perhaps, have gratified the vanity of a few literary *Frisseurs*: but he has certainly prevented all sensible men from attempting any improvement on his plan. For in history, nothing is more pleasing than a correct and elegant brevity of expression. With your leave, however, it is high time to return to those Orators who have quitted the stage of life. C. Sicinius then, who was a grandson of the Censor Q. Pompey, by one of his daughters, died after his advancement to the Quaestorship. He was a Speaker of some merit and reputation, which he derived from the system of Hermagoras; who, though he furnished but little assistance for acquiring an ornamental style, gave many useful precepts to expedite and improve the invention of an Orator. For in this System we have a collection of fixed and determinate rules for public speaking; which are delivered indeed without any shew or parade, (and, I might have added, in a trivial and homely form) but yet are so plain and methodical, that it is almost impossible to mistake the road. By keeping close to these, and always digesting his subject before he ventured to speak upon it, (to which we may add, that he had a tolerable fluency of expression) he so far succeeded, without any other assistance, as to be ranked among the pleaders of the day.—As to C. Visellius Varro, who was my cousin, and a cotemporary of Sicinius, he was a man of great learning. He died while he was a member of the Court of Inquests, into which he had been admitted after the expiration of his Aedileship. The public, I confess, had not the same opinion of his abilities that I have; for he never passed as a man of Sterling Eloquence among the people. His style was excessively quick and rapid, and consequently obscure; for, in fact, it was embarrassed and blinded by the celerity of its course: and yet, after all, you will scarcely find a man who had a better choice of words, or a richer vein of sentiment. He had besides a complete fund of polite literature, and a thorough knowledge of the principles of jurisprudence, which he learned from his father Aculeo. To proceed in our account of the dead, the next that presents himself is L. Torquatus, whom you will not so readily pronounce a connoisseur in the Art of Speaking (though he was by no means destitute of elocution) as, what is called by the Greeks, *a political Adept*. He had a plentiful stock of learning, not indeed of the common sort, but of a more abstruse and curious nature: he had likewise an admirable memory, and a very sensible and elegant turn of expression; all which qualities derived an additional grace from the dignity of his deportment, and the integrity of his manners. I was also highly pleased with the style of his cotemporary Triarius, which expressed to perfection, the character of a worthy old gentleman, who had been thoroughly polished by the refinements of Literature.—What a venerable severity was there in his look! What forcible solemnity in his language! and how thoughtful and deliberate every word he spoke!"—At the mention of Torquatus and Triarius, for each of whom he had the most affectionate veneration,—"It fills my heart with anguish," said Brutus, "(to omit a thousand other circumstances) when I reflect, as I cannot help doing, on your mentioning the names of these worthy men, that your long-respected authority was insufficient to procure an accommodation of our differences. The Republic would not otherwise have been deprived of these, and many other excellent Citizens."—"Not a word more," said I, on this melancholy subject, which can only aggravate our sorrow: for as the remembrance of what is already past is painful enough, the prospect of what is yet to come is still more cutting. Let us, therefore, drop our unavailing complaints, and (agreeably to our plan) confine our attention to the forensic merits of our deceased friends. Among those, then, who lost their lives in this unhappy war, was M. Bibulus, who, though not a professed orator, was a very accurate writer, and a solid and experienced advocate: and Appius

Claudius, your father-in-law, and my colleague and intimate acquaintance, who was not only a hard student, and a man of learning, but a practised Orator, a skilful Augurist and Civilian, and a thorough Adept in the Roman History.—As to L. Domitius, he was totally unacquainted with any rules of art; but he spoke his native language with purity, and had a great freedom of address. We had likewise the two Lentuli, men of consular dignity; one of whom, (I mean Publius) the avenger of my wrongs, and the author of my restoration, derived all his powers and accomplishments from the assistance of Art, and not from the bounty of Nature: but he had such a great and noble disposition, that he claimed all the honours of the most illustrious Citizens, and supported them with the utmost dignity of character.—The other (L. Lentulus) was an animated Speaker, for it would be saying too much, perhaps, to call him an Orator— but, unhappily, he had an utter aversion to the trouble of thinking. His voice was sonorous; and his language, though not absolutely harsh and forbidding, was warm and rigorous, and carried in it a kind of terror. In a judicial trial, you would probably have wished for a more agreeable and a keener advocate: but in a debate on matters of government, you would have thought his abilities sufficient.—Even Titus Postumius had such powers of utterance, as were not to be despised: but in political matters, he spoke with the same unbridled ardour he fought with: in short, he was much too warm; though it must be owned he possessed an extensive knowledge of the laws and constitution of his country."—"Upon my word," cried Atticus, "if the persons you have mentioned were still living, I should be apt to imagine, that you was endeavouring to solicit their favour. For you introduce every body who had the courage to stand up and speak his mind: so that I almost begin to wonder how M. Servilius has escaped your notice."—"I am, indeed, very sensible," replied I, "that there have been many who never spoke in public, that were much better qualified for the talk, than those Orators I have taken the pains to enumerate: [Footnote: This was probably intended as an indirect Compliment to

Atticus.] but I have, at least, answered one purpose by it, which is to shew you, that in this populous City, we have not had very many who had the resolution to speak at all; and that even among these, there have been few who were entitled to our applause. I cannot, therefore, neglect to take some notice of those worthy knights, and my intimate friends, very lately deceased, P. Comminius Spoletinus, against whom I pleaded in defence of C. Cornelius, and who was a methodical, a spirited, and a ready Speaker; and T. Accius, of Pisaurum, to whom I replied in behalf of A. Cluentius, and who was an accurate, and a tolerably copious Advocate: he was also well instructed in the precepts of Hermagoras, which, though of little service to embellish and enrich our Elocution, furnish a variety of arguments, which, like the weapons of the light infantry, may be readily managed, and are adapted to every subject of debate. I must add, that I never knew a man of greater industry and application. As to C. Piso, my son-in-law, it is scarcely possible to mention any one who was blessed with a finer capacity. He was constantly employed either in public speaking, and private declamatory exercises, or, at least, in writing and thinking: and, consequently, he made such a rapid progress, that he rather seemed to fly than to run. He had an elegant choice of expression, and the structure of his periods was perfectly neat and harmonious; he had an astonishing variety and strength of argument, and a lively and agreeable turn of sentiment: and his gesture was naturally so graceful, that it appeared to have been formed (which it really was not) by the nicest rules of art. I am rather fearful, indeed, that I should be thought to have been prompted by my affection for him to have given him a greater character than he deserved: but this is so far from being the case, that I might justly have ascribed to him many qualities of a different and more valuable nature: for in continence, social piety, and every other kind of virtue, there was scarcely any of his cotemporaries who was worthy to be compared with him.—M. Caelius too must not pass unnoticed, notwithstanding the unhappy change, either of his fortune or disposition, which marked the latter part of his life. As long as he was directed by my influence, he behaved himself so well as a Tribune of the people, that no man supported the interests of the Senate, and of all the good and virtuous, in opposition to the factious and unruly madness of a set of abandoned citizens, with more firmness than *he* did: a part in which he was enabled to exert himself to great advantage, by the force and dignity of his language, and his lively humour, and genteel address. He spoke several harangues in a very sensible style, and three spirited invectives, which originated from our political disputes: and his defensive speeches, though not equal to the former, were yet tolerably good, and had a degree of merit which was far from being contemptible. After he had been advanced to the Aedileship, by the hearty approbation of all the better sort of citizens, as he had lost my company (for I was then abroad in Cilicia) he likewise lost himself; and entirely sunk his credit, by imitating the conduct of those very men, whom he had before so successfully opposed.—But M. Calidius has a more particular claim to our notice for the singularity of his character; which cannot so properly be said to have entitled him to a place among our other Orators, as to distinguish him from the whole fraternity; for in him we beheld the most uncommon, and the most delicate sentiments, arrayed in the softest and finest language imaginable. Nothing could be so easy as the turn and compass of his periods; nothing so ductile; nothing more pliable and obsequious to his will, so that he had a greater command of it than any Orator whatever. In short, the flow of his language was so pure and limpid, that nothing could be clearer; and so free, that it was never clogged or obstructed. Every word was exactly in the place where it should be, and disposed (as Lucilius expresses it) with as much nicety as in a curious piece of Mosaic-work. We may add, that he had not a single expression which was either harsh, unnatural, abject, or far-fetched; and yet he was so far from confining himself to the plain and ordinary mode of speaking, that he abounded greatly in the metaphor,—but such metaphors as did not appear to usurp a post that belonged to another, but only to occupy their own. These delicacies were displayed not in a loose and disfluent style; but in such a one as was strictly *numerous*, without *either* appearing to be so, or running on with a dull uniformity of sound. He was likewise master of the various ornaments of language and sentiment which the Greeks call *figures*, whereby he enlivened and embellished his style as with so many forensic decorations. We may add that he readily discovered, upon all occasions, what was the real point of debate, and where the stress of the argument lay; and that his method of ranging his ideas was extremely artful, his action genteel, and his whole manner very engaging and very sensible. In short, if to speak agreeably is the chief merit of an Orator, you will find no one who was better qualified than Calidius. But as we have observed a little before, that it is the business of an Orator to instruct, to please, and *to move the passions*; he was, indeed, perfectly master of the two first; for no one could better elucidate his subject, or charm the attention of his audience. But as to the third qualification,—the moving and alarming the passions,—which is of much greater efficacy than the two former, he was wholly destitute of it. He had no force,—no exertion;—either by his own choice, and from an opinion that those who had a loftier turn of expression, and a more warm and spirited action, were little betther than madmen; or because it was contrary to his natural temper, and habitual practice; or, lastly, because it was beyond the strength of his abilities. If, indeed, it is a useless quality, his want of it was a real excellence: but if otherwise, it was certainly a defect. I particularly remember, that when he prosecuted Q. Gallius for an attempt to poison him, and pretended that he had the plainest proofs of it, and could produce many letters, witnesses, informations, and other evidences to put the truth of his charge beyond a doubt, interspersing many sensible and ingenious remarks on the nature of the crime;—I remember, I say, that when it came to my turn to reply to him, after urging every argument which the case itself suggested, I insisted upon it as a material circumstance in favour of my client, that the prosecutor, while he charged him with a design against his life, and assured us that he had the most indubitable proofs of it then in his hands, related his story with as much ease, and as much calmness, and indifference, as if nothing had happened."—"Would it have been possible," said I, (addressing myself to Calidius) "that you should speak with this air of unconcern, unless the charge was purely an invention of your own? and, above all, that you, whose Eloquence has often vindicated the wrongs of other people with so much spirit, should speak so coolly of a crime which threatened your life? Where was that expression of resentment which is so natural to the injured? Where that ardour, that eagerness, which extorts the most pathetic language even from men of the dullest capacities? There was no visible disorder in your mind, no emotion in your looks and gesture, no smiting of the thigh or the forehead, nor even a single stamp of the foot. You was, therefore, so far from interesting our passions in your favour, that we could scarcely keep our eyes open, while you was relating the dangers you had so narrowly escaped. Thus we employed the natural defect, or if you please, the sensible calmness of an excellent Orator, as an argument to invalidate his charge."—"But is it possible to doubt," cried Brutus, "whether this was a sensible quality, or a defect? For as the greatest merit of an Orator is to be able to inflame the passions, and give them such a biass as shall best answer his purpose; he who is destitute of this must certainly be deficient in the most capital part of his profession."—"I am of the same opinion," said I; "but let us now proceed to him (Hortensius) who is the only remaining Orator worth noticing; after which, as you may seem to insist upon it, I shall say something of myself. I must first, however, do justice to the memory of two promising youths, who, if they had lived to a riper age, would have acquired the highest reputation for their Eloquence."—"You mean, I suppose," said Brutus, "C. Curio, and C. Licinius Calvus."—"The very same," replied I. "One of them, besides his plausible manner, had such an easy and voluble flow of expression, and such an inexhaustible variety, and sometimes accuracy of sentiment, that he was one of the most ready and ornamental speakers of his time. Though he had received but little instruction from the professed masters of the art, Nature had furnished him with an admirable capacity of the practice of it. I never, indeed, discovered in him any great degree of application; but he was certainly very ambitious to distinguish himself; and if he had continued to listen to my advice, as he had begun to do, he would have preferred the acquisition of real honour to that of untimely grandeur."— "What do you mean," said Brutus? "Or in what manner are these two objects to be distinguished?"—"I distinguish them thus," replied I: "As honour is the reward of virtue, conferred upon a man by the choice and affection of his fellow-citizens, he who obtains it by their free votes and suffrages is to be considered, in my opinion, as an honourable member of the community. But he who acquires his power and authority by taking advantage of every unhappy incident, and without the consent of his fellow-citizens, as Curio aimed to do, acquires only the name of honour, without the substance. Whereas, if he had hearkened to me, he would have risen to the highest dignity, in an honourable manner, and with the hearty approbation of all men, by a gradual advancement to public offices, as his father and many other eminent citizens had done before. I often gave the same advice to P. Crassus, the son of Marcus, who courted my friendship in the early part of his life; and recommended it to him very warmly, to consider *that* as the truest path to honour which had been already marked out to him by the example of his ancestors. For he had been extremely well educated, and was perfectly versed in every branch of polite literature: he had likewise a penetrating genius, and an elegant variety of expression; and appeared grave and sententious without arrogance, and modest and diffident without dejection. But like many other young men he was carried away by the tide of ambition; and after serving a short time with reputation as a volunteer, nothing could satisfy him but to try his fortune as a General,—an employment which was confined by the wisdom of our ancestors to men who had arrived at a certain age, and who, even then, were obliged to submit their pretensions to the uncertain issue of a public decision. Thus, by exposing himself to a fatal catastrophe, while he was endeavouring to rival the fame of Cyrus and Alexander, who lived to finish their desperate career, he lost all resemblance of L. Crassus, and his other worthy Progenitors.

"But let us return to Calvus whom we have just mentioned,—an Orator who had received more literary improvements than Curio, and had a more accurate and delicate manner of speaking, which he conducted with great taste and elegance; but, (by being too minute and nice a critic upon himself,) while he was labouring to correct and refine his language, he suffered all the force and spirit of it to evaporate. In short, it was so exquisitely polished, as to charm the eye of every skilful observer; but it was little noticed by the common people in a crowded Forum, which is the proper theatre of Eloquence."—"His aim," said Brutus, "was to be admired as an *Attic* Orator: and to this we must attribute that accurate exility of style, which he constantly affected."—"This, indeed, was his professed character," replied I: "but he was deceived himself, and led others into the same mistake. It is true, whoever supposes that to speak in the *Attic* taste, is to avoid every awkward, every harsh, every vicious expression, has, in this sense, an undoubted right to refuse his approbation to every thing which is not strictly *Attic*. For he must naturally detest whatever is insipid, disgusting, or invernacular; while he considers a correctness and propriety of language as the religion, and good-manners of an Orator:—and every one who pretends to speak in public should adopt the same opinion. But if he bestows the name of Atticism on a half-starved, a dry, and a niggardly turn of expression, provided it is neat, correct, and genteel, I cannot say, indeed, that he bestows it improperly; as the Attic Orators, however, had many qualities of a more important nature, I would advise him to be careful that he does not overlook their different kinds and degrees of merit, and their great extent and variety of character. The Attic Speakers, he will tell me, are the models upon which he wishes to form his Eloquence. But which of them does he mean to fix upon? for they are not all of the same cast. Who, for instance, could be more unlike each other than Demosthenes and Lysias? or than Demosthenes and Hyperides? Or who more different from either of them, than Aeschines? Which of them, then, do you propose to imitate? If only *one*, this will be a tacit implication, that none of the rest were true masters of Atticism: if *all*, how can you possibly succeed, when their characters are so opposite? Let me further ask you, whether Demetrius Phalereus spoke in the Attic style? In my opinion, his Orations have the very smell of Athens. But he is certainly more florid than either Hyperides or Lysias; partly from the natural turn of his genius, and partly by choice. There were likewise two others, at the time we are speaking of, whose characters were equally dissimilar; and yet both of them were truly *Attic*. The first (Charisius) was the author of a number of speeches, which he composed for his friends, professedly in imitation of Lysias:—and the other (Demochares, the nephew of Demosthenes) wrote several Orations, and a regular History of what was transacted in Athens under his own observation; not so much, indeed, in the style of an Historian, as of an Orator. Hegesias took the former for his model, and had so vain a conceit of his own taste for Atticism, that he considered his predecessors, who were really masters of it, as mere rustics in comparison of himself. But what can be more insipid, more frivolous, or more puerile, than that very concinnity of expression which he actually acquired?"—"*But still we wish to resemble the Attic Speakers.*"—"Do so, by all means. But were not those, then, true Attic Speakers, we have just been mentioning?"—"*Nobody denies it; and these are the men we imitate.*"—"But how? when they are so very different, not only from each other, but from all the rest of their contemporaries?"—"*True; but Thucydides is our leading pattern.*"—"This too I can allow, if you design to compose histories, instead of pleading causes. For Thucydides was both an exact, and a stately historian: but he never intended to write models for conducting a judicial process. I will even go so far as to add, that I have often commended the speeches which he has inserted into his history in great numbers; though I must frankly own, that I neither *could* imitate them, if I *would,* nor indeed *would,* if I *could;* like a man who would neither choose his wine so new as to have been turned off in the preceding vintage, nor so excessively old as to date its age from the consulship of Opimius or Anicius."—"*The latter,* you'll say, *bears the highest price.*" "Very probable; but when it has too much age, it has lost that delicious flavour which pleases the palate, and, in my opinion, is scarcely tolerable."—"*Would you choose, then, when you have a mind to regale yourself, to apply to a fresh, unripened cask?*" "By no means; but still there is a certain age, when good wine arrives at its utmost perfection. In the same manner, I would recommend neither a raw, unmellowed style, which, (if I may so express myself) has been newly drawn off from the vat; nor the rough, and antiquated language of the grave and manly Thucydides. For even *he,* if he had lived a few years later, would have acquired a much softer and mellower turn of expression."—"*Let us, then, imitate Demosthenes.*"—"Good Gods! to what else do I direct all my endeavours, and my wishes! But it is, perhaps, my misfortune not to succeed. These *Atticisers,* however, acquire with ease the paltry character they aim at; not once recollecting that it is not only recorded in history, but must have been the natural consequence of his superior fame, that when Demosthenes was to speak in public, all Greece flocked in crowds to hear him. But when our *Attic* gentry venture to speak, they are presently deserted not only by the little throng around them who have no interest in the dispute, (which alone is a mortifying proof of their insignificance) but even by their associates and fellow-advocates. If to speak, therefore, in a dry and lifeless manner, is the true criterion of Atticism, they are heartily welcome to enjoy the credit of it: but if they wish to put their abilities to the trial, let them attend the Comitia, or a judicial process of real importance. The open Forum demands a fuller, and more elevated tone: and *he* is the Orator for me, who is so universally admired that when he is to plead an interesting cause, all the benches are filled beforehand, the tribunal crowded, the clerks and notaries busy in adjusting their seats, the populace thronging about the rostra, and the judge brisk, and vigilant;—*he*, who has such a commanding air, that when he rises up to speak, the whole audience is hushed into a profound silence, which is soon interrupted by their repeated plaudits, and acclamations, or by those successive bursts of laughter, or violent transports of passion, which he knows how to excite at his pleasure; so that even a distant observer, though unacquainted with the subject he is speaking upon, can easily discover that his hearers are pleased with him, and that a *Roscius* is performing his part on the stage. Whoever has the happiness to be thus followed and applauded is, beyond dispute, an *Attic* speaker: for such was Pericles,—such was Hyperides, and Aeschines,—and such, in the most eminent degree, was the great Demosthenes! If indeed, these connoisseurs, who have so much dislike to every thing bold and ornamental, only mean to say that an accurate, a judicious, and a neat, and compact, but unembellished style, is really an *Attic* one, they are not mistaken. For in an art of such wonderful extent and variety as that of speaking, even this subtile and confined character may claim a place: so that the conclusion will be, that it is very possible to speak in the *Attic* taste, without deserving the name of an Orator; but that all in general who are truly eloquent, are likewise *Attic* Speakers.—It is time, however, to return to Hortensius."—" Indeed, I think so," cried Brutus: "though I must acknowledge that this long digression of yours has entertained me very agreeably."

"But I made some remarks," said Atticus, "which I had several times a mind to mention; only I was loath to interrupt you. As your discourse, however, seems to be drawing towards an end, I think I may venture to out with them."—"By all means," replied I.—"I readily grant, then," said he, "that there is something very humourous and elegant in that continued *Irony*, which Socrates employs to so much advantage in the dialogues of Plato, Xenophon, and Aeschines. For when a dispute commences on the nature of wisdom, he professes, with a great deal of humour and ingenuity, to have no pretensions to it himself; while, with a kind of concealed raillery, he ascribes the highest degree of it to those who had the arrogance to lay an open claim to it. Thus, in Plato, he extols Protagoras, Hippias, Prodicus, Gorgias, and several others, to the skies: but represents himself as a mere ignorant. This in *him* was peculiarly becoming; nor can I agree with Epicurus, who thinks it censurable. But in a professed History, (for such, in fact, is the account you have been giving us of the Roman Orators) I shall leave you to judge, whether an application of the *Irony* is not equally reprehensible, as it would be in giving a judicial evidence."—"Pray, what are you driving at," said I,— "for I cannot comprehend you."—"I mean," replied he, "in the first place, that the commendations which you have bestowed upon some of our Orators, have a tendency to mislead the opinion of those who are unacquainted with their true characters. There were likewise several parts of your account, at which I could scarcely forbear laughing: as, for instance, when you compared old Cato to Lysias. He was, indeed, a great, and a very extraordinary man. Nobody, I believe, will say to the contrary. But shall we call him an Orator? Shall we pronounce him the rival of Lysias, who was the most finished character of the kind? If we mean to jest, this comparison of your's would form a pretty *Irony*: but if we are talking in real earnest, we should pay the same scrupulous regard to truth, as if we were giving evidence upon oath. As a Citizen, a Senator, a General, and, in short, a man who was distinguished by his prudence, his activity, and every other virtue, your favourite Cato has my highest approbation. I can likewise applaud his speeches, considering the time he lived in. They exhibit the out-lines of a great genius; but such, however, as are evidently rude and imperfect. In the same manner, when you represented his *Antiquities* as replete with all the graces of Oratory, and compared Cato with Philistus and Thucydides, did you really imagine, that you could persuade me and Brutus to believe you? or would you seriously degrade those, whom none of the Greeks themselves have been able to equal, into a comparison with a stiff country, gentleman, who scarcely suspected that there was any such thing in being, as a copious and ornamental style? You have likewise said much in commendation of Galba;—if as the best Speaker of his age, I can so far agree with you, for such was the character he bore:—but if you meant to recommend him as an *Orator*, produce his Orations (for they are still extant) and then tell me honestly, whether you would wish your friend Brutus here to speak as *he*? Lepidus too was the author of several Speeches, which have received your approbation; in which I can partly join with you, if you consider them only as specimens of our ancient Eloquence. The same might be said of Africanus and Laelius, than whose language (you tell us) nothing in the world can be sweeter: nay, you have mentioned it with a kind of veneration, and endeavoured to dazzle our judgment by the great character they bore, and the uncommon elegance of their manners. Divest it of these adventitious Graces, and this sweet language of theirs will appear so homely, as to be scarcely worth noticing. Carbo too was mentioned as one of our capital Orators; and for this only reason,—that in speaking, as in all other professions, whatever is the best of its kind, for the time being, how deficient soever in reality, is always admired and applauded. What I have said of Carbo, is equally true of the Gracchi: though, in some particulars, the character you have given them was no more than they deserved. But to say nothing of the rest of your Orators, let us proceed to Antonius and Crassus, your two paragons of Eloquence, whom I have heard myself, and who were certainly very able Speakers. To the extraordinary commendation you have bestowed upon them, I can readily give my assent; but not, however, in such an unlimited manner as to persuade myself that you have received as much improvement from the Speech in support of the Servilian Law, as Lysippus said he had done by studying the famous [Footnote: *Doryphorus*. A Spear- man.] statue of Polycletus. What you have said on *this* occasion I consider as an absolute *Irony:* but I shall not inform you why I think so, lest you should imagine I design to flatter you. I shall therefore pass over the many fine encomiums you have bestowed upon *these*; and what you have said of Cotta and Sulpicius, and but very lately of your pupil Caelius. I acknowledge, however, that we may call them Orators: but as to the nature and extent of their merit, let your own judgment decide. It is scarcely worth observing, that you have had the additional good-nature to crowd so many daubers into your list, that there are some, I believe, who will be ready to wish they had died long ago, that you might have had an opportunity to insert *their* names among the rest."—"You have opened a wide field of enquiry," said I, "and started a subject which deserves a separate discussion; but we must defer it to a more convenient time. For, to settle it, a great variety of authors must be examined, and especially *Cato*: which could not fail to convince you, that nothing was wanting to complete his pieces, but those rich and glowing colours which had not then been invented. As to the above Oration of Crassus, he himself, perhaps, could have written better, if he had been willing to take the trouble; but nobody else, I believe, could have mended it. You have no reason, therefore, to think I spoke *ironically*, when I mentioned it as the guide and *tutoress* of my Eloquence: for though you seem to have a higher opinion of my capacity, in its present state, you must remember that, in our youth, we could find nothing better to imitate among the Romans. And as to my admitting so *many* into my list of Orators, I only did it (as I have already observed) to shew how few have succeeded in a profession, in which all were desirous to excel. I therefore insist upon it that you do not consider *me* in the present case, as an *Ironist*; though we are informed by C. Fannius, in his History, that *Africanus* was a very excellent one."—"As you please about *that*," cried Atticus: "though, by the bye, I did not imagine it would have been any disgrace to you, to be what Africanus and Socrates have been before you."—"We may settle *this* another time," interrupted Brutus: "but will you be so obliging," said he, (addressing himself to *me*) "as to give us a critical analysis of some of the old speeches you have mentioned?"—"Very willingly," replied I; "but it must be at Cuma, or Tusculum, when opportunity offers: for we are near neighbours, you know, in both places. At present, let us return to *Hortensius*, from whom we have digressed a second time."

"Hortensius, then, who began to speak in public when he was very young, was soon employed even in causes of the greatest moment: and though he first appeared in the time of Cotta and Sulpicius, (who were only ten years older) and when Crassus and Antonius, and afterwards Philip and Julius, were in the height of their reputation, he was thought worthy to be compared with either of them in point of Eloquence. He had such an excellent memory as I never knew in any person; so that what he had composed in private, he was able to repeat, without notes, in the very same words he had made use of at first. He employed this natural advantage with so much readiness, that he not only recollected whatever he had written or premeditated himself, but remembered every thing that had been said by his opponents, without the help of a prompter. He was likewise inflamed with such a passionate fondness for the profession, that I never saw any one, who took more pains to improve himself; for he would not suffer a day to elapse, without either speaking in the Forum, or composing something at home; and very often he did both in the same day. He had, besides, a turn of expression which was very far from being low and unelevated; and possessed two other accomplishments, in which no one could equal him,—an uncommon clearness and accuracy in stating the points he was to speak to; and a neat and easy manner of collecting the substance of what had been said by his antagonist, and by himself. He had likewise an elegant choice of words, an agreeable flow in his periods, and a copious Elocution, which he was partly indebted for to a fine natural capacity, and partly acquired by the most laborious rhetorical exercises. In short, he had a most retentive view of his subject, and always divided and parcelled it out with the greatest exactness; and he very seldom overlooked any thing which the case could suggest, that was proper either to support his *own* allegations, or to refute those of his opponent. Lastly, he had a sweet and sonorous voice; and his gesture had rather more art in it, and was more exactly managed, than is requisite to an Orator.

"While *he* was in the height of his glory, Crassus died, Cotta was banished, our public trials were intermitted by the Marsic war, and I myself made my first appearance in the Forum. Hortensius joined the army, and served the first campaign as a volunteer, and the second as a military Tribune: Sulpicius was made a lieutenant general; and Antonius was absent on a similar account. The only trial we had, was that upon the Varian Law; the rest, as I have just observed, having been intermitted by the war. We had scarcely any body left at the bar but L. Memmius, and Q. Pompeius, who spoke mostly on their own affairs; and, though far from being Orators of the first distinction, were yet tolerable ones, (if we may credit Philippus, who was himself a man of some Eloquence) and in supporting an evidence, displayed all the poignancy of a prosecutor, with a moderate freedom of Elocution. The rest, who were esteemed our capital Speakers, were then in the magistracy, and I had the benefit of hearing their harangues almost every day. C. Curio was chosen a Tribune of the people; though he left off speaking after being once deserted by his whole audience. To him I may add Q. Metellus Celer, who, though certainly no Orator, was far from being destitute of utterance: but Q. Varius, C. Carbo, and Cn. Pomponius, were men of real Elocution, and might almost be said to have lived upon the Rostra. C. Julius too, who was then a Curule Aedile, was daily employed in making Speeches to the people, which were composed with great neatness and accuracy. But while I attended the Forum with this eager curiosity, my first disappointment was the banishment of Cotta: after which I continued to hear the rest with the same assiduity as before; and though I daily spent the remainder of my time in reading, writing, and private declamation, I cannot say that I much relished my confinement to these preparatory exercises. The next year Q. Varius was condemned, and banished, by his own law: and I, that I might acquire a competent knowledge of the principles of jurisprudence, then attached myself to Q. Scaevola, the son of Publius, who, though he did not choose to undertake the charge of a pupil, yet by freely giving his advice to those who consulted him, he answered every purpose of instruction to such as took the trouble to apply to him. In the succeeding year, in which Sylla and Pompey were Consuls, as Sulpicius, who was elected a Tribune of the people, had occasion to speak in public almost every day, I had an opportunity to acquaint myself thoroughly with his manner of speaking. At this time Philo, a philosopher of the first name *in the Academy*, with many of the principal Athenians, having deserted their native home, and fled to Rome, from the fury of Mithridates, I immediately became his scholar, and was exceedingly taken with his philosophy; and, besides the, pleasure I received from the great variety and sublimity of his matter, I was still more inclined to confine, my attention to that study; because there was reason to apprehend that our laws and judicial proceedings would be wholly overturned by the continuance of the public disorders. In the same year Sulpicius lost his life; and Q. Catulus, M. Antonius, and C. Julius, three Orators, who were partly cotemporary with each other, were most inhumanly put to death. Then also I attended the lectures of Molo the Rhodian, who was newly come to Rome, and was both an excellent Pleader, and an able Teacher of the Art. I have mentioned these particulars, which, perhaps, may appear foreign to our purpose, that *you*, my Brutus, (for Atticus is already acquainted with them) may be able to mark my progress, and observe how closely I trod upon the heels of Hortensius.

"The three following years the city was free from the tumult of arms; but either by the death, the voluntary retirement, or the flight of our ablest Orators (for even M. Crassus, and the two Lentuli, who were then in the bloom of youth, had all left us) Hortensius, of course, was the first Speaker in the Forum. Antistius too was daily rising into reputation,— Piso pleaded pretty often,—Pomponius not so frequently,—Carbo very seldom,—and Philippus only once or twice. In the mean while I pursued my studies of every kind, day and night, with unremitting application. I lodged and boarded at my own house [where he lately died] Diodotus the Stoic; whom I employed as my preceptor in various other parts of learning, but particularly in Logic, which may be considered as a close and contracted species of Eloquence; and without which, you yourself have declared it impossible to acquire that full and perfect Eloquence, which they suppose to be an open and dilated kind of Logic. Yet with all my attention to Diodotus, and the various arts he was master of, I never suffered even a single day to escape me, without some exercise of the oratorial kind. I constantly declaimed in private with M. Piso, Q. Pompeius, or some other of my acquaintance; pretty often in Latin, but much oftener in Greek; because the Greek furnishes a greater variety of ornaments, and an opportunity of imitating and introducing them into the Latin; and because the Greek masters, who were far the best, could not correct and improve us, unless we declaimed in that language. This time was distinguished by a violent struggle to restore the liberty of the Republic:—the barbarous slaughter of the three Orators, Scaevola, Carbo, and Antistius;—the return of Cotta, Curio, Crassus, Pompey, and the Lentuli;—the re-establishment of the laws and courts of judicature;—and the intire restoration of the Commonwealth: but we lost Pomponius, Censorinus, and Murena, from the roll of Orators.

"I now began, for the *first* time, to undertake the management of causes, both private and public; not, as most did, with a view to learn my profession, but to make a trial of the abilities which I had taken so much pains to acquire. I had then a second opportunity of attending the instructions of Molo; who came to Rome, while Sylla was Dictator, to sollicit the payment of what was due to his countrymen, for their services in the Mithridatic war. My defence of Sext. Roscius, which was the first cause I pleaded, met with such a favourable reception, that, from that moment, I was looked upon as an advocate of the first class, and equal to the greatest and most important causes: and after this I pleaded many others, which I pre-composed with all the care and accuracy I was master of.

"But as you seem desirous not so much to be acquainted with any incidental marks of my character, or the first sallies of my youth, as to know me thoroughly, I shall mention some particulars, which otherwise might have seemed unnecessary. At this time my body was exceedingly weak and emaciated; my neck long, and slender; a shape and habit, which I thought to be liable to great risk of life, if engaged in any violent fatigue, or labour of the lungs. And it gave the greater alarm to those who had a regard for me, that I used to speak without any remission or variation, with the utmost stretch of my voice, and a total agitation of my body. When my friends, therefore, and physicians, advised me to meddle no more with forensic causes, I resolved to run any hazard, rather than quit the hopes of glory, which I had proposed to myself from pleading: but when I considered, that by managing my voice, and changing my way of speaking, I might both avoid all future danger of that kind, and speak with greater ease, I took a resolution of travelling into Asia, merely for an opportunity to correct my manner of speaking. So that after I had been two years at the Bar, and acquired some reputation in the Forum, I left Rome. When I came to Athens, I spent six months with Antiochus, the principal and most judicious Philosopher of *the old Academy*; and under this able master, I renewed those philosophical studies which I had laboriously cultivated and improved from my earliest youth. At the same time, however, I continued my *rhetorical Exercises* under Demetrius the Syrian, an experienced and reputable master of the Art of Speaking.

"After leaving Athens, I traversed every part of Asia, where I was voluntarily attended by the principal Orators of the country with whom I renewed my rhetorical Exercises. The chief of them was Menippus of Stratonica, the most eloquent of all the Asiatics: and if to be neither tedious nor impertinent is the characteristic of an Attic Orator, he may be justly ranked in that class. Dionysius also of Magnesia, Aeschilus of Cnidos, and Xenocles of Adramyttus, who were esteemed the first Rhetoricians of Asia, were continually with me. Not contented with these, I went to Rhodes, and applied myself again to Molo, whom I had heard before at Rome; and who was both an experienced pleader, and a fine writer, and particularly judicious in remarking the faults of his scholars, as well as in his method of teaching and improving them. His principal trouble with me, was to restrain the luxuriancy of a juvenile imagination, always ready to overflow its banks, within its due and proper channel. Thus, after an excursion of two years, I returned to Italy, not only much improved, but almost changed into a new man. The vehemence of my voice and action was considerably abated; the excessive ardour of my language was corrected; my lungs were strengthened; and my whole constitution confirmed and settled.

"Two Orators then reigned in the Forum; (I mean Cotta and Hortensius) whose glory fired my emulation. Cotta's way of speaking was calm and easy, and distinguished by the flowing elegance and propriety of his language. The other was splendid, warm, and animated; not such as you, my Brutus, have seen him when he had shed the blossom of his eloquence, but far more lively and pathetic both in his style and action. As Hortensius, therefore, was nearer to me in age, and his manner more agreeable to the natural ardour of my temper, I considered him as the proper object of my competition. For I observed that when they were both engaged in the same cause, (as for instance, when they defended M. Canuleius, and Cn. Dolabella, a man of consular dignity) though Cotta was generally employed to open the defence, the most important parts of it were left to the management of Hortensius. For a crowded audience, and a clamorous Forum, require an Orator who is lively, animated, full of action, and able to exert his voice to the highest pitch. The first year, therefore, after my return from Asia, I undertook several capital causes; and in the interim I put up as a candidate for the Quaestorship, Cotta for the Consulate, and Hortensius for the Aedileship. After I was chosen Quaestor, I passed a year in Sicily, the province assigned to me by lot: Cotta went as Consul into Gaul: and Hortensius, whose new office required his presence at Rome, was left of course the undisputed sovereign of the Forum. In the succeeding year, when I returned from Sicily, my oratorial talents, such as they were, displayed themselves in their full perfection and maturity.

"I have been saying too much, perhaps, concerning myself: but my design in it was not to make a parade of my eloquence and ability, which I have no temptation to do, but only to specify the pains and labour which I have taken to improve it. After spending the five succeeding years in pleading a variety of causes, and with the ablest Advocates of the time, I was declared an Aedile, and undertook the patronage of the Sicilians against Hortensius, who was then one of the Consuls elect. But as the subject of our conversation not only requires an historical detail of Orators, but such preceptive remarks as may be necessary to elucidate their characters; it will not be improper to make some observations of this kind upon that of Hortensius. After his appointment to the consulship (very probably, because he saw none of consular dignity who were able to rival him, and despised the competition of others of inferior rank) he began to remit that intense application which he had hitherto persevered in from his childhood; and having settled himself in very affluent circumstances, he chose to live for the future what he thought an *easy* life, but which, in truth, was rather an indolent one. In the three succeeding years, the beauty of his colouring was so much impaired, as to be very perceptible to a skilful connoisseur, though not to a common observer. After that, he grew every day more unlike himself than before, not only in other parts of Eloquence, but by a gradual decay of the former celerity and elegant texture of his language. I, at the same time, spared no pains to improve and enlarge my talents, such as they were, by every exercise that was proper for the purpose, but particularly by that of writing. Not to mention several other advantages I derived from it, I shall only observe, that about this time, and but a very few years after my Aedileship, I was declared the first Praetor, by the unanimous suffrages of my fellow- citizens. For, by my diligence and assiduity as a Pleader, and my accurate way of speaking, which was rather superior to the ordinary style of the Bar, the novelty of my Eloquence had engaged the attention, and secured the good wishes of the public. But I will say nothing of myself: I will confine my discourse to our other Speakers, among whom there is not one who has gained more than a common acquaintance with those parts of literature, which feed the springs of Eloquence:—not one who has been thoroughly nurtured at the breast of Philosophy, which is the mother of every excellence either in deed or speech:—not one who has acquired an accurate knowledge of the Civil Law, which is so necessary for the management even of private causes, and to direct the judgment of an Orator:—not one who is a complete master of the Roman History, which would enable us, on many occasions, to appeal to the venerable evidence of the dead:—not one who can entangle his opponent in such a neat and humourous manner, as to relax the severity of the Judges into a smile or an open laugh:—not one who knows how to dilate and expand his subject, by reducing it from the limited considerations of time, and person, to some general and indefinite topic;—not one who knows how to enliven it by an agreeable digression: not one who can rouse the indignation of the Judge, or extort from him the tear of compassion;—or who can influence and bend his soul (which is confessedly the capital perfection of an Orator) in such a manner as shall best suit his purpose.

"When Hortensius, therefore, the once eloquent and admired Hortensius, had almost vanished from the Forum, my appointment to the Consulship, which happened about six years after his own promotion to that office, revived his dying emulation; for he was unwilling that after I had equalled him in rank and dignity, I should become his superior in any other respect. But in the twelve succeeding years, by a mutual deference to each other's abilities, we united our efforts at the Bar in the most amicable manner: and my Consulship, which at first had given a short alarm to his jealousy, afterward cemented our friendship, by the generous candor with which he applauded my conduct. But our emulous efforts were exerted in the most conspicuous manner, just before the commencement of that unhappy period, when Eloquence herself was confounded and terrified by the din of arms into a sudden and a total silence: for after Pompey had proposed and carried a law, which allowed even the party accused but three hours to make his defence, I appeared, (though comparatively as a mere *noviciate* by this new regulation) in a number of causes which, in fact, were become perfectly the same, or very nearly so; most of which, my Brutus, you was present to hear, as having been my partner and fellow-advocate in many of them, though you pleaded several by yourself; and Hortensius, though he died a short time afterwards, bore his share in these limited efforts. He began to plead about ten years before the time of your birth; and in his sixty-fourth year, but a very few days before his death, he was engaged with you in the defence of Appius, your father-in-law. As to our respective talents, the Orations we have published will enable posterity to form a proper judgment of them. But if we mean to inquire, why Hortensius was more admired for his Eloquence in the younger part of his life, than in his latter years, we shall find it owing to the following causes. The first was, that an *Asiatic* style is more allowable in a young man than in an old one. Of this there are two different kinds.

"The former is sententious and sprightly, and abounds in those turns of sentiment which are not so much distinguished by their weight and solidity as by their neatness and elegance; of this cast was Timaeus the Historian, and the two Orators so much talked of in our younger days, Hierocles the Alabandean, and his brother Menecles, but particularly the latter; both whose Orations may be reckoned master-pieces of the kind. The other sort is not so remarkable for the plenty and richness of its sentiments, as for its rapid volubility of expression, which at present is the ruling taste in Asia; but, besides it's uncommon fluency, it is recommended by a choice of words which are peculiarly delicate and ornamental:—of this kind were Aeschylus the Cnidian, and my cotemporary Aeschines the Milesian; for they had an admirable command of language, with very little elegance of sentiment. These showy kinds of eloquence are agreeable enough in young people; but they are entirely destitute of that gravity and composure which befits a riper age. As Hortensius therefore excelled in both, he was heard with applause in the earlier part of his life. For he had all that fertility and graceful variety of sentiment which distinguished the character of Menecles: but, as in Menecles, so in him, there were many turns of sentiment which were more delicate and entertaining than really useful, or indeed sometimes convenient. His language also was brilliant and rapid, and yet perfectly neat and accurate; but by no means agreeable to men of riper years. I have often seen it received by Philippus with the utmost derision, and, upon some occasions, with a contemptuous indignation: but the younger part of the audience admired it, and the populace were highly pleased with it. In his youth, therefore, he met the warmest approbation of the public, and maintained his post with ease as the first Orator in the Forum. For the style he chose to speak in, though it has little weight, or authority, appeared very suitable to his age: and as it discovered in him the most visible marks of genius and application, and was recommended by the numerous cadence of his periods, he was heard with universal applause. But when the honours he afterwards rose to, and the dignity of his years required something more serious and composed, he still continued to appear in the same character, though it no longer became him: and as he had, for some considerable time, intermitted those exercises, and relaxed that laborious attention which had once distinguished him, though his former neatness of expression, and luxuriancy of sentiment still remained, they were stripped of those brilliant ornaments they had been used to wear. For this reason, perhaps, my Brutus, he appeared less pleasing to you than he would have done, if you had been old enough to hear him, when he was fired with emulation and flourished in the full bloom of his Eloquence.

"I am perfectly sensible," said Brutus, "of the justice of your remarks; and yet I have always looked upon Hortensius as a great Orator, but especially when he pleaded for Messala, in the time of your absence."—"I have often heard of it," replied I, "and his Oration, which was afterwards published, they say, in the very same words in which he delivered it, is no way inferior to the character you give it. Upon the whole, then, his reputation flourished from the time of Crassus and Scaevola (reckoning from the Consulship of the former) to the Consulship of Paullus and Marcellus: and I held out in the same career of glory from the Dictatorship of Sylla, to the period I have last, mentioned. Thus the Eloquence of Hortensius was extinguished by his *own* death, and mine by that of the Commonwealth."—"Ominate more favourably, I beg of you," cried Brutus. —"As favourably as you please," said I, "and that not so much upon my own account, as your's. But *his* death was truly fortunate, who did not live to behold the miseries, which he had long foreseen. For we often lamented, between ourselves, the misfortunes which hung over the State, when we discovered the seeds of a civil war in the insatiable ambition of a few private Citizens, and saw every hope of an accommodation excluded by the rashness and precipitancy of our public counsels. But the felicity which always marked his life, seems to have exempted him, by a seasonable death, from the calamities that followed. But, as after the decease of Hortensius, we seem to have been left, my Brutus, as the sole guardians of an *orphan* Eloquence, let us cherish her, within our own walls at least, with a generous fidelity: let us discourage the addresses of her worthless, and impertinent suitors; let us preserve her pure and unblemished in all her virgin charms, and secure her, to the utmost of our ability, from the lawless violence of every armed ruffian. I must own, however, though I am heartily grieved that I entered so late upon the road of life, as to be overtaken by a gloomy night of public distress, before I had finished my journey; that I am not a little relieved by the tender consolation which you administered to me in your very agreeable letters;— in which you tell me I ought to recollect my courage, since my past transactions are such as will speak for me when I am silent, and survive my death,—and such as, if the Gods permit, will bear an ample testimony to the prudence and integrity of my public counsels, by the final restoration of the Republic:—or, if otherwise, by burying me in the ruins of my country. But when I look upon *you*, my Brutus, it fills me with anguish to reflect that, in the vigour of your youth, and when you was making the most rapid progress in the road to fame, your career was suddenly stopped by the fatal overthrow of the Commonwealth. This unhappy circumstance has stung me to the heart; and not *me* only; but my worthy friend here, who has the same affection for you, and the same esteem for your merit which I have. We have the warmest wishes for your happiness, and heartily pray that you may reap the rewards of your excellent virtues, and live to find a Republic in which you will be able, not only to revive, but even to add to the fame of your illustrious ancestors. For the Forum was your birth-right, your native theatre of action; and you was the only person that entered it, who had not only formed his Elocution by a rigorous course of private practice, but enriched his Oratory with the furniture of philosophical Science, and thus united the highest virtue to the most consummate Eloquence. Your situation, therefore, wounds us with the double anxiety, that *you* are deprived of the *Republic*, and the Republic of *you*. But still continue, my Brutus, (notwithstanding the career of your genius has been checked by the rude shock of our public distresses) continue to pursue your favourite studies, and endeavour (what you have almost, or rather intirely effected already) to distinguish yourself from the promiscuous crowd of Pleaders with which I have loaded the little history I have been giving you. For it would ill befit you, (richly furnished as you are with those liberal Arts, which, unable to acquire at home, you imported from that celebrated city which has always been revered as the seat of learning) to pass after all as an ordinary Pleader. For to what purposes have you studied under Pammenes, the most eloquent man in Greece; or what advantage have you derived from the discipline of *the old* Academy, and it's hereditary master Aristus (my guest, and very intimate acquaintance) if you still rank yourself in the common class of Orators? Have we not seen that a whole age could scarcely furnish two Speakers who really excelled in their profession? Among a crowd of cotemporaries, Galba, for instance, was the only Orator of distinction: for old Cato (we are informed) was obliged to yield to his superior merit, as were likewise his two juniors Lepidus, and Carbo. But, in a public Harangue, the style of his successors the Gracchi was far more easy and lively: and yet, even in their time, the Roman Eloquence had not reached its perfection. Afterwards came Antonius, and Crassus; and then Cotta, Sulpicius, Hortensius, and—but I say no more: I can only add, that if I had been so fortunate, &c, &c,"—[*Caetera defunt.*]

THE ORATOR,
BY MARCUS TULLIUS CICERO;
ADDRESSED TO MARCUS BRUTUS;
And now first translated from the Original Latin.

"Song charms the Sense, but Eloquence the Soul."

MILTON.

THE ORATOR.

Which, my Brutus, would be the most difficult talk,—to decline answering a request which you have so often repeated, or to gratify it to your satisfaction,—I have long been at a loss to determine. I should be extremely sorry to deny any thing to a friend for whom I have the warmest esteem, and who, I am sensible, has an equal affection for me;— especially, as he has only desired me to undertake a subject which may justly claim my attention. But to delineate a character, which it would be very difficult, I will not say to *acquire*, but even to *comprehend* in its full extent, I thought was too bold an undertaking for him who reveres the censure of the wife and learned. For considering the great diversity of manner among the ablest Speakers, how exceedingly difficult must it be to determine which is best, and give a finished model of Eloquence? This, however, in compliance with your repeated solicitations, I shall now attempt;—not so much from any hopes of succeeding, as from a strong inclination to make the trial. For I had rather, by yielding to your wishes, give you room to complain of my insufficiency; than, by a peremptory denial, tempt you to question my friendship.

You desire to know, then, (and you have often repeated your request) what kind of Eloquence I most approve, and can look upon to be so highly finished, as to require no farther improvement. But should I be able to answer your expectations, and display, in his full perfection, the Orator you enquire after; I am afraid I shall retard the industry of many, who, enfeebled by despair, will no longer attempt what they think themselves incapable of attaining. It is but reasonable, however, that all those who covet what is excellent, and which cannot be acquired without the greatest application, should exert their utmost. But if any one is deficient in capacity, and destitute of that admirable force of genius which Nature bestows upon her favourites, or has been denied the advantages of a liberal education, *let him make the progress he is able*. For while we are driving to overtake the foremost, it is no disgrace to be found among the *second* class, or even the *third*. Thus, for instance, among the poets, we respect the merit not only of a *Homer* (that I may confine myself to the Greeks) or of *Archilochus, Sophocles*, or *Pindar*, but of many others who occupied the second, or even a lower place. In Philosophy also the diffusive majesty of Plato has not deterred *Aristotle* from entering the list; nor has *Aristotle* himself, with all his wonderful knowledge and fertility of thought, disheartened the endeavours of others. Nay, men of an elevated genius have not only disdained to be intimidated from the pursuit of literary fame;—but the very artists and mechanics have never relinquished their profession, because they were unable to equal the beauty of that *Iasylus* which we have seen at Rhodes, or of the celebrated *Venus* in the island of *Coos*:—nor has the noble image of Olympian *Jove*, or the famous statue of the Man at Arms, deterred others from making trial of their abilities, and exerting their skill to the utmost. Accordingly, such a large number of them has appeared, and each has performed so well in his own way, that we cannot help being pleased with their productions, notwithstanding our admiration at the nobler efforts of the great masters of the chissel.

But among the Orators, I mean those of Greece, it is astonishing how much one of them has surpassed the rest:—and yet, though there was a *Demosthenes*, there were even *then* many other Orators of considerable merit;—and such there were before he made his appearance, nor have they been wanting since. There is, therefore, no reason why those who have devoted themselves to the study of Eloquence, should suffer their hopes to languish, or their industry to flag. For, in the first place, even that which is most excellent is not to be despaired of;—and, in all worthy attempts, that which is next to what is best is great and noble.

But in sketching out the character of a compleat Orator, it is possible I may exhibit such a one as hath never *yet* existed. For I am not to point out the *Speaker*, but to delineate the *Eloquence* than which nothing can be more perfect of the kind:—an Eloquence which hath blazed forth through a whole Harangue but seldom, and, it may be, never; but only here and there like a transient gleam, though in some Orators more frequently, and in others, perhaps, more sparingly.

My opinion, then, is,—that there is no human production of any kind, so compleatly beautiful, than which there is not a *something* still more beautiful, from which the other is copied like a portrait from real life, and which can be discerned neither by our eyes nor ears, nor any of our bodily senses, but is visible only to thought and imagination. Though the statues, therefore, of Phidias, and the other images above-mentioned, are all so wonderfully charming, that nothing can be found which is more excellent of the kind; we may still, however, *suppose* a something which is more exquisite, and more compleat. For it must not be thought that the ingenious artist, when he was sketching out the form of a Jupiter, or a Minerva, borrowed the likeness from any particular object;—but a certain admirable semblance of beauty was present to his mind, which he viewed and dwelt upon, and by which his skill and his hand were guided. As, therefore, in mere bodily shape and figure there is a kind of perfection, to whose ideal appearance every production which falls under the notice of the eye is referred by imitation; so the semblance of what is perfect in Oratory may become visible to the mind, and the ear may labour to catch a likeness.

These primary forms of thing are by Plato (the father of science and good language) called *Ideas*; and he tells us they have neither beginning nor end, but are co-eval with reason and intelligence; while every thing besides has a derived, and a transitory existence, and passes away and decays, so as to cease in a short time to be the thing it was. Whatever, therefore, may be discussed by reason and method, should be constantly reduced to the primary form or semblance of it's respective genus.

I am sensible that this introduction, as being derived not from the principles of Eloquence, but from the deepest recesses of Philosophy, will excite the censure, or at least the wonder of many, who will think it both unfashionable and intricate. For they will either be at a loss to discover it's connection with my subject, (though they will soon be convinced by what follows, that, if it appears to be far-fetched, it is not so without reason;)—or they will blame me, perhaps, for deserting the beaten track, and striking out into a new one. But I am satisfied that I often appear to advance novelties, when I offer sentiments which are, indeed, of a much earlier date, but happen to be generally unknown: and I frankly acknowledge that I came forth an Orator, (if indeed I am one, or whatever else I may be deemed) not from the school of the Rhetoricians, but from the spacious walks of the Academy. For these are the theatres of diversified and extensive arguments which were first impressed with the foot-steps of Plato; and his Dissertations, with those of other Philosophers, will be found of the greatest utility to an Orator, both for his exercise and improvement; because all the fertility, and, as it were, the materials of Eloquence, are to be derived from thence;—but not, however, sufficiently prepared for the business of the Forum, which, as themselves have frequently boasted, they abandoned to the *rustic Muses* of the vulgar! Thus the Eloquence of the Forum, despised and rejected by the Philosophers, was bereaved of her greatest advantages:—but, nevertheless, being arrayed in all the brilliance of language and sentiment, she made a figure among the populace, nor feared the censure of the judicious few. By this means, the learned became destitute of a popular Eloquence, and the Orators of polite learning.

We may, therefore, consider it as a capital maxim, (the truth of which will be more easily understood in the sequel) that the eloquent Speaker we are enquiring after, cannot be formed without the assistance of Philosophy. I do not mean that this alone is sufficient; but only (for it is sometimes necessary to compare great things to small) that it will contribute to improve him in the same manner as the *Palaestra* [Footnote: The *Palaestra* was a place set apart for public exercises, such as wrestling, running, fencing, &c. the frequent performance of which contributed much to a graceful carriage of the body, which is a necessary accomplishment in a good Actor.] does an Actor; because without Philosophy, no man can speak fully and copiously upon a variety of important subjects which come under the notice of an Orator. Accordingly, in the *Phaedrus* of Plato, it is observed by Socrates that the great *Pericles* excelled all the Speakers of his time, because he had been a hearer of *Anaxagoras* the Naturalist, from whom he supposes that he not only borrowed many excellent and sublime ideas, but a certain richness and fertility of language, and (what in Eloquence is of the utmost consequence) the various arts either of soothing or alarming each particular passion. The same might be said of *Demosthenes*, whose letters will satisfy us, how assiduously he attended the Lectures of Plato. For without the instruction of Philosophy, we can neither discover what is the *Genus* or the *Species* to which any thing belongs, nor explain the nature of it by a just definition, or an accurate analysis of its parts;— nor can we distinguish between what is true and false, or foresee the consequences, point out the inconsistencies, and dissolve the ambiguities which may lie in the case before us. But as to Natural Philosophy (the knowledge of which will supply us with the richest treasures of Elocution;)—and as to life, and it's various duties, and the great principles of morality,—what is it possible either to express or understand aright, without a large acquaintance with these? To such various and important accomplishments we must add the innumerable ornaments of language, which, at the time above mentioned, were the only weapons which the Masters of Rhetoric could furnish. This is the reason why that genuine, and perfect Eloquence we are speaking of, has been yet attained by no one; because the Art of *Reasoning* has been supposed to be one thing, and that of *Speaking* another; and we have had recourse to different Instructors for the knowledge of things and words.

Antonius, [Footnote: A celebrated Orator, and grandfather to M. Antonius The Triumvir.] therefore, to whom our ancestors adjudged the palm of Eloquence, and who had much natural penetration and sagacity, has observed in the only book he published, "*that he had seen many good Speakers, but not a single Orator*." The full and perfect semblance of Eloquence had so thoroughly possessed his mind, and was so completely visible there, though no where exemplified in practice, that this consummate Genius, (for such, indeed, he was) observing many defects in both himself and others, could discover no one who merited the name of *eloquent*. But if he considered neither himself, nor Lucius Crassus, as a genuine Orator, he must have formed in his mind a sublime idea of Eloquence, under which, because there was nothing wanting to compleat it, he could not comprehend those Speakers who were any ways deficient. Let us then, my Brutus, (if we are able) trace out the Orator whom Antonius never saw, and who, it may be, has never yet existed; for though we have not the skill to copy his likeness in real practice, (a talk which, in the opinion of the person above- mentioned, would be almost too arduous for one of the Gods,) we may be able, perhaps, to give some account of what he *ought* to be.

Good Speaking, then, may be divided into three characters, in each of which there are some who have made an eminent figure: but to be equally excellent in all (which is what we require) has been the happiness of few.

The *lofty* and *majestic* Speaker, who distinguishes himself by the energy of his sentiments, and the dignity of his expression, is impetuous,—diversified,—copious,—and weighty,—and abundantly qualified to alarm and sway the passions;—which some effect by a harsh, and a rough, gloomy way of speaking, without any harmony or measure; and others, by a smooth, a regular, and a well-proportioned style.

On the other hand, the *simple* and *easy* Speaker is remarkably dexterous and keen, and aiming at nothing but our information, makes every thing he discourses upon, rather clear and open than great and striking, and polishes it with the utmost neatness and accuracy. But some of this kind of Speakers, who are distinguished by their peculiar artificie, are designedly unpolished, and appear rude and unskilful, that they may have the better opportunity of deceiving us:—while others, with the same poverty of style, are far more elegant and agreeable,—that is, they are pleasant and facetious, and sometimes even florid, with here and there an easy ornament.

But there is likewise a *middle* kind of Oratory, between the two above-mentioned, which neither has the keenness of the latter, nor hurls the thunder of the former; but is a mixture of both, without excelling in either, though at the same time it has something of each, or (perhaps, more properly) is equally destitute of the true merit of both. This species of Eloquence flows along in a uniform course, having nothing to recommend it, but it's peculiar smoothness and equability; though at the same time, it intermingles a number of decorations, like the tufts of flowers in a garland, and embellishes a discourse from beginning to end with the moderate and less striking ornaments of language and sentiment.

Those who have attained to any degree of perfection in either of the above characters, have been distinguished as eminent Orators: but the question is whether any of them have compassed what we are seeking after, and succeeded equally in all. For there have been several who could speak nervously and pompously, and yet, upon occasion, could express themselves with the greates address, and simplicity. I wish I could refer to such an Orator, or at least to one who nearly resembles him, among the Romans; for it would certainly have been more to our credit to be able to refer to proper examples of our own, and not be necessitated to have recourse to the Greeks. But though in another treatis of mine, which bears the name of *Brutus*, [Footnote: A very excellent Treatise in the form of a Dialogue. It contains a critical and very instructive account of all the noted Orators of *Greece* and *Rome* and might be called, with great propriety, *the History of Eloquence*. Though it is perhaps the most entertaining of all Cicero's performances, the Public have never been obliged before with a translation of it into English; which, I hope, will sufficiently plead my excuse for preforming to undertake it.] I have said much in favour of the Romans, partly to excite their emulation, and, in some measure, from a partial fondness for my country; yet I must always remember to give the preference to *Demosthenes*, who alone has adapted his genius to that perfect species of Eloquence of which I can readily form an idea, but which I have never yet seen exemplified in practice. Than *him*, there has never hitherto existed a more nervous, and at the same time, a more subtle Speaker, or one more cool and temperate. I must, therefore, caution those whose ignorant discourse is become so common, and who wish to pass for *Attic* Speakers, or at least to express themselves in the *Attic* taste, —I must caution them to take *him* for their pattern, than whom it is impossible that Athens herself should be more completely Attic: and, as to genuine Atticism, that them learn what it means, and measure the force of Eloquence, not by their own weakness and incapacity, but by his wonderful energy and strength. For, at present, a person bestows his commendation upon just so much as he thinks himself capable of imitating. I therefore flatter myself that it will not be foreign to my purpose, to instruct those who have a laudable emulation, but are not thoroughly settled in their judgment, wherein the merit of an Attic Orator consists.

The taste of the Audience, then, has always governed and directed the Eloquence of the Speaker: for all who wish to be applauded, consult the character, and the inclinations of those who hear them, and carefully form and accommodate themselves to their particular humours and dispositions. Thus in Caria, Phrygia, and Mysia, because the inhabitants have no relish for true elegance and politeness, the Orators have adopted (as most agreeable to the ears of their audience) a luxuriant, and, if I may so express myself, a corpulent style; which their neighbours the Rhodians, who are only parted from them by a narrow straight, have never approved, and much less the Greeks; but the Athenians have entirely banished it; for their taste has always been so just and accurate that they could not listen to any thing but what was perfectly correct and elegant. An Orator, therefore, to compliment their delicacy, was forced to be always upon his guard against a faulty or a distasteful expression.

Accordingly, *he*, whom we have just mentioned as surpassing the rest, has been careful in his Oration for Ctesiphon, (which is the best he ever composed) to set out very cooly and modestly: when he proceeds to argue the point of law, he grows more poignant and pressing; and as he advances in his defence, he takes still greater liberties; till, at last, having warmed the passions of his Judges, he exults at his pleasure through the reamining part of his discourse. But even in *him*, thus carefully weighing and poising his every word *Aeschines* [Footnote: *Aeschines* was a cotemporary, and a professed rival of Demosthenes. He carried his animosity so far as to commence a litigious suit against him, at a time when the reputation of the latter was at the lowest ebb. But being overpowered by the Eloquence of Demosthenes, he was condemned to perpetual banishment.] could find several expressions to turn into ridicule:—for giving a loose to his raillery, he calls them harsh, and detestable, and too shocking to be endured; and styling the author of them a very *monster*, he tauntingly asks him whether such expressions could be considered as *words* or not rather as absolute *frights* and *prodigies*. So that to AEschines not even *Demosthenes* himself was perfectly *Attic*; for it is an easy matter to catch a *glowing* expression, (if I may be allowed to call it so) and expose it to ridicule when the fire of attention is extinguished. Demosthenes, therefore, when he endeavours to excuse himself, condescends to jest, and denies that the fortune of Greece was in the least affected by the singularity of a particular expression, or by his moving his hand either this way or that.

With what patience, then, would a Mysian or a Phrygian have been heard at Athens, when even Demosthenes himself was reproached as a nuisance? But should the former have begun his whining sing-song, after the manner of the Asiatics, who would have endured it? or rather, who would not have ordered him to be instantly torn from the Rostrum? Those, therefore, who can accommodate themselves to the nice and critical ears of an Athenian audience, are the only persons who should pretend to Atticism.

But though Atticism may be divided into several kinds, these mimic Athenians suspect but one. They imagine that to discourse plainly, and without any ornament, provided it be done correctly, and clearly, is the only genuine Atticism. In confining it to this alone, they are certainly mistaken; though when they tell us that this is really Attic, they are so far in the right. For if the only true Atticism is what they suppose to be, not even *Pericles* was an Attic Speaker, though he was universally allowed to bear away the palm of Eloquence; nor, if he had wholly attached himself to this plain and simple kind of language, would he ever have been said by the Poet Aristophanes *to thunder and lighten, and throw all Greece into a ferment.*

Be it allowed, then, that Lysias, that graceful and most polite of Speakers, was truly Attic: for who can deny it? But let it also be remembered that Lysias claims the merit of Atticism, not so much for his simplicity and want of ornament, as because he has nothing which is either faulty or impertinent. But to speak floridly, nervously, and copiously, this also is true Atticism:—otherwise, neither Aeschines nor even Demosthenes himself were Attic Speakers.

There are others who affect to be called *Thucydideans,*—a strange and novel race of Triflers! For those who attach themselves to Lysias, have a real Pleader for their pattern;—not indeed a stately, and striking Pleader, but yet a dextrous and very elegant one, who might appear in the Forum with reputation.

Thucydides, on the contrary, is a mere Historian, who ('tis true) describes wars, and battles with great dignity and precision; but he can supply us with nothing which is proper for the Forum. For his very speeches have so many obscure and intricate periods, that they are scarcely intelligible; which in a public discourse is the greatest fault of which an Orator can be guilty. But who, when the use of corn has been discovered, would be so mad as to feed upon acorns? Or could the Athenians improve their diet, and bodily food, and be incapable of cultivating their language? Or, lastly, which of the Greek Orators has copied the style of Thucydides? [Footnote: Demosthenes indeed took the pains to transcribe the History of Thucydides several times. But he did this, no so much to copy the *form* as the energy of his language.] "True," they reply, "but Thucydides was universally admired." And so, indeed, he was; but only as a sensible, an exact, and a grave Historian;—not for his address in public debates, but for his excellence in describing wars and battles. Accordingly, he was never mentioned as an Orator; nor would his name have been known to posterity, if he had not composed his History, notwithstanding the dignity of his birth, and the honourable share he held in the Government. But none of these Pretenders have copied his energy; and yet when they have uttered a few mutilated and broken periods (which they might easily have done without a master to imitate) we must rever them, truly, as so many genuine *Thucydideses*. I have likewise met with a few who were professed imitators of Xenophon; whose language, indeed, is sweeter than honey, but totally unqualified to withstand the clamours of the Forum.

Let us return then to the Orator we are seeking after, and furnish him with those powers of Elocution, which Antonius could not discover in any one: an arduous task, my Brutus, and full of difficulty:—yet nothing, I believe, is impossible to him whose breast is fired with the generous flame of friendship! But I affectionately admire (and have always admired) your genius, your inclinations, and your manners. Nay, I am daily more inflamed and ravished, not only with a desire (which, I assure you, is a violent one) to renew our friendly intercourses, our social repasts, and your improving conversation, but by the wonderful fame of your incredible virtues, which, though different in kind, are readily united by your superior wisdom and good-sense. For what is so remote from severity of manners as gentleness and affability? and yet who more venerable than yourself, or who more agreeable? What can be more difficult than to decide a number of suits, so as to be equally esteemed and beloved by the parties on both sides? You, however, possess the admirable talent of sending away perfectly easy and contented even those against whom your are forced to give judgment: thus bringing it to bear that, while you do nothing from a partial favour to any man, whatever you do is favourably received. Hence it happens, that the only country upon earth, which is not involved in the present confusion, is the province of Gaul; where you are now enjoying yourself in a happy tranquillity, while you are universally respected at home, and live in the hearts of the flower and strength of your fellow- citizens. It is equally amazing, though you are always engaged in the most important offices of

Government, that your studies are never intermitted; and that you are constantly either composing something of your own, or finding employment for me! Accordingly I began this Essay, at your request, as soon as I had finished my *Cato*; which last also I should never have attempted (especially at a time when the enemies of virtue were so numerous) if I had not considered it as a crime to disobey my friend, when he only urged me to revive the memory of a man whom I always loved and honoured in his life-time. But I have now ventured upon a task which you have frequently pressed upon me, and I as often refused: for, if possible, I would share the fault between us, that if I should prove unequal to the subject, you may have the blame of loading me with a burden which is beyond my strength, and I the censure of presuming to undertake it:—though after all, the single merit of gratifying such a friend as Brutus, will sufficiently atone for any defects I may fall into.

But in every accomplishment which may become the object of pursuit, it is excessively difficult to delineate the form (or, as the Greeks call it, the *character* [Footnote: [Greek: charachtaer].]) of what is *best*; because some suppose it to consist in one thing, and some in another. Thus, for instance, "I am for *Ennius*," says one; "because he confines himself to the style of conversation:"—"and I," says another, "give the preference to *Pacuvius*, because his verses are embellished and well- wrought; whereas Ennius is rather too "negligent." In the same manner we may suppose a third to be an admirer of Attius; for, as among the Greeks, so it happens with us, "*different men have different opinions*;"—nor is it easy to determine which is best. Thus also in painting, some are pleased with a rough, a wild, and a dark and cloudy style; while others prefer that which is clear, and lively, and well covered with light. How then shall we strike out a general *rule* or *model*, when there are several manners, and each of them has a certain perfection of its own? But this difficulty has not deterred me from the undertaking; nor have I altered my opinion that in all things there is a *something* which comprehends the highest excellence of the kind, and which, though not generally discernible, is sufficiently conspicuous to him, who is skilled in the subject.

"But as there are several kinds of Eloquence which differ considerably from each other, and therefore cannot be reduced to one common form;—for this reason, as to mere laudatory Orations, Essays, Histories, and such suasory performances as the Panegyric of Isocrates, and the speeches of many others who were called *Sophists*;—and, in short, as to every thing which is unconnected with the Forum, and the whole of that species of discourse which the Greeks call the *demonstrative* [Footnote: The *demonstrative* species of Eloquence is that which was solely employed either in *praising* or *dispraising*. Besides this, there are two others, viz. the *deliberative*, and the *judicial*; the former was employed in political debates, where it's whole business was either to *persuade* or *dissuade*; and the latter, in judicial suits and controversies, where the Speaker was either to *accuse* or *defend*. But, on many occasions, they were all three intermingled in the same discourse.];—the form, or leading character of these I shall pass over; though I am far from considering it as a mere trifle, or a subject of no consequence; on the contrary, we may regard it as the nurse and tutoress of the Orator we are now delineating. For *here*, a fluency of expression is confessedly nourished and cultivated; and the easy construction, and harmonious cadence of our language is more openly attended to. *Here*, likewise, we both allow and recommend a studious elegance of diction, and a continued flow of melodious and well-turned periods;—and *here*, we may labour visibly, and without concealing our art, to contrast word to word, and to compare similar, and oppose contrary circumstances, and make several sentences (or parts of a sentence) conclude alike, and terminate with the same cadence; —ornaments, which in real pleadings, are to be used more sparingly, and with less appearance of art. Isocrates, therefore, confesses in his *Panathenaicus*, that these were beauties which he industriously pursued;

for he composed it not for victory in a suit at law (where such a confession must have greatly injured his cause) but merely to gratify the ear.

"It is recorded that the first persons who practised this species of composition [Footnote: The *composition* here mentioned consisted of three parts, The *first* regarded the structure; that is, the *connection* of our words, and required that the last syllable of every preceding, and the first of every succeeding word should be so aptly united as to produce an agreeable sound; which was effected by avoiding a collision of vowels or of inamicable consonants. It likewise required that those words should be constantly made choice of, whose separate sounds were most harmonious and most agreeable to the sense. The *second* part consisted in the use of particular forms of expression, such as contrasts and antithesises, which have an appearance of order and regularity in their very texture. The *third* and last regarded that species of harmony which results not so much from the sound, as from the time and quantity of the several syllables in a sentence. This was called *number*, and sometimes *rhyme*; and was in fact a kind of *prosaic metre*, which was carefully attended to by the ancients in every part of a sentence, but more particularly at the beginning and end of it. In this part they usually included the *period*, or the rules for determining the length of their sentences. I thought it necessary to give this short account of their composition, because our author very frequently alludes to it, before he proceeds to explain it at large.] were *Thrasymachus* the Chalcedonian, and *Gorgias* the Leontine; and that these were followed by *Theodorus* the Byzantine, and a number of others, whom Socrates, in the Phaedrus of Plato, calls [Greek: logodaidalos] *Speech-wrights*; many of whole discourses are sufficiently neat and entertaining; but, being the first attempts of the kind, were too minute and puerile, and had too poetical an air, and too much colouring. On this account, the merit of *Herodotus*, and *Thucydides* is the more conspicuous: for though they lived at the time we are speaking of, they carefully avoided those studied decorations, or rather futilities. The former rolls along like a deep, still river without any rocks or shoals to interrupt it's course; and the other describes wars and battles, as if he was founding a charge on the trumpet; so that history (to use the words of *Theophrastus*) caught the first alarm from these, and began to express herself with greater dignity and spirit.

"After these came *Socrates*, whom I have always recommended as the most accomplished writer we have in the way I am speaking of; though sometimes, my Brutus, you have objected to it with a great deal of pleasantry and erudition. But when you are better informed for what it is I recommend him, you will then think of him perhaps as favourably as I do. Thrasymachus and Gorgias (who are said to have been the first who cultivated the art of prosaic harmony) appeared to him to be too minutely exact; and Thucydides, he thought, was as much too loose and rugged, and not sufficiently smooth, and full-mouthed; and from hence he took the hint to give a scope to his sentences by a more copious and unconfined flow of language, and to fill up their breaks and intervals with the softer and more agreeable numbers. By teaching this to the most celebrated Speakers, and Composers of the age, his house came at last to be honoured as the *School of Eloquence*. Wherefore as I bore the censure of others with indifference, when I had the good fortune to be applauded by Cato; thus Isocrates, with the approbation of Plato, may slight the judgment of inferior critics. For in the last page of the Phaedrus, we find *Socrates* thus expressing himself;—'Now, indeed, my dear Phaedrus,' said he, 'Isocrates is but a youth: but I will discover to you what I think of him.'—'And what is that?' replied the other.—'He appears to me,' said the Philosopher, 'to have too elevated a genius to be placed on a level with the arid speeches of Lysias. Besides, he has a stronger turn for virtue; so that I shall not wonder, as he advances in years, if in the species of Eloquence to which he now applies himself, he should exceed all, who have hitherto pursued it, like so many infants. Or, if this should not content him, I shall not be astonished to behold him with a godlike ardour pursuing higher and more important studies; for I plainly see that he has a natural bent to Philosophy!'"

Thus Socrates presaged of him when he was but a youth. But Plato recorded this eulogium when he was older; and he recorded it, though he was one of his equals and cotemporaries, and a professed enemy to the whole tribe of Rhetoricians! *Him* he admires, and *him* alone! So that such who despise Isocrates, must suffer me to err with Socrates and Plato.

The manner of speaking, then, which is observed in the *demonstrative* or ornamental species of Eloquence, and which I have before remarked, was peculiar to the Sophists, is sweet, harmonious, and flowing, full of pointed sentiments, and arrayed in all the brilliance of language. But it is much fitter for the parade than the field; and being, therefore, consigned to the Palaestra, and the schools, has been long banished from the Forum. As Eloquence, however, after she had been fed and nourished with this, acquires a fresher complexion, and a firmer constitution; it would not be amiss, I thought, to trace our Orator from his very *cradle*.

But these things are only for shew and amusement: whereas it is our business to take the field in earnest, and prepare for action. As there are three particulars, then, to be attended to by an Orator,—viz. *what* he is to say, in *what order*, and *how*; we shall consider what is most excellent in each; but after a different manner from what is followed in delivering a system of the Art. For we are not to furnish a set of precepts (this not being the province we have undertaken) but to exhibit a portrait of Eloquence in her full perfection: neither is it our business to explain the methods by which we may acquire it, but only to shew what opinion we ought to form of it.

The two first articles are to be lightly touched over; for they have not so much a remarkable as a necessary share in forming the character of a compleat Orator, and are likewise common to *his* with many other professions;—and though, to invent, and judge with accuracy, what is proper to be said, are important accomplishments, and the same as the soul is to the body, yet they rather belong to *prudence* than to Eloquence. In what cause, however, can *prudence* be idle? Our Orator, therefore, who is to be all perfection, should be thoroughly acquainted with the sources of argument and proof. For as every thing which can become the subject of debate, must rest upon one or another of these particulars, viz.—whether a fact has been really committed, or what name it ought to bear in law, or whether it is agreeable or contrary to justice; and as the reality of a fact must be determined by force of evidence, the true name of it by it's definition, and the quality of it by the received notions of right and wrong; —an Orator (not an ordinary one, but the finished Speaker we are describing) will always turn off the controversy, as much as possible, from particular persons and times, (for we may argue more at liberty concerning general topics than about circumstances) in such a manner that what is proved to be true *universally*, may necessarily appear to be so in all *subordinate* cases. The point in debate being thus abstracted from particular persons and times, and brought to rest upon general principles, is called a *thesis*. In *this* the famous Aristotle carefully practised his scholars;—not to argue with the formal precision of Philosophers, but to canvass a point handsomely and readily on both sides, and with all the copiousness so much admired in the Rhetoricians: and for this purpose he delivered a set of *common places* (for so he calls them) which were to serve as so many marks or characters for the discovery of arguments, and from which a discourse might be aptly framed on either side of a question.

Our Orator then, (for I am not speaking of a mere school-declaimer, or a noisy ranter in the Forum, but of a well-accomplished and a finished Speaker)—our Orator, as there is such a copious variety of common-places, will examine them all, and employ those which suit his purpose in as general and indefinite a manner as his cause will permit, and carefully trace and investigate them to their inmost sources. But he will use the plenty before him with discretion, and weighing every thing with the utmost accuracy, select what is best: for the stress of an argument does not always, and in every cause, depend upon similar topics. He will, therefore, exercise his judgment; and not only discover what *may* be said, but thoroughly examine the *force* of it. For nothing is more fertile than the powers of genius, and especially those which have been blessed with the cultivation of science. But as a rich and fruitful soil not only produces corn in abundance, but also weeds to choak and smother it; so from the common-places we are speaking of, many arguments will arise, which are either trivial, or foreign to our purpose, or entirely useless. An Orator, therefore, should carefully examine each, that he may be able to select with propriety. Otherwise, how can he enlarge upon those which are most pertinent, and dwell upon such as more particularly affect his cause? Or how can he soften a harsh circumstance, or conceal, and (if possible) entirely suppress what would be deemed unanswerable, or steal off the attention of the hearer to a different topic? Or how alledge another argument in reply, which shall be still more plausible than that of his antagonist?

But after he has thus *invented* what is proper to be said, with what accuracy must he *methodize* it? For this is the second of the three articles above-mentioned. Accordingly, he will give the portal of his Harangue a graceful appearance, and make the entrance to his cause as neat and splendid as the importance of it will permit. When he has thus made himself master of the hearer's good wishes at the first onset, he will endeavour to invalidate what makes against him; and having, by this means, cleared his way, his strongest arguments will appear some of them in the front, and others at the close of his discourse; and as to those of more trifling consequence, he will occasionally introduce [Footnote: In the Original it is *inculcabit*, he will *tread them in*, (like the sand or loose dust in a new pavement) to support and strengthen the whole.] them here and there, where he judges them likely to be most serviceable. Thus, then, we have given a cursory view of what he ought to be, in the two first departments of Oratory. But, as we before observed, these, though very important in their consequences, require less art and application.

After he has thus invented what is proper to be said, and in what order, the greatest difficulty is still behind;—namely to consider *how* he is to say it, and *in what manner*. For the observation of our favourite *Carneades* is well-known,—"That *Clitomachus* had a perpetual sameness of sentiment, and Charmidas a tiresome uniformity of expression." But if it is a circumstance of so much moment in Philosophy, *in what manner* we express ourselves, where the matter, and not the language, is principally regarded; what must we think of public debates, which are wholly ruled and swayed by the powers of Elocution? Accordingly, my Brutus, I am sensible from your letters, that you mean to inquire what are my notions of a finished Speaker, not so much with respect to his Invention and Disposition, as to his talents of *Elocution*:—a severe task! and the most difficult you could have fixed upon! For as language is ever soft and yielding, and so amazingly pliable that you may bend and form it at your pleasure; so different natures and dispositions have given rise to different kinds of Elocution. Some, for instance, who place the chief merit of it in it's rapidity, are mightily pleased with a torrent of words, and a volubility of expression. Others again are better pleased with regular, and measured intervals, and frequent stops, and pauses. What can be more opposite? and yet both have their proper excellence. Some also confine their attention to the smoothness and equability of their periods, and aim at a style which is perfectly neat and clear: while others affect a harshness, and severity of diction, and to give a gloomy cast to their language:—and as we have already observed that some endeavour to be nervous and majestic, others neat and simple, and some to be smooth and florid, it necessarily follows that there must be as many different kinds of Orators, as there are of Eloquence. But as I have already enlarged the talk you have imposed upon me;—(for though your enquiries related only to Elocution, I have ventured a few hints on the arts of Invention and Disposition;)—I shall now treat not only of *Elocution*, but of *action*. By this means, every part of Oratory will be attended to: for as to *memory*, which is common to this with many other arts, it is entirely out of the question.

The Art of Speaking then, so far as it regards only the *manner* in which our thoughts should be expressed, consists in *action* and *Elocution*; for action is the Eloquence of the body, and implies the proper management of our *voice* and *gesture*. As to the inflexions of the voice, they are as numerous as the various passions it is capable of exciting. The finished Orator, therefore, who is the subject of this Essay, in whatever manner he would appear to be affected himself, and touch the heart of his hearer, will employ a suitable and corresponding tone of voice:—a topic which I could willingly enlarge upon, if delivering precepts was any part of my present design, or of your request. I should likewise have treated concerning *gesture*, of which the management of the countenance is a material part: for it is scarcely credible of what great importance it is to an Orator to recommend himself by these external accomplishments. For even those who were far from being masters of good language, have many times, by the sole dignity of their action, reaped the fruits of Eloquence; while others who had the finest powers of Elocution, have too often, by the mere awkwardness of their delivery, led people to imagine that they were scarcely able to express themselves:—so that Demosthenes, with sufficient reason, assigned the first place, and likewise the second and third to *pronunciation*. For if Eloquence without this is nothing, but this, even without Eloquence, has such a wonderful efficacy, it must be allowed to bear the principal sway in the practice of Speaking.

If an Orator, then, who is ambitious to win the palm of Eloquence, has any thing to deliver which is warm and cutting, let his voice be strong and quick;—if what is calm and gentle, let it be mild and easy;—if what is grave and sedate, let it be cool and settled;—and if what is mournful and affecting, let his accents be plaintive and flexible. For the voice may be raised or depressed, and extended or contracted to an astonishing degree; thus in Music (for instance) it's three tones, the *mean*, the *acute*, and the *grave*, may be so managed by art, as to produce a pleasing and an infinite variety of sounds. Nay, even in Speaking, there may be a concealed kind of music:—not like the whining epilogue of a Phrygian or a Carian declaimer, but such as was intended by *Aeschines*, and *Demosthenes*, when the one upbraids and reproaches the other with the artificial modulations of his voice. *Demosthenes*, however, says most upon this head, and often speaks of his accuser as having a sweet and clear pronunciation. There is another circumstance, which may farther enforce our attention to the agreeable management of the voice; for Nature herself, as if she meant to harmonize the speech of man, has placed an accent on every word, and one accent only, which never lies farther than the third syllable from the last. Why, therefore, should we hesitate to follow her example, and to do our best to gratify the ear? A good voice, indeed, though a desirable accomplishment, is not in our power to acquire:—but to exercise, and improve it, is certainly in the power of every person.

The Orator, then, who means to be the prince of his profession, will change and vary his voice with the most delicate propriety; and by sometimes raising, and sometimes depressing it, pursue it gradually through all it's different tones, and modulations. He will likewise regulate his *gesture*, so as to avoid even a single motion which is either superfluous or impertinent. His posture will be erect and manly:— he will move from his ground but seldom, and not even then too precipitately; and his advances will be few and moderate. He will practise no languishing, no effeminate airs of the head, no finical playing of the fingers, no measured movement of the joints. The chief part of his gesture will consist in the firm and graceful sway of his body, and in extending his arm when his arguments are pressing, and drawing it again when his vehemence abates. But as to the *countenance*, which next to the voice has the greatest efficacy, what dignity and gracefulness is it not capable of supporting! and when you have been careful that it may neither be unmeaning, nor ostentatious, there is still much to be left to the expression of the *eyes*. For if the countenance is the *image* of the mind, the eyes are it's *interpreters*, whose degree of pleasantry or sadness must be proportioned to the importance of our subject.

But we are to exhibit the portrait of a finished Orator, whose chief excellence must be supposed, from his very name, to consist in his *Elocution*; while his other qualifications (though equally complete) are less conspicuous. For a mere inventor, a mere digester, or a mere actor, are titles never made use of to comprize the whole character; but an Orator derives his name, both in Greek and Latin, from the single talent of Elocution. As to his other qualifications, every man of sense may claim a share of them: but the full powers of language are exerted by himself alone. Some of the philosophers, indeed, have expressed themselves in a very handsome manner: for *Theophrastus* derived his name from the divinity of his style; *Aristotle* rivalled the glory of *Isocrates*; and the Muses themselves are said to have spoken from the lips of *Xenophon*; and, to say no more, the great *Plato* is acknowledged in majesty and sweetness to have far exceeded all who ever wrote or spoke. But their language has neither the nerves nor the sting which is required in the Orator's, when he harangues the crowded Forum. They speak only to the learned, whose passions they rather choose to compose than disturb; and they discourse about matters of calm and untumultuous speculation, merely as teachers, and not like eager antagonists: though even *here*, when they endeavour to amuse and delight us, they are thought by some to exceed the limits of their province. It will be easy, therefore, to distinguish this species of Elocution from the Eloquence we are attempting to delineate. For the language of philosophy is gentle and composed, and entirely calculated for the shady walks of the Academy;—not armed with those forcible sentiments, and rapid turns of expression, which are suited to move the populace, nor measured by exact numbers and regular periods, but easy, free, and unconfined. It has nothing resentful belonging to it, nothing invidious, nothing fierce and flaming, nothing exaggerated, nothing marvellous, nothing artful and designing; but resembles a chaste, a bashful, and an unpolluted virgin. We may, therefore, consider it as a kind of polite conversation, rather than a species of Oratory.

As to the *Sophists*, whom I have already mentioned, the resemblance ought to be more accurately distinguished: for they industriously pursue the same flowers which are used by an Orator in the Forum. But they differ in this,—that, as their principal aim is not to disturb the passions, but rather to allay them, and not so much to persuade as to please,—they attempt the latter more openly, and more frequently than we do. They seek for agreeable sentiments, rather than probable ones; they use more frequent digressions, intermingle tales and fables, employ more shewy metaphors, and work them into their discourses with as much fancy and variety as a painter does his colours; and they abound in contrasts and antitheses, and in similar and corresponding cadences.

Nearly allied to these is *History*, which conducts her narratives with elegance and ease, and now and then sketches out a country, or a battle. She likewise diversifies her story with short speeches, and florid harangues: but in these, only neatness and fluency is to be expected, and not the vehemence and poignant severity of an Orator [Footnote: In the Original it is,—*sed in his tracta quaedam et fluens expetitur, nan haec contorta, et acris Oratorio*; upon which Dr. Ward has made the following remark: —"Sentences, with respect to their form or composition, are distinguished into two sorts, called by Cicero *tracta*, strait or direct, and *contorta*, bent or winding. By the former are meant such, whose members follow each other in a direct order, without any inflexion; and by the latter, those which strictly speaking are called periods."].

There is much the same difference between Eloquence and *Poetry*; for the Poets likewise have started the question, What it is which distinguishes them from the Orators? It was formerly supposed to be their *number* and *metre*: but numbers are now as familiar to the Orator, as to the Poet; for whatever falls under the regulation of the ear, though it bears no resemblance to verse (which in Oratory would be a capital fault) is called *number*, and by the Greeks *rhyme*. [Footnote: [Greek: Ruthmos]] In the opinion of some, therefore, the style of *Plato* and *Democritus*, on account of it's majestic flow, and the splendor of it's ornaments, though it is far from being verse, has a nearer resemblance to poetry than the style of the Comedians, who, excepting their metre, have nothing different from the style of conversation. Metre, however, is far from being the principal merit of the Poets; though it is certainly no small recommendation, that, while they pursue all the beauties of Eloquence, the harmony of their numbers is far more regular and exact. But, though the language of Poetry is equally grand and ornamental with that of an Orator, she undoubtedly takes greater liberties both in making and compounding word; and frequently administers to the pleasure of her hearers, more by the pomp and lustre of her expressions, than by the weight and dignity of her sentiments. Though judgment, therefore, and a proper choice of words, is alike common to both, yet their difference in other respects is sufficiently discernible: but if it affords any matter of doubt (as to some, perhaps, it may) the discussion of it is no way necessary to our present purpose.

We are, therefore, to delineate the Orator who differs equally from the Eloquence of the Philosopher, the Sophist, the Historian, and the Poet. He, then, is truly eloquent, (for after *him* we must search, by the direction of Antonius) who in the Forum, and in public debates, can so speak, as to *prove, delight,* and *force the passions.* To *prove,* is a matter of necessity:—to *delight,* is indispensably requisite to engage the attention:—and to *force the passions,* is the surest means of victory; for this contributes more effectually than both the others to get a cause decided to our wishes. But as the duties of an Orator, so the kinds of Elocution are three. The neat and accurate is used in *proving;* the moderately florid in *delighting* apd the vehement and impetuous in *forcing the passions,* in which alone all the power of Eloquence consists. Great, therefore, must be the judgment, and wonderful the talents of the man, who can properly conduct, and, as it were, temper this threefold variety: for he will at once determine what is suitable to every case; and be always able to express himself as the nature of his subject may require.

Discretion, therefore, is the basis of Eloquence, as well as of every other accomplishment. For, as in the conduct of life, so in the practice of Speaking, nothing is more difficult than to maintain a propriety of character. This is called by the Greeks [Greek: to prepon], *the becoming,* but we shall call it *decorum;*—a subject which has been excellently and very copiously canvassed, and richly merits our attention. An unacquaintance with this has been the source of innumerable errors, not only in the business of life, but in Poetry and Eloquence. An Orator, therefore, should examine what is becoming, as well in the turn of his language, as in that of his sentiments. For not every condition, not every rank, not every character, nor every age, or place, or time, nor every hearer is to be treated with the same invariable train either of sentiment or expression:—but we should always consider in every part of a public Oration, as well as of life, what will be most becoming,—a circumstance which naturally depends on the nature of the subject, and the respective characters of the Speaker and Hearer. Philosophers, therefore, have carefully discussed this extensive and important topic in the doctrine of Ethics, (though not, indeed, when they treat of right and wrong, because those are invariably the fame:)—nor is it less attended to by the Critics in their poetical Essays, or by men of Eloquence in every species and every part of their public debates. For what would be more out of character, than to use a lofty style, and ransack every topic of argument, when we are speaking only of a petty trespass in some inferior court? Or, on the other hand, to descend to any puerile subtilties, and speak with the indifference and simplicity of a frivolous narrative, when we are lashing treason and rebellion?

Here, the indecorum would arise from the very nature and quality of the subject: but others are equally guilty of it, by not adapting their discourse either to their own characters, or to that of their hearers, and, in some cafes, to that of their antagonists; and they extend the fault not only to their sentiments, but to the turn of their expression. It is true, indeed, that the force of language is a mere nothing, when it is not supported by a proper solidity of sentiment: but it is also equally true that the same thing will be either approved or rejected, according as it is this or that way expressed. In all cases, therefore, we cannot be too careful in examining the *how far*? for though every thing has it's proper mean, yet an *excess* is always more offensive and disgusting than a proportionable *defect*. *Apelles*, therefore, justly censures some of his cotemporary artists, because they never knew when they had performed enough.

This, my Brutus, as your long acquaintance with it must necessarily inform you, is a copious subject, and would require an extensive volume to discuss. But it is sufficient to our present purpose to observe, that in all our words and actions, as well the smallest as the greatest, there is a something which will appear either becoming or unbecoming, and that almost every one is sensible of it's confluence. But what is becoming, and what *ought to be*, are very different considerations, and belong to a different topic:—for the *ought to be* points out the perfection of duty, which should be attended to upon all occasions, and by all persons: but the *becoming* denotes that which is merely *proper*, and suited to time and character, which is of great importance not only in our actions and language, but in our very looks, our gesture, and our walk; and that which is contrary to it will always be *unbecoming*, and disagreeable. If the Poet, therefore, carefully guards against any impropriety of the kind, and is always condemned as guilty of a fault, when he puts the language of a worthy man into the mouth of a ruffian, or that of a wife man into the mouth of a fool:—if, moreover, the artist who painted the sacrifice of *Iphigenia*, [Footnote: Agamemnon, one of the Grecian chiefs, having by accident slain a deer belonging to Diana, the Goddess was so enraged at this profanation of her honours, that she kept him wind-bound at Aulis with the whole fleet. Under this heavy disaster, having recourse to the Oracle, (their usual refuge in such cases) they were informed that the only atonement which the angry Goddess would accept, was the sacrifice of one of the offender's children. Ulysses having, by a stratagem, withdrawn *Iphigenia* from her mother for that purpose, the unhappy Virgin was brought to the altar. But, as the story goes, the Goddess relenting at her hard fate, substituted a deer in her stead, and conveyed her away to serve her as a Priestess. It must be farther remarked that *Menelaus* was the Virgin's uncle, and Calchas the Priest who was to officiate at this horrid sacrifice.] could see that *Chalcas* should appear greatly concerned, *Ulysses* still more so, and *Menelaus* bathed in tears, but that the head of Agamemnon (the virgin's father) should be covered with his robe, to intimate a degree of anguish which no pencil could express: lastly, if a mere actor on the stage is ever cautious to keep up the character he appears in, what must be done by the Orator? But as this is a matter of such importance, let him consider at his leisure, what is proper to be done in particular causes, and in their several parts and divisions:—for it is sufficiently evident, not only that the different parts of an Oration, but that entire causes ought to be managed, some in one manner, and some in another.

We must now proceed to delineate the form and character of each of the three species of Eloquence above-mentioned; a great and an arduous talk, as I have already observed more than once; But we should have considered the difficulty of the voyage before we embarked: for now we have ventured to set sail, we must run boldly before the wind, whether we reach our port or not.

The first character, then, to be described, is the Orator who, according to some, is the only one that has any just pretensions to *Atticism.* He is distinguished by his modest simplicity; and as he imitates the language of conversation, he differs from those who are strangers to Eloquence, rather in reality than in appearance. For this reason, those who hear him, though totally unskilled in the art of Speaking, are apt to persuade themselves that they can readily discourse in the same manner [Footnote: There is a pretty remark to the same purpose in the fifteenth number of *The Guardian*, which, as it may serve to illustrate the observation of Cicero, I shall beg leave to insert.

"From what I have advanced, it appears how difficult it is to write *easily*. But when easy writings fall into the hands of an ordinary reader, they appear to him so natural and unlaboured, that he immediately resolves to write, and fancies that all he has to do is to take no pains. Thus he thinks indeed simply, but the thoughts not being chosen with judgment, are not beautiful. He, it is true, expresses himself plainly, but flatly withal. Again, if a man of vivacity takes it into his head to write this way, what self-denial must he undergo, when bright points of wit occur to his fancy? How difficult will he find it to reject florid phrases, and pretty embellishments of style? So true it is, that simplicity of all things is the hardest to be copied, and case to be acquired with the greatest labour."];—and the unaffected simplicity of his language appears very imitable to an ignorant observer; though nothing will be found less so by him who makes the trial. For, if I may so express myself, though his veins are not over-stocked with blood, his juices must be found and good; and though he is not possessed of any extraordinary strength, he must have a healthy constitution. For this purpose, we must first release him from the shackles of *number*; for there is (you know) a kind of *number* to be observed by an Orator, which we shall treat of in the sequel:—but this is to be used in a different species of Eloquence, and to be relinquished in the present. His language, therefore, must be free and unconfined, but not loose and irregular, that he may appear to walk at ease, without reeling or tottering. He will not be at the pains to cement word to word with a scrupulous exactness: for those breaks which are made by a collision of vowels, have now and then an agreeable effect, and betray the not unpleasing negligence of a man who is more felicitous about things than words. But though he is not to labour at a measured flow, and a masterly arrangement of his words, he must be careful in other respects. For even these limited and unaspiring talents are not to be employed carelessly, but with a kind of industrious negligence: for as some females are most becoming in a dishabille, so this artless kind of Eloquence has her charms, though she appears in an undress. There is something in both which renders them agreeable, without striking the eye. Here, therefore, all the glitter of ornament, like that of jewels and diamonds, must be laid aside; nor must we apply even the crisping-iron to adjust the hair. There must be no colouring, no artful washes to heighten the complexion: but elegance and neatness must be our only aim. Our style muft be pure, and correct;—we must speak with clearness and perspicuity; —and be always attentive to appear in character. There is one thing, however, which must never be omitted, and which is reckoned by Theophrastus to be one of the chief beauties of composition;—I mean that sweet and flowing ornament, a plentiful intermixture of lively sentiments, which seem to result from a natural fund of good sense, and are peculiarly graceful in the Orator we are now describing. But he will be very moderate in using the *furniture* of Eloquence: for (if I may be allowed such an expression) there is a species of furniture belonging to us, which consists in the various ornaments of sentiment and language. The ornaments of language are two-fold; the one sort relates to words as they stand singly, and the other as they are connected together. A *single* word (I speak of those which are *proper*, and in common use) is then said to be well chosen, when it founds agreeably, and is the best which could have been taken to express our meaning. Among borrowed and *translatitious* [Footnote: Words which are transferred from their primitive meaning to a metaphorical one.] words, (or those which are not used in their proper sense) we may reckon the metaphor, the metonymy, and the rest of the tropes; as also compounded and new-made words, and such as are obsolete and out of date; but obsolete words should rather be considered as proper ones, with this only difference, that we seldom make use of them. As to words in connection, these also may be considered as ornamental, when they have a certain gracefulness which would be destroyed by changing their order, though the meaning would still remain the same. For as to the ornaments of sentiment, which lose nothing of their beauty, by varying the position of the words,—these, indeed, are very numerous, though only a few of them are remarkably striking.

The Orator, then, who is distinguished by the simplicity of his manner, provided he is correct and elegant, will be sparing in the use of new words; easy and modest in his metaphors; and very cautious in the use of words which are antiquated;—and as to the other ornaments of language and sentiment, here also he will be equally plain and reserved. But in the use of metaphors, he will, perhaps, take greater liberties; because these are frequently introduced in conversation, not only by Gentlemen, but even by rustics, and peasants: for we often hear them say that the vine *shoots out* it's buds, that the fields are *thirsty*, the corn *lively*, and the grain *rich* and flourishing. Such expressions, indeed, are rather bold: but the resemblance between the metaphor and the object is either remarkably obvious; or else, when the latter has no proper name to express it, the metaphor is so far from appearing to be laboured, that we seem to use it merely to explain our meaning. This, therefore, is an ornament in which our artless Orator may indulge himself more freely; but not so openly as in the more diffusive and lofty species of Eloquence. For that *indecorum*, which is best understood by comparing it with its opposite quality, will even here be viable when a metaphor is too conspicuous;—or when this simple and dispassionate sort of language is interrupted by a bold ornament, which would have been proper enough in a different kind of Elocution.

As to that sort of ornament which regards the position of words, and embellishes it with those studied graces, which are considered by the Greeks as so many *attitudes* of language, and are therefore called *figures*, (a name which is likewise extended to the flowers of sentiment;)—the Orator before us, who may justly be regarded as an *Attic* Speaker, provided the title is not confined to him, will make use even of *this*, though with great caution and moderation. He will conduct himself as if he was setting out an entertainment, and while he carefully avoids a splendid magnificence, he will not only be plain and frugal, but neat and elegant, and make his choice accordingly. For there is a kind of genteel parsimony, by which his character is distinguished from that of others. He will, therefore, avoid the more conspicuous ornaments above- mentioned, such as the contracting word to word,—the concluding the several members of a sentence with the same cadence, or confining them to the same measure,—and all the studied prettiness which are formed by the change of a letter, or an artful play of found;—that, if possible, there may not be the slightest appearance, or even suspicion, of a design to please. As to those repetitions which require an earnest and forcible exertion of the voice, these also would be equally out of character in this lower species of Eloquence; but he may use the other ornaments of Elocution at his pleasure, provided he checks and interrupts the flow of his language, and softens it off by using familiar expressions, and such metaphors as are plain and obvious. Nay, even as to the figures of sentiment, he may sometimes indulge himself in those which are not remarkably bold and striking. Thus, for instance, we must not allow him to introduce the Republic as speaking, nor to fetch up the dead from their graves, nor to crowd a multitude of ideas into the same period. These efforts demand a firmer constitution, and should be neither required nor expected from the simple Orator before us; for as in his voice, so likewise in his language, he should be ever easy and composed. But there are many of the nobler ornaments which may be admitted even here, though always in a plainer and more artless habit than in any other species of Eloquence; for such is the character we have assigned him. His gesture also will be neither pompous, nor theatrical, but consist in a moderate and easy sway of the body, and derive much of it's efficacy from the countenance,—not a stiff and affected countenance, but such a one as handsomely corresponds with his sentiments.

This kind of Oratory will likewise be frequently enlivened by those turns of wit and pleasantry, which in Speaking have a much greater effect than is imagined. There are two sorts of them; the one consisting in smart sayings and quick repartees, and the other in what is called *humour*. Our Orator will make use of both;—of the latter in his narratives, to make them lively and entertaining;—and of the other, either in giving or retorting a stroke of ridicule, of which there are several kinds; but at present it is not our business to specify them. It will not be amiss, however, to observe by way of caution, that the powers of *ridicule* are not to be employed too often, lest we sink into scurrility;—nor in loose and indecent language, lest we degenerate into wantonness and buffoonery; —nor with the least degree of petulance and abuse, lest we appear audacious and ill-bred;—nor levelled against the unfortunate, lest we incur the censure of inhumanity;—nor against atrocious crimes, lest we raise a laugh where we ought to excite abhorrence;—nor, in the last place, should they be used unseasonably, or when the characters either of the Speaker, or the Hearer, and the circumstances of time and place forbid it;—otherwise we should grossly fail in that decorum of which we have already said so much. We should likewise avoid all affected witticisms, which appear not to be thrown out occasionally, but to be dragged from the closet; for such are generally cold and insipid. It is also improper to jest upon our friends, or upon persons of quality, or to give any strokes of wit which may appear ill-natured, or malicious. We should aim only at our enemies; and even at these, not upon every occasion, or without any distinction of character, or with the same invariable turn of ridicule. Under these restrictions our artless Orator will play off his wit and humour, as I have never seen it done by any of the modern pretenders to Atticism, though they cannot deny that this is entirely in the Attic taste.

Such, then, is the idea which I have formed of a *simple and an easy Speaker*, who is likewise a very masterly one, and a genuine Athenian; for whatever is smart and pertinent is unquestionably *Attic*, though some of the Attic Speakers were not remarkable for their wit. *Lysias*, indeed, and *Hyperides* were sufficiently so; and *Demades*, it is said, was more so than all the others. Demosthenes, however, is thought by many to have but little merit of the kind; but to me nothing can be more genteel than he is; though, perhaps, he was rather smart than humourous. The one requires a quicker genius, but the other more art and address.

But there is a second character, which is more diffusive, and somewhat stronger than the simple and artless, one we have been describing,—though considerably inferior to that copious and all-commanding Eloquence we shall notice in the sequel. In this, though there is but a moderate exertion of the nerves and sinews of Oratory, there is abundance of melody and sweetness. It is much fuller and richer than the close and accurate style above-mentioned; but less elevated than the pompous and diffusive. In *this* all the ornaments of language may be employed without reserve; and *here* the flow of our numbers is ever soft and harmonious. Many of the Greeks have pursued it with success: but, in my opinion, they must all yield the palm to *Demetrius Phalereus*, whose Eloquence is ever mild and placid, and bespangled with a most elegant variety of metaphors and other tropes, like so many *stars*. By *metaphors*, as I have frequently observed, I mean expressions which, either for the sake of ornament, or through the natural poverty of our language, are removed and as it were *transplanted* from their proper objects to others, by way of similitude. As to *tropes* in general, they are particular forms of expression, in which the proper name of a thing is supplied by another, which conveys the same meaning, but is borrowed from its adjuncts or effects: for, though, in this case, there is a kind of metaphor, (because the word is shifted from its primary object) yet the remove is performed by *Ennius* in a different manner, when he says metaphorically,—"*You bereave the citadel and the city of their offspring*,"—from what it would have been, if he had put the citadel alone for the whole state: and thus again, when he tells us that,—"*rugged Africa was shaken by a dreadful tumult*,"—he puts Africa for the inhabitants. The Rhetoricians call this an *Hypallage*, because one word is substituted for another: but the Grammarians call it a *Metonymy*, because the words are shifted and interchanged. Aristotle, however, subjoins it to the metaphor, as he likewise does the *Abuse* or *Catachresis*; by which, for instance, we say a *narrow, contracted soul,* instead of a *mean* one, and thus steal an expression which has a kindred meaning with the proper one, either for the sake of ornament or decency. When several metaphors are connected together in a regular chain, the form of speaking is varied. The Greeks call this an *Allegory*, which indeed is proper enough if we only attend to the etymology; but if we mean to refer it to its particular *genus* or kind, he has done better who comprehends the whole under the general name of metaphors. These, however, are frequently used by *Phalereus,* and have a soft and pleasing effect: but though he abounds in the metaphor, he also makes use of the other tropes with as much freedom as any writer whatever.

This species of Eloquence (I mean the *middling*, or temperate) is likewise embellished with all the brilliant figures of language, and many of the figures of sentiment. By this, moreover, the most extensive and refined topics of science are handsomely unfolded, and all the weapons of argument are employed without violence. But what need have I to say more? Such Speakers are the common offspring of Philosophy; and were the nervous, and more striking Orator to keep out of sight, these alone would fully answer our wishes. For they are masters of a brilliant, a florid, a picturesque, and a well-wrought Elocution, which is interwoven with all the beautiful embroidery both of language and sentiment. This character first streamed from the limpid fountains of the *Sophists* into the Forum; but being afterwards despised by the more simple and refined kind of Speakers, and disdainfully rejected by the nervous and weighty; it was compelled to subside into the peaceful and unaspiring mediocrity we are speaking of.

The *third character* is the extensive,—the copious,—the nervous,—the majestic Orator, who possesses the powers of Elocution in their full extent. *This* is the man whose enchanting and diffusive language is so much admired by listening nations, that they have tamely suffered Eloquence to rule the world;—but an Eloquence whose course is rapid and sonorous!—an Eloquence which every one gazes at, and admires, and despairs to equal! This is the Eloquence that bends and sways the passions!—*this* the Eloquence that alarms or sooths them at her pleasure! This is the Eloquence that sometimes tears up all before it like a whirlwind; and, at other times, steals imperceptibly upon the senses, and probes to the bottom of the heart!—the Eloquence which ingrafts opinions that are new, and eradicates the old; but yet is widely different from the two characters of Speaking before-mentioned.

He who exerts himself in the simple and accurate character, and speaks neatly and smartly without aiming any higher!—*he*, by this alone, if carried to perfection, becomes a great, if not the greatest of Orators; nor does he walk upon slippery ground, so that if he has but learned to tread firm, he is in no danger of falling. Also the middle kind of Orator, who is distinguished by his equability, provided he only draws up his forces to advantage, fears not the perilous and doubtful hazards of a public Harangue; and, though sometimes he may not succeed to his wishes, yet he is never exposed to an absolute defeat; for as he never soars, his fall must be inconsiderable. But the Orator, whom we regard as the prince of his profession,—the nervous,—the fierce,—the flaming Orator, if he is born for this alone, and only practices and applies himself to this, without tempering his copiousness with the two inferior characters of Eloquence, is of all others the most contemptible. For the plain and simple Orator, as speaking acutely and expertly, has an appearance of wisdom and good-sense; and the middle kind of Orator is sufficiently recommended by his sweetness:—but the copious and diffusive Speaker, if he has no other qualification, will scarcely appear to be in his senses. For he who can say nothing calmly,—nothing gently—nothing methodically, —nothing clearly, distinctly, or humourously, (though a number of causes should be so managed throughout, and others in one or more of their parts:)—he, moreover, who proceeds to amplify and exaggerate without preparing the attention of his audience, will appear to rave before men of understanding, and to vapour like a person intoxicated before the sober and sedate.

Thus then, my Brutus, we have at last discovered the finished Orator we are seeking for: but we have caught him in imagination only;—for if I could have seized him with my hands, not all his Eloquence should persuade me to release him. We have at length, however, discovered the eloquent Speaker, whom Antonius never saw.—But who, then, is he?—I will comprize his character in a few words, and afterwards unfold it more at large.—He, then, is an Orator indeed! who can speak upon trivial subjects with simplicity and art, upon weighty ones with energy and pathos, and upon those of middling import with calmness and moderation. You will tell me, perhaps, that such a Speaker has never existed. Be it so:—for I am now discoursing not upon what I *have* seen, but upon what I could *wish* to see; and must therefore recur to that primary semblance or ideal form of Plato which I have mentioned before, and which, though it cannot be seen with our bodily eyes, may be comprehended by the powers of imagination. For I am not seeking after a living Orator, or after any thing which is mortal and perishing, but after that which confers a right to the title of *eloquent*; in other words, I am seeking after Eloquence herself, who can be discerned only by the eye of the mind.

He then is truly an *Orator*, (I again repeat it,) who can speak upon trivial subjects with simplicity, upon indifferent ones with moderation, and upon weighty subjects with energy and pathos. [Footnote: Our Author is now going to indulge himself in the *Egotism*,—a figure, which, upon many occasions, he uses as freely as any of the figures of Rhetoric. How the Reader will relish it, I know not; but it is evident from what follows, and from another passage of the same kind further on, that Cicero had as great a veneration for his own talents as any man living. His merit, however, was so uncommon both as a Statesman, a Philosopher, and an Orator, and he has obliged posterity with so many useful and amazing productions of genius, that we ought in gratitude to forgive the vanity of the *man*. Although he has ornamented the socket in which he has *set* his character, with an extravagant (and I had almost said ridiculous) profusion of self-applause, it must be remembered that the diamond it contains is a gem of inestimable value.] The cause I pleaded for Caecina related entirely to the bare letter of the Interdict: here, therefore, I explained what was intricate by a definition,—spoke in praise of the Civil Law,—and dissolved the ambiguities which embarrassed the meaning of the Statute.—In recommending the Manilian Law, I was to blazon the character of *Pompey*, and therefore indulged myself in all that variety of ornament which is peculiar to the second species of Eloquence. In the cause of Rabirius, as the honour of the Republic was at stake, I blazed forth in every species of amplification. But these characters are sometimes to be intermingled and diversified. Which of them, therefore, is not to be met with in my seven Invectives against *Verres*? or in the cause of *Habitus*? or in that of *Cornelius*? or indeed in most of my Defences? I would have specified the particular examples, did I not believe them to be sufficiently known; or, at least, very easy to be discovered by those who will take the trouble to seek for them. For there is nothing which can recommend an Orator in the different characters of speaking, but what has been exemplified in my Orations,—if not to perfection, yet at least it has been attempted, and faintly delineated. I have not, indeed, the vanity to think I have arrived at the summit; but I can easily discern what Eloquence ought to be. For I am not to speak of myself, but to attend to my subject; and so far am I from admiring my own productions, that, on the contrary, I am so nice and difficult, as not to be entirely satisfied with Demosthenes himself, who, though he rises with superior eminence in every species of Eloquence, does not always fill my ear;—so eager is it, and so insatiable, as to be ever coveting what is boundless and immense. But as, by the assistance of *Pammenes*, who is very fond of that Orator, you made yourself thoroughly acquainted with him when you was at *Athens*, and to this day scarcely ever part with him from your hands, and yet frequently condescend to peruse what has been written by *me*; you must certainly have taken notice that he hath *done* much, and that I have *attempted* much,—that he has been *happy* enough, and I *willing* enough to speak, upon every occasion, as the nature of the subject required. But he, beyond dispute, was a consummate Orator; for he not only succeeded several eminent Speakers, but had many such for his cotemporaries:—and I also, if I could have reached the perfection I aimed at, should have made no despicable figure in a city, where (according to Antonius) the voice of genuine Eloquence was never heard.

But if to Antonius neither Crassus, nor even himself, appeared to be *eloquent*, we may presume that neither Cotta, Sulpicius, nor Hortensius would have succeeded any better. For *Cotta* had no expansion, *Sulpicius* no temper, and *Hortensius* too little dignity. But the two former (I mean Crassus and Antonius) had a capacity which was better adapted to every species of Oratory. I had, therefore, to address myself to the ears of a city which had never been filled by that multifarious and extensive Eloquence we are discoursing of; and I first allured them (let me have been what you please, or what ever were my talents) to an incredible desire of hearing the finished Speaker who is the subject of the present Essay. For with what acclamations did I deliver that passage in my youth concerning the punishment of parricides [Footnote: Those unnatural and infamous wretches, among the Romans, were sown into a leathern sack, and thus thrown into the sea; to intimate that they were unworthy of having the lead communication with the common elements of water, earth, and air.], though I was afterwards sensible it was too warm and extravagant? —"What is so common, said I, as air to the living, earth to the dead, the sea to floating corpses, and the shore to those who are caft upon it by the waves! But these wretches, as long as life remains, so live as not to breathe the air of heaven; —they so perish, that their limbs are not suffered to touch the earth;—they are so tossed to and fro' by the waves, as never to be warned by them;—and when they are cast on the shore, their dead, carcases cannot rest upon the surface of the rocks!" All this, as coming from a youth, was much applauded, not for it's ripeness and solidity, but for the hopes it gave the Public of my future improvement. From the same capacity came those riper expressions,—"She was the spouse of her son-in-law, the step-mother of her own offspring? and the mistress of her daughter's husband [Footnote: This passage occurs in the peroration of his Defence of Cluentius]."

But I did not always indulge myself in this excessive ardour of expression, or speak every thing in the same manner: for even that youthful redundance which was so visible in the defence of *Roscius*, had many passages which were plain and simple, and some which were, tolerably humourous. But the Orations in defence of *Habitus*, and *Cornelius*, and indeed many others; (for no single Orator, even among the peaceful and speculative Athenians, has composed such a number as I have;)—these, I say, have all that variety which I so much approve. For have *Homer* and *Ennius*, and the rest of the Poets, but especially the tragic writers, not expressed themselves at all times with the same elevation, but frequently varied their manner, and sometimes lowered it to the style of conversation; and shall I oblige myself never to descend from that highest energy of language? Bit why do I mention the Poets whose talents are divine! The very actors on the stage, who have most excelled in their profession, have not only succeeded in very different characters, though still in the same province; but a comedian has often acted tragedies, and a tragedian comedies so as to give us universal satisfaction. Wherefore, then, should not *I* also exert my efforts? But when I say *myself*, my worthy Brutus I mean *you*: for as to *me*, I have already done all, I was capable of doing. Would *you*, then, plead every cause in the same manner? Or is there any sort of causes which your genius would decline? Or even in the same cause, would you always express yourself in the same strain, and without any variety? Your favourite *Demosthenes*, whose brazen statue I lately beheld among your own, and your family images, when I had the pleasure to visit you at Tusculanum,—Demosthenes, I say, was nothing inferior to *Lysias* in simplicity; to *Hyperides* in smartness and poignancy, or to *Aeschines* in the smoothness and splendor of his language. There are many of his Orations which are entirely of the close and simple character, as that against *Lepsines*; many which are all nervous, and striking, as those against *Philip*; and many which are of a mixed character, as that against *Aeschines*, concerning the false embassy, and another against the same person in defence of *Ctesiphon*. At other times he strikes into the *mean* at his pleasure, and quitting the nervous character, descends to this with all the ease imaginable. But he raises the acclamations of his audience, and his Oratory is then most weighty and powerful, when he applies himself to the *nervous*.

But as our enquiries relate to the art, and not to the artist, let us leave *him* for the present, and consider the nature and the properties of the object before us,—that is, of *Eloquence*. We must keep in mind, however, what I have already hinted,—that we are not required to deliver a system of precepts, but to write as judges and critics, rather than teachers. But I have expatiated so largely upon the subject, because I foresee that you (who are, indeed, much better versed in it, than I who pretend to inform you) will not be my only reader; but that my little essay, though not much perhaps to my credit, will be made public, and with your name prefixed to it.

I am of opinion, therefore, that a finished Orator should not only possess the talent (which, indeed, is peculiar, to himself) of speaking copiously and diffusively: but that he should also borrow the assistance of it's nearest neighbour, the art of Logic. For though public speaking is one thing, and disputing another; and though there is a visible difference between a private controversy, and a public Harangue; yet both the one and the other come under the notion of reasoning. But mere discourse and argument belongs to the Logician, and the art of Speaking gracefully and ornamentally is the prerogative of the Orator. *Zeno*, the father of the *Stoics*, used to illustrate the difference between the two by holding up his hand;—for when he clenched his fingers, and presented a close fist,— "*that*," he said, "was an emblem of Logic:"—but when he spread them out again, and displayed his open hand, —"this," said he, "resembles Eloquence." But Aristotle observed before him, in the introduction to his Rhetoric, that it is an art which has a near resemblance to that of Logic;—and that the only difference between them is, that the method of reasoning in the former is more diffusive, and in the latter more close and contracted.

I, therefore, advise that our finished Orator make himself master of every thing in the art of Logic, which is applicable to his profession:—an art (as your thorough knowledge of it has already informed you) which is taught after two methods. For Aristotle himself has delivered a variety of precepts concerning the art of Reasoning:—and besides these, the *Dialecticians* (as they are called) have produced many intricate and thorny speculations of their own. I am, therefore, of opinion, that he who is ambitious to be applauded for his Eloquence, should not be wholly unacquainted with this branch of Erudition; but that he ought (at least) to be properly instructed either in the old method, or in that of *Chrysippus*. In the first place, he should understand the force, the extension, and the different species of words as they stand singly, or connected into sentences. He should likewise be acquainted with the various modes and forms in which any conception of the mind may be expressed—the methods of distinguishing a true proposition from a false one;—the different conclusions which result from different premises;—the true consequences and opposites to any given proposition;—and, if an argument is embarrassed by ambiguities, how to unravel each of them by an accurate distinction. These particulars, I say, should be well understood by an Orator, because they are such as frequently occur: but as they are naturally rugged and unpleasing, they should be relieved in practice by an easy brilliance of expression.

But as in every topic which is discussed by reason and method, we should first settle what it is we are to discourse upon,—(for unless the parties in a dispute are agreed about the subject of it, they can neither reason with propriety, nor bring the argument to an issue;)—it will frequently be necessary to explain our notions of it, and, when the matter is intricate, to lay it open by a *definition*;—for a *definition* is only a sentence, or explanation, which specifies, in as few words as possible, the nature of the object we propose to consider. After the *genus*, or kind, has been sufficiently determined, we must then proceed (you know) to examine into it's different species, or subordinate parts, that our whole discourse may be properly distributed among them. Our Orator, then, should be qualified to make a just definition;—though not in such a close and contracted form, as in the critical debates of the Academy, but more explicitly and copiously, and as will be best adapted to the common way of thinking, and the capacity of the vulgar. He is likewise, as often as occasion requires, to divide the genus into it's proper species, so as to be neither defective, nor redundant. But *how* and *when* this should be done, is not our present business to consider: because, as I observed before, I am not to assume the part of a teacher, but only of a critic and a judge.

But he ought to acquaint himself not only with the art of Logic, but with all the common and most useful branches of Morality. For without a competent knowledge of these, nothing can be advanced and unfolded with any spirit and energy, or with becoming dignity and freedom, either concerning religion,—death,—filial piety,—the love of our country,—things good or evil,—the several virtues and vices,—the nature of moral obligation,—grief or pleasure, and the other emotions of the mind,—or the various errors and frailties of humanity,—and a variety of important topics which are often closely connected with forensic causes; though *here*(it is true) they must be touched upon more slightly and superficially. I am now speaking of the *materials* of Eloquence, and not of the *art* itself:—for an Orator should always be furnished with a plentiful stock of sentiments,—(I mean such as may claim the attention of the learned, as well as of the vulgar)—before he concerns himself about the language and the manner in which he ought to express himself.

That he may make a still more respectable and elevated figure (as we have already observed of *Pericles*) he should not be unacquainted with the principles of Natural Philosophy. For when he descends, as it were, from the starry heavens, to the little concerns of humanity, he will both think and speak with greater dignity and splendor. But after acquainting himself with those divine and nobler objects of contemplation, I would have him attend to human concerns. In particular, let him make himself master of the *Civil Law*, which is of daily, and indeed necessary use in every kind of causes. For what can be more scandalous, than to undertake the management of judicial suits and controversies, without a proper knowledge of the laws, and of the principles of Equity and Jurisprudence? He should also be well versed in History and the venerable records of Antiquity, but particularly those of his own country: not neglecting, however, to peruse the annals of other powerful nations, and illustrious monarchs;—a toil which has been considerably shortened by our friend *Atticus*, who (though he has carefully specified the time of every event, and omitted no transaction of consequence) has comprized the history of seven hundred years in a single volume. To be unacquainted with what has passed in the world, before we came into it ourselves, is to be always children. For what is the age of a single mortal, unless it is connected, by the aid of History, with the times of our ancestors? Besides, the relation of past occurrences, and the producing pertinent and striking examples, is not only very entertaining, but adds a great deal of dignity and weight to what we say.

Thus furnished and equipped our Orator may undertake the management of causes. But, in the first place, he should be well acquainted with their different kinds. He should know, for instance, that every judicial controversy must turn either upon a matter of *fact*, or upon the meaning of some particular expression. As to the former, this must always relate either to the *reality* of a fast, the *equity* of it, or the *name* it bears in law. As to forms of expression, these may become the subject of controversy, when they are either *ambiguous*, or *contradictory*. For when the *spirit* of a law appears to be at variance with the *letter* of it, this must cause an ambiguity which commonly arises from some of the preceding terms; so that in this case (for such is the nature of an ambiguity) the law will appear to have a double meaning.

As the kinds of causes are so few, the rules for the invention of arguments must be few also. The topics, or common places from which those arguments are derived, are twofold,—the one *inherent* in the subject, and the other *assumptive*. A skilful management of the former contributes most to, give weight to a discourse, and strike the attention of the hearer: because they are easy, and familiar to the understanding.

What farther remains (within the province of the Art) but that we should begin our discourses so as to conciliate the hearer's good-will, or raise his expectation, or prepare him to receive what follows?—to state the case before us so concisely, and yet so plausibly and clearly, as that the substance of it may be easily comprehended?—to support our own proofs, and refute those of our antagonist, not in a confused and disorderly manner, but so that every inference may be fairly deducible from the premises?—and, in the last place, to conclude the whole with a peroration either to inflame or allay the passions of the audience? How each of these parts should be conducted is a subject too intricate and extensive for our present consideration: for they are not always to be managed in the same manner.

But as I am not seeking a pupil to instruct, but an Orator who is to be the model of his profession, *he* must have the preference who can always discern what is proper and becoming. For Eloquence should, above all, things, have that kind of discretion which makes her a *perfect mistress of time and character*: because we are not to speak upon every occasion, or before every audience, or against every opponent, or in defence of every client, and to every Judge, in the same invariable manner. He, therefore, is the man of genuine Eloquence, who can adapt his language to what is most suitable to each. By doing this, he will be sure to say every thing as it ought to be said. He will neither speak drily upon copious subjects, nor without dignity and spirit upon things of importance; but his language will always be proportioned, and equal to his subject. His introduction will be modest, —not flaming with all the glare of expression, but composed of quick and lively turns of sentiment, either to wound the cause of his antagonist, or recommend his own. His narratives will be clear and plausible,—not delivered with the grave formality of an Historian, but in the style of polite conversation. If his cause be slight, the thread of his argument, both in proving and refuting, will be so likewise, and he will so conduct it in every part, that his language may rise and expand itself, as the dignity of his subject encreases. But when his cause will admit a full exertion of the powers of Eloquence, he will then display himself more openly;—he will then rule, and bend the passions, and direct them, at his pleasure,—that is, as the nature of his cause and the circumstances of the time shall require.

But his powers of ornament will be chiefly exerted upon two occasions; I mean that striking kind of ornament, from which Eloquence derives her greatest glory. For though every part of an Oration should have so much merit, as not to contain a single word but what is either weighty or elegant; there are two very interesting parts which are susceptible of the greatest variety of ornament. The one is the discussion of an indefinite question, or general truth, which by the Greeks (as I have before observed) is called a *thesis*: and the other is employed in amplifying and exaggerating, which they call an *auxesis*. Though the latter, indeed, should diffuse itself more or less through the whole body of a discourse, it's powers will be more conspicuous in the use and improvement of the *common places*:—which are so called, as being alike *common* to a number of causes, though (in the application of them) they are constantly appropriated to a single one. But as to the other part, which regards universal truths, or indefinite questions, this frequently extends through a whole cause:—for the leading point in debate, or that which the controversy hinges upon, is always most conveniently discussed when it can be reduced to a general question, and considered as an universal proposition:—unless, indeed, when the mere truth of a matter of fact: is the object: of disquisition: for then the case must be wholly conjectural. We are not, however, to argue like the *Peripatetics* (who have a neat method of controversy which they derive from *Aristotle*) but more nervously and pressingly; and general sentiments must be so applied to particular cases, as to leave us room to say many extenuating things in behalf of the Defendant, and many severe ones against the Plaintiff. But in heightening or softening a circumstance, the powers of language are unlimited, and may be properly exerted, even in the middle of an argument, as often as any thing presents itself which may be either exaggerated, or extenuated; but, in, controul.

There are two parts, however, which must not be omitted;—for when these are judiciously conducted, the sorce of Eloquence will be amazing. The one is a certain *propriety of manner* (called the *ethic* by the Greeks) which readily adapts itself to different dispositions and humours, and to every station of life:—and the other is the pathetic, which rouses and alarms the passions, and may be considered as the *scepter* of Eloquence. The former is mild and insinuating, and entirely calculated to conciliate the good-will of the hearer: but the latter is all energy and fire, and snatches a cause by open violence;—and when it's course is rapid and unrestrained, the shock is irresistible. I [footnote: Here follows the second passage above-referred to, in which there is a long string of *Egotisms*. But as they furnish some very instructive hints, the Reader will peruse them with more pleasure than pain] myself have possessed a tolerable share of this, or, it may be, a trifling one:—but as I always spoke with uncommon warmth and impetuosity, I have frequently forced my antagonist to relinquish the field. *Hortensius*, an eminent Speaker, once declined to answer me, though in defence of an intimate friend. *Cataline*, a most audacious traitor, being publicly accused by me in the Senate-house, was struck dumb with shame: and *Curio*, the father, when he attempted to reply to me in a weighty and important cause which concerned the honour of his family, sat suddenly down, and complained that I had *bewitched* him out of his memory. As to moving the pity of my audience, it will be unnecessary to mention this. I have frequently attempted it with good success, and when several of us have pleaded on the same side, this part of the defence was always resigned to me; in which my supposed excellence was not owing to the superiority of my genius, but to the real concern I felt for the distresses of my client. But what in this respect have been my talents (for I have had no reason to complain of them) may be easily discovered in my Orations:—though a book, indeed, must lose much of the spirit which makes a speech delivered in public appear to greater advantage than when it is perused in the closet.

But we are to raise not only the pity of our judges, (which I have endeavoured so passionately, that I once took up an infant in my arms while I was speaking;—and, at another time, calling up the nobleman in whose defence I spoke, and holding up a little child of his before the whole assembly, I filled the Forum with my cries and lamentations:)—but it is also necessary to rouse the judge's indignation, to appease it, to excite his jealousy, his benevolence, his contempt, his wonder, his abhorrence, his love, his desire, his aversion, his hope, his fear, his joy, and his grief:—in all which variety, you may find examples, in many accusatory speeches, of rousing the harsher passions; and my Defences will furnish instances enough of the methods of working upon the gentler. For there is no method either of alarming or soothing the passions, but what has been attempted by *me*. I would say I have carried it to perfection, if I either thought so, or was not afraid that (in this case) even truth itself might incur the charge of arrogance. But (as I have before observed) I have been so much transported, not by the force of my genius, but by the real fervor of my heart, that I was unable to restrain myself: —and, indeed, no language will inflame the mind of the hearer, unless the Speaker himself first catches the ardor, and glows with the importance of his subject. I would refer to examples of my own, unless you had seen them already; and to those of other Speakers among the Romans, if I could produce any, or among the Greeks, if I judged it proper. But *Crassus* will only furnish us with a few, and those not of the forensic kind:— *Antonius*, *Cotta*, and *Sulpicius* with none:—and as to *Hortensius*, he spoke much better than he wrote. We may, therefore, easily judge how amazing must be the force of a talent, of which we have so few examples:

— but if we are resolved to seek for them, we must have recourse to *Demosthenes*, in whom we find almost a continued succession of them, in that part of his Oration for *Ctesiphon*, where he enlarges on his own actions, his measures, and his good services to the State, For that Oration, I must own, approaches so near to the primary form or semblance of Eloquence which exists in my mind, that a more complete and exalted pattern is scarcely desirable. But still, there will remain a general model or character, the true nature and excellence of which may be easily collected from the hints I have already offered.

We have slightly touched upon the ornaments of language, both in single words, and in words as they stand connected with each other;—in which our Orator will so indulge himself, that not a single expression may escape him, but what is either elegant or weighty. But he will most abound in the *metaphor*; which, by an aptness of similitude, conveys and transports the mind from object to object, and hurries it backwards and forwards through a pleasing variety of images;—a motion which, in its own nature, (as being full of life and action) can never fail to be highly delightful. As to the other ornaments of language which regard words as they are connected with each other, an Oration will derive much of its lustre from these. They are like the decorations in the Theatre, or the Forum, which not only embellish, but surprize. [Footnote: In the following Abstract of the Figures of *Language* and *Sentiment*, I have often paraphrased upon my author, to make him intelligible to the English reader;—a liberty which I have likewise taken in several other places, where I judged it necessary.] For such also is the effect of the various *figures* or decorations of language;—such as the doubling or repetition of the same word;—the repeating it with a slight variation; —the beginning or concluding several sentences in the same manner, or both at once;—the making a word, which concludes a preceding sentence, to begin the following;—the concluding a sentence with the same expression which began it;—the repeating the same word with a different meaning; —the using several corresponding words in the same case, or with the same termination;—the contrasting opposite expressions;—the using words whose meaning rises in gradation;—the leaving out the conjunctive particles to shew our earnestness;—the passing by, or suddenly dropping a circumstance we were going to mention, and assigning a reason for so doing; —[Footnote: We have an instance of this, considered as a figure of language, in the following line of Virgil; Quos ego—, sed praestat motos componere fluctus. Aeneid. I. Whom I—, but let me still the raging waves. This may likewise serve as an example of the figure which is next mentioned.] the pretending to correct or reprove ourselves, that we may seem to speak without artifice or partiality;—the breaking out into a sudden exclamation, to express our wonder, our abhorrence, or our grief;— and the using the same noun in different cases.

But the figures of *sentiment* are more weighty and powerful; and there are some who place the highest merit of *Demosthenes* in the frequent use he makes of them. For be his subject what it will, almost all his sentences have a figurative air: and, indeed, a plentiful intermixture of this sort of figures is the very life and soul of a popular Eloquence. But as you are thoroughly acquainted with these, my Brutus, what occasion is there to explain and exemplify them? The bare mention of them will be sufficient.—Our Orator, then, will sometimes exhibit an idea in different points of view, and when he has started a good argument, he will dwell upon it with an honest exultation;—he will extenuate what is unfavourable, and have frequent recourse to raillery;—he will sometimes deviate from his plan, and seem to alter his first purpose:—he will inform his audience beforehand, what are the principal points upon which he intends to rest his cause;—he will collect and point out the force of the arguments he has already discussed; he will check an ardent expression, or boldly reiterate what he has said;—he will close a lively paragraph with some weighty and convincing sentiment; —he will press upon his adversary by repeated interrogations;—he will reason with himself, and answer questions of his own proposing;—he will throw out expressions which he designs to be otherwise understood than they seem to mean;—he will pretend to doubt what is most proper to be said, and in what order;— he will divide an action, &c. into its several parts and circumstances, to render it more striking;—he will pretend to pass over and relinquish a circumstance which might have been urged to advantage; —he will secure himself against the known prejudices of his audience;—he will turn the very circumstance which is alledged against him to the prejudice of his antagonist;—he will frequently appeal to his hearers, and sometimes to his opponent;—he will represent the very language and manners of the persons he is speaking of;—he will introduce irrational and even inanimate beings, as addressing themselves to his audience;—he will (to serve some necessary purpose) steal off their attention from the point in debate;—he will frequently move them to mirth and laughter;—he will answer every thing which he foresees will be objected;—he will compare similar incidents,—refer to past examples,—and by way of amplification assign their distinguishing qualities to opposite characters and circumstances;—he will check an impertinent plea which may interrupt his argument;—he will pretend not to mention what he might have urged to good purpose;—he will caution his hearers against the various artifices and subterfuges which may be employed to deceive them;—he will sometimes appear to speak with an honest, but unguarded freedom;—he will avow his resentment;—he will entreat;—he will earnestly supplicate;—he will apologize;—he will seem for a moment to forget himself;—he will express his hearty good wishes for the deserving, and vent his execrations against notorious villainy;—and now and then he will descend imperceptibly to the most tender and insinuating familiarities. There are likewise Other beauties of composition which he will not fail to pursue;—such as brevity where the subject requires it;—a lively and pathetic description of important occurrences;—a passionate exaggeration of remarkable circumstances;—an earnestness of expression which implies more than is said;—a well-timed variety of humour;—and a happy imitation of different characters and dispositions. Assisted and adorned by such figures as these, which are very numerous, the force of Eloquence will appear in its brightest lustre. But even these, unless they are properly formed and regulated, by a skilful disposition of their constituent words, will never attain the merit we require;—a subject which I shall be obliged to treat of in the sequel, though I am restrained partly by the circumstances already mentioned, but much more so by the following. For I am sensible not only that there are some invidious people, to whom every improvement appears vain and superfluous; but that even those, who are well-wishers to my reputation, may think it beneath the dignity of a man whose public services have been so honourably distinguished by the Senate, and the whole body of the Roman people, to employ my pen so largely upon the art of Speaking. [Footnote: The long apology which our author is now going to make for bestowing his time in composing a treatise of Oratory, is in fact a very artful as well as an elegant digression; to relieve the dryness and intricacy of the abstract he has just given us of the figures of rhetoric, and of the subsequent account of the rules of prosaic harmony. He has also enlivened that account (which is a very long one) in the same manner, by interspersing it, at convenient distances, with fine examples, agreeable companions, and short historical digressions to elucidate the subject.]

If, however, I was to return no other answer to the latter, but that I was unwilling to deny any thing to the request of Brutus, the apology must be unexceptionable; because I am only aiming at the satisfaction of an intimate friend, and a worthy man, who desires nothing of me but what is just and honourable.

But was I even to profess (what I wish I was capable of) that I mean to give the necessary precepts, and point out the road to Eloquence to those who are desirous to qualify themselves for the Forum, what man of sense could blame me for it? For who ever doubted that in the decision of political matters, and in time of peace, Eloquence has always borne the sway in the Roman state, while Jurisprudence has possessed only the second post of honour? For whereas the former is a constant source of authority and reputation, and enables us to defend ourselves and our friends in the most effectual manner;—the other only furnishes us with formal rules for indictments, pleas, protests, &c. in conducting which she is frequently obliged to sue for the assistance of Eloquence;—but if the latter condescends to oppose her, she is scarcely able to maintain her ground, and defend her own territories. If therefore to teach the Civil Law has always been reckoned a very honourable employment, and the houses of the most eminent men of that profession, have been crowded with disciples; who can be reasonably censured for exciting our youth to the study of Eloquence, and furnishing them with all the assistance in his power? If it is a fault to speak gracefully, let Eloquence be for ever banished from the state. But if, on the contrary, it reflects an honour, not only upon the man who possesses it, but upon the country which gave him birth, how can it be a disgrace to *learn*, what it is so glorious to *know*? Or why should it not be a credit to *teach* what it is the highest honour to have *learned*?

But, in one case, they will tell me, the practice has been sanctified by custom, and in the other it has not. This I grant: but We may easily account for both. As to the gentlemen of the law, it was sufficient to hear them, when they decided upon such cases as were laid before them in the course of business;—so that when they taught, they did not set apart any particular time for that purpose, but the same answers satisfied their clients and their pupils. On the other hand, as our Speakers of eminence spent their time, while at home, in examining and digesting their causes, and while in the Forum in pleading them, and the remainder of it in a seasonable relaxation, what opportunity had they for teaching and instructing others? I might venture to add that most of our Orators have been more distinguishied by their *genius*, than by their *learning*; and for that reason were much better qualified to be *Speakers* than *Teachers*; which it is possible may be the reverse of my case.—"True," say they; "but teaching is an employment which is far from being recommended by its dignity." And so indeed it is, if we teach like mere pedagogues. But if we only direct, encourage, examine, and inform our pupils; and sometimes accompany them in reading or hearing the performances of the most eminent Speakers;—if by these means we are able to contribute to their improvement, what should hinder us from communicating a few instructions, as opportunity offers? Shall we deem it an honourable employment, as indeed with us it is, to teach the form of a legal process, or an excommunication from the rites and privileges of our religion; and shall it not be equally honourable to teach the methods by which those privileges may be defended and secured?—"Perhaps it may," they will reply; "but even those who know scarcely any thing of the law are ambitious to be thought masters of it; whereas those who are well furnished with the powers of Eloquence pretend to be wholly unacquainted with them; because they are sensible that useful knowledge is a valuable recommendation, whereas an artful tongue is suspected by every one." But is it possible, then, to exert the powers of Eloquence without discovering them? Or is an Orator really thought to be no Orator, because he disclaims the title? Or is it likely that, in a great and noble art, the world will judge it a scandal to *teach* what it is the greatest honour to *learn*? Others, indeed, may have been more reserved; but, for my part, I have always owned my profession. For how could I do otherwise, when, in my youth, I left my native land, and crossed the sea, with no other view but to improve myself in this kind of knowledge; and, when afterwards my house was crowded with the ablest professors, and my very style betrayed some traces of a liberal education? Nay, when my own writings were in every body's hands, with what face could I pretend that I had not studied? Or what excuse could

I have for submitting my abilities to the judgment of the public, if I had been apprehensive that they would think I had studied to no purpose? [Footnote: This sentence in the original runs thus;—*Quid erat cur probarem* (i.e. scripta nostra), *nisi quod parum fortasse profeceram*?—"Wherefore did I approve of them," (that is, of my writings, so far as to make them public) "but because I had," (in my own opinion) "made a progress, though perhaps a small one, in useful literature?" This, at least, is the only meaning I am able to affix to it; and I flatter myself, that the translation I have given of it, will be found to correspond with the general sense of my author.] But the points we have already discussed are susceptible of greater dignity and elevation, than those which remain to be considered. For we are next to treat of the arrangement of our words; and, indeed, I might have said, of the art of numbering and measuring our very syllables; which, though it may, in reality, be a matter of as much consequence as I judge it to be, cannot however be supposed to have such a striking appearance in precept as in practice. This, indeed, might be said of every other branch of useful knowledge; but it is more remarkably true with respect to this. For the actual growth and improving height of all the sublimer arts, like that of trees, affords a pleasing prospect; whereas the roots and stems are scarcely beheld with indifference: and yet the former cannot subsist without the latter. But whether I am restrained from dissembling the pleasure I take in the subject, by the honest advice of the Poet, who says,

"Blush not to own the art you love to practise."

or whether this treatise has been extorted from me by the importunity of my friend, it was proper to obviate the censures to which it will probably expose me. And yet, even supposing that I am mistaken in my sentiments, who would shew himself so much of a savage, as to refuse me his indulgence (now all my forensic employments and public business are at an end) for not resigning myself to that stupid inactivity which is contrary to my nature, or to that unavailing sorrow which I do my best to overcome, rather than devote myself to my favourite studies? These first conducted me into the Forum and the Senate-House, and they are now the chief comforts of my retirement. I have, however, applied myself not only to such speculations as form the subject of the present Essay, but to others more sublime and interesting; and if I am able to discuss them in a proper manner, my private studies will be no disparagement to my forensic employments.

But it is time to return to our subject.—Our words, then, should be so disposed that every following one may be aptly connected with the preceding, so as to make an agreeable sound;—or that the mere form and *concinnity* of our language may give our sentences their proper measure and dimensions;—or, lastly, that our periods may have a numerous and measured cadence.

The first thing, then, to be attended to, is the *structure* of our language, or the agreeable connection of one word with another; which, though it certainly requires care, ought not to be practised with a laborious nicety. For this would be an endless and puerile attempt, and is justly ridiculed by *Lucilius*, when he introduces *Scaevola* thus reflecting upon *Albucius*:

"As in the checquer'd pavement ev'ry square
Is nicely fitted by the mason's care:
So all thy words are plac'd with curious art,
And ev'ry syllable performs its part."

But though we are not to be minutely exact in the *structure* of our language, a moderate share of practice will habituate us to every thing of this nature which is necessary. For as the eye in *reading*, so the mind in *speaking*, will readily discern what ought to follow,—that, in connecting our words, there may neither be a chasm, nor a disagreeable harshness. The most lively and interesting sentiments, if they are harshly expressed, will offend the ear, that delicate and fastidious judge of rhetorical harmony. This circumstance, therefore, is so carefully attended to in the Roman language, that there is scarcely a rustic among us who is not averse to a collision of vowels,—a defect which, in the opinion of some, was too scrupulously avoided by *Theopompus*, though his master *Isocrates* was equally cautious. But *Thucydides* was not so exact; nor was Plato, (though a much better writer)—not only in his *Dialogues*, in which it was necessary to maintain an easy negligence, to resemble the style of conversation, but in the famous *Panegyric*, in which (according to the custom of the Athenians) he celebrated the praises of those who fell in battle, and which was so greatly esteemed, that it is publicly repeated every year. In that Oration a collision of vowels occurs very frequently; though *Demosthenes* generally avoids it as a fault.

But let the Greeks determine for themselves: we Romans are not allowed to interrupt the connection of our words. Even the rude and unpolished Orations of *Cato* are a proof of this; as are likewise all our poets, except in particular instances, in which they were obliged to admit a few breaks, to preserve their metre. Thus we find in *Naevius*,

"*Vos* QUI ACCOLITIS *histrum* FLUVIUM ATQUE ALGIDUM."

And in another place,

"*Quam nunquam vobis* GRAII ATQUE *Barbari*."

But *Ennius* admits it only once, when he says,

"*Scipio invicte*;"

and likewise I myself in

"*Hoc motu radiantis* ETESIAE IN *Vada Ponti*."

This, however, would seldom be suffered among us, though the Greeks often commend it as a beauty.

But why do I speak of a collision of vowels? for, omitting this, we have frequently *contracted* our words for the sake of brevity; as in *multi' modis, vas' argenteis, palm' et crinibus, tecti' fractis*, &c. We have sometimes also contracted our proper *names*, to give them a smoother sound: for as we have changed *Duellum* into *Bellum*, and *duis* into *bis*, so *Duellius*, who defeated the Carthagenians at sea, was called *Bellius*, though all his ancestors were named *Duellii*. We likewise abbreviate our words, not only for convenience, but to please and gratify the ear. For how otherwise came *axilla* to be changed into *ala*, but by the omission of an unweildy consonant, which the elegant pronunciation of our language has likewise banished from the words *maxillae, taxillae, vexillum*, and *paxillum*?

Upon the same principle, two or more words have been contracted into one, as *sodes* for *si audes*, *sis* for *si vis*, *capsis* for *cape si vis*, *ain'* for *aisne*, *nequire* for *non quire*, *malle* for *magis velle*, and *nolle* for *non velle*; and we often say *dein'* and *exin'* for *deinde* and *exinde*. It is equally evident why we never say *cum nobis*, but *nobiscum*; though we do not scruple to say *cum illis*;—*viz.* because, in the former case, the union of the consonants *m* and *n* would produce a jarring sound: and we also say *mecum* and *tecum*, and not *cum me* and *cum te*, to correspond with *nobiscum* and *vobiscum*. But some, who would correct antiquity rather too late, object to these contractions: for, instead of *prob* DEÛM *atque hominum fidem*, they say *Deorum*. They are not aware, I suppose, that custom has sanctified the licence. The same Poet, therefore, who, almost without a precedent, has said *patris mei MEÛM FACTÛM pudet*, instead of *meorum factorum*,—and *textitur exitiûm examen rapit* for *exitiorum*, does not choose to say *liberum*, as we generally do in the expressions *cupidos liberûm*, and *in liberûm loco*, but, as the literary virtuosos above-mentioned would have it,

neque tuum unquam in gremium extollas LIBERORUM *ex te genus*,

and,

namque Aesculapî LIBERORUM.

But the author before quoted says in his Chryses, not only

Cives, antiqui amici majorum MEÛM,

which was common enough—, but more harshly still,

CONSILIÛM, AUGURIÛM, *atque* EXTÛM *interpretes*;

and in another place,

Postquam PRODIGIÛM HORRIFERÛM PORTENTÛM *pavos*.

a licence which is not customary in all neuters indifferently: for I should not be so willing to say armûm *judicium*, as *armorum*; though in the same writer we meet with *nihilne ad te de judicio* armûm *accidit*? And yet (as we find it in the public registers) I would venture to say *fabrûm*, and *procûm*, and not *fabrorum* and *procorum*. But I would never say duorum virorum *judicium*, or *trium* virorum *capitalium*, or *decem* virorum *litibus judicandis*. In Accius, however, we meet with

Video sepulchra duo duorum *corporum*;

though in another place he says,

Mulier una duum virum.

I know, indeed, which is most conformable to the rules of grammar: but yet I sometimes express myself as the freedom of our language allows me, as when I say at pleasure, either *prob deum*, or *prob deorum*;—and, at other times, as I am obliged by custom, as when I say *trium* virum for *virorum*, or sestertium nummum for *nummorum*: because in the latter case the mode of expression is invariable.

But what shall we say when these humourists forbid us to say *nosse* and *judicasse* for *novisse* and *judicavisse*; as if we did not know, as well as themselves, that, in these instances, the verb at full length is most agreeable to the laws of grammar, though custom has given the preference to the contracted verb? Terence, therefore, has made use of both, as when he says, *eho tu cognatum tuum non norâs*? and afterwards,

Stilphonem, inquam, noveras?

Thus also, *fiet* is a perfect verb, and *fit* a contracted one; and accordingly we find in the same Comedian,

Quam cara SINTQUE *post carendo intelligunt*,

and

Quamque attinendi magni dominatus SIENT.

In the same manner I have no objection to *scripsere alii rem*, though I am sensible that *scripserunt* is more grammatical; because I submit with pleasure to the indulgent laws of custom which delights to gratify the ear. *Idem campus habet*, says Ennius; and in another place, *in templis îsdem*; *eisdem*, indeed, would have been more grammatical, but not sufficiently harmonious; and *iisdem* would have sounded still worse.

But we are allowed by custom even to dispense with the rules of etymology to improve the sweetness of our language; and I would therefore rather say, *pomeridianas Quadrigas*, than *postmeridianas*; and *mehercule*, than *mehercules*. For the same reason *non scire* would now be deemed a barbarism, becaule *nescire* has a smoother sound; and we have likewise substituted *meridiem* for *medidiem*, because the latter was offensive to the ear. Even the preposition *ab*, which so frequently occurs in our compound verbs is preserved entire only in the formality of a Journal, and, indeed, not always there: in every other sort of language it is frequently altered. Thus we say *amovit*, *abegit*, and *abstulit*; so that you can scarcely determine whether the primitive preposition should be *ab* or *abs*. We have likewise rejected even *abfugit*, and *abfer*, and introduced *aufugit* and *aufer* in their stead;—thus forming a new preposition, which is to be found in no other verb but these. *Noti*, *navi*, and *nari*, have all been words in common use: but when they were afterwards to be compounded with the preposition *in*, it was thought more harmonious to say *ignoti*, *ignavi*, and *ignari*, than to adhere strictly to the rules of etymology. We likewise say *ex usu*, and *e Republicâ*; because, in the former case, the preposition is followed by a vowel, and, in the latter, it would have sounded harshly without omitting the consonant; as may also be observed in *exegit, edixit, refecit, retulit*, and *reddidit*.

Sometimes the preposition alters or otherwise affects the first letter of the verb with which it happens to be compounded; as in *subegit, summutavit*, and *sustutit*. At other times it changes one of the subsequent letters; as when we say *insipientem* for *insapientem*, *iniquum* for inaequum_, *tricipitem* for *tricapitem*, and *concisum* for *concaesum*: and from hence some have ventured to say *pertisum* for *pertaesum*, which custom has never warranted.

But what can be more delicate than our changing even the natural quantity of our syllables to humour the ear? Thus in the adjectives *inclytus*, and *inhumanus*, the first syllable after the preposition is short, whereas *insanus* and *infelix* have it long; and, in general, those words whose first letters are the same as in *sapiens* and *felix*, have their first syllable long in composition, but all others have the same syllable short, as *composuit, consuevit, concrepuit, confecit*. Examine these liberties by the strict rules of etymology, and they must certainly be condemned; but refer them to the decision of the ear, and they will be instantly approved.—What is the reason? Your ear will inform you they have an easier sound; and every language must submit to gratify the ear. I myself, because our ancestors never admitted the aspirate, unless where a syllable began with a vowel, used to say *pulcros, Cetegos, triumpos*, and *Cartaginem*: but some time afterwards, though not very soon, when this grammatical accuracy was wrested from me by the censure of the ear, I resigned the mode of language to the vulgar, and reserved the theory to myself. But we still say, without any hesitation, *Orcivios, Matones, Otones, coepiones, sepulcra, coronas*, and *lacrymas*, because the ear allows it. *Ennius* always uses *Burrum*, and never *Pyrrhum*; and the ancient copies of the same author have

Vi patefecerunt BRUGES,

not *Phryges*; because the Greek vowel had not then been adopted, though we now admit both that and the aspirate:—and, in fact, when we had afterwards occasion to say *Phrygum* and *Phrygibus*, it was rather absurd to adopt the Greek letter without adopting their cases, [Footnote: This passage, as it stands in the original, appears to me unintelligible: I have therefore taken the liberty to give it a slight alteration.] or at least not to confine it to the nominative; and yet (in the accusative) we say *Phryges*, and *Pyrrhum*, to please the ear. Formerly it was esteemed an elegancy, though it would now be considered as a rusticism, to omit the *s* in all words which terminate in *us*, except when they were followed by a vowel; and the same elision which is so carefully avoided by the modern Poets, was very far from being reckoned a fault among the ancient: for they made no scruple to say,

Qui est OMNIBU' princeps,

not, as we do, OMNIBUS princeps; and,

Vitâ illâ DIGNU' locoque,

not *dignus.*

But if untaught custom has been so ingenious in the formation of agreeable sounds, what may we not expect from the improvements of art and erudition? I have, however, been much shorter upon this subject, than I should have been if I had written upon it professedly: for a comparison of the natural and customary laws of language would have opened a wide field for speculation: but I have already enlarged upon it sufficiently, and more, perhaps, than the nature of my design required.

To proceed then;—as the choice of proper matter, and of suitable words to express it, depends upon the judgment of the Speaker, but that of agreeable sounds, and harmonious numbers, upon the decision of the ear; and because the former is intended for information, and the latter for pleasure; it is evident that reason must determine the rules of art in one case, and mere sensation in the other. For we must either neglect the gratification of those by whom we wish to be approved, or apply ourselves to invent the most likely methods to promote it.

There are two things which contribute to gratify the ear,—agreeable *sounds*, and harmonious *numbers*. We shall treat of numbers in the sequel, and at present confine ourselves to *sound*.—Those words, then, as we have already observed, are to have the preference which sound agreeably;—not such as are exquisitely melodious, like those of the Poets, but such as can be found to our purpose in common language.—*Quà Pontus Helles* is rather beyond the mark:—but in

Auratos aries Colchorum,

the verse glitters with a moderate harmony of expression; whereas the next, as ending with a letter which is remarkably flat, is unmusical,

Frugifera et ferta arva Alfiae tenet,

Let us, therefore, rather content ourselves with the agreeable mediocrity of our own language, than emulate the splendor of the Greeks; unless we are so bigotted to the latter as to hesitate to say with the poet,

Quà tempestate Paris Helenam, &c.

we might even imitate what follows, and avoid, as far as possible, the smallest asperity of sound,

habeo istam ego PERTERRICREPAM;

or say, with the same author, in another passage,

versutiloquas MALITIAS.

But our words must have a proper *compass*, as well as be connected together in an agreeable manner; for this, we have observed, is another circumstance which falls under the notice of the ear. They are confined to a proper compass, either by certain rules of composition, as by a kind of natural pause, or by the use of particular forms of expression, which have a peculiar *concinnity* in their very texture; such as a succession of several words which have the same termination, or the comparing similar, and contrasting opposite circumstances, which will always terminate in a measured cadence, though no immediate pains should be taken for that purpose. Gorgias, it is said, was the first Orator who practised this species of *concinnity*. The following passage in my Defence of *Milo* is an example.

"Est enim, Judices, haec non *scripta*, fed *nata* Lex; quam non *didicimus, accepimus, legimus,* verum ex Naturâ ipsâ *arripuimus, hausimus, expressimus*; ad quam non *docti*, sed *facti*; non *instituti*, sed *imbuti* simus."

"For this, my Lords, is a law not written upon tables, but impressed upon our hearts;—a law which we have not learned, or heard, or read, but eagerly caught and imbibed from the hand of Nature;—a law to which we have not been train'd, but originally form'd; and with the principles of which we have not been furnished by education, but tinctured and impregnated from the moment of our birth."

In these forms of expression every circumstance is so aptly referred to some other circumstance, that the regular turn of them does not appear to have been studied, but to result entirely from the sense. The same effect is produced by contrasting opposite circumstances; as in the following lines, where it not only forms a measured sentence, but a verse:

Eam, quam nihil accusas, damnas,

Her, whom you ne'er accus'd, you now condemn;

(in prose we should say *condemnas*) and again,

Bene quam meritam esse autumas, dicis male mereri,

Her merit, once confess'd, you now deny; and,

Id quod scis, prodest nihil; id quod nescis, obest,

From what you've learnt no real good accrues,
But ev'ry ill your ignorance pursues.

Here you see the mere opposition of the terms produces a verse; but in prosaic composition, the proper form of the last line would be, *quod scis nihil prodest; quod nescis multum obest.* This contrasting of opposite circumstances, which the Greeks call an Antithesis, will necessarily produce what is styled *rhetorical metre,* even without our intending it. The ancient Orators, a considerable time before it was practised and recommended by *Isocrates*, were fond of using it; and particularly *Gorgias*, whose measured cadences are generally owing to the mere *concinnity* of his language. I have frequently practised it myself; as, for instance, in the following passage of my fourth Invective against *Verres*:

"Conferte *hanc Pacem* cum *illo Bello*;—*hujus* Praetoris *Adventum*, cum *illius* Imperatoris *Victoriâ*;—hujas *Cohortem impuram*, cum illius *Exercitu invicto*;—hujus *Libidines*, cum illius *Continentiâ*;—ab illo qui cepit *conditas*; ab hoc, qui constitutas accepit, *captas* dicetis Syracusas."

"Compare this detestable *peace* with that glorious *war,*—the *arrival* of this governor with the *victory* of that commander,—his *ruffian guards*, with the *invincible forces* of the other;—the brutal luxury of the former, with the modest temperance of the latter;—and you will say, that Syracuse was really *founded* by him who *stormed* it, and *stormed* by him who received it already *founded* to his hands."—So much, then, for that kind of measure which results from particular forms of expression, and which ought to be known by every Orator.

We must now proceed to the third thing proposed,—that *numerous* and well-adjusted style; of the beauty of which, if any are so insensible as not to feel it, I cannot imagine what kind of ears they have, or what resemblance of a human Being! For my part, my ears are always fond of a complete and full-measured flow of words, and perceive in an instant what is either defective or redundant. But wherefore do I say *mine*? I have frequently seen a whole assembly burst into raptures of applause at a happy period: for the ear naturally expects that our sentences should be properly tuned and measured. This, however, is an accomplishment which is not to be met with among the ancients. But to compensate the want of it, they had almost every other perfection: for they had a happy choice of words, and abounded in pithy and agreeable sentiments, though they had not the art of harmonizing and completing their periods. This, say some, is the very thing we admire. But what if they should take it into their heads to prefer the ancient *peinture*, with all its poverty of colouring, to the rich and finished style of the moderns? The former, I suppose, must be again adopted, to compliment their delicacy, and the latter rejected. But these pretended connoisseurs regard nothing but the mere *name* of antiquity. It must, indeed, be owned that antiquity has an equal claim to authority in matters of imitation, as grey hairs in the precedence of age. I myself have as great a veneration for it as any man: nor do I so much upbraid antiquity with her defects, as admire the beauties she was mistress of:—especially as I judge the latter to be of far greater consequence than the former. For there is certainly more real merit in a masterly choice of words and sentiments, in which the ancients are allowed to excell, than in those measured periods with which they were totally unacquainted. This species of composition was not known among the Romans till lately: but the ancients, I believe, would readily have adopted it, if it had then been discovered: and we accordingly find, that it is now made use of by all Orators of reputation. "But when *number*, or (as the Greeks call it) prosaic *metre*, is professedly introduced into judicial and forensic discourses, the very name, say they, has a suspicious sound: for people will conclude that there is too much artifice employed to sooth and captivate their ears, when the Speaker is so over-exact as to attend to the harmony of his periods." Relying upon the force of this objection, these pretenders are perpetually grating our ears with their broken and mutilated sentences; and censure those, without mercy, who have the presumption to utter an agreeable and a well-turned period. If, indeed, it was our design to spread a varnish over empty words and trifling sentiments, the censure would be just: but when the matter is good, and the words are proper and expressive, what reason can be assigned why we should prefer a limping and imperfect period to one which terminates and keeps pace with the sense? For this invidious and persecuted *metre* aims at nothing more than to adapt the compass of our words to that of our thoughts; which is sometimes done even by the ancients,—though generally, I believe, by mere accident, and often by the natural delicacy of the ear; and the very passages which are now most admired in them, commonly derive their merit from the agreeable and measured flow of the language.

This is an art which was in common use among the Greek Orators, about four hundred years ago, though it has been but lately introduced among the Romans. Ennius, therefore, when he ridicules the inharmonious numbers of his predecessors, might be allowed to say,

"*Such verses as the rustic Bards and Satyrs sung*:"

But I must not take the same liberty; especially as I cannot say with him,

Before this bold adventurer, &c.

(meaning himself:) nor, as he afterwards exults to the same purpose,

I first have dar'd t'unfold, &c.

for I have both read and heard several who were almost complete masters of the numerous and measured style I am speaking of: But many, who are still absolute strangers to it, are not content to be exempted from the ridicule they deserve, but claim a right to our warmest applause. I must own, indeed, that I admire the venerable patterns, of which those persons pretend to be the faithful imitators, notwithstanding the defects I observe in them: but I can by no means commend the folly of those who copy nothing but their blemishes, and have no pretensions even to the most distant resemblance in what is truly excellent.

But if their own ears are so indelicate and devoid of taste, will they pay no deference to the judgment of others, who are universally celebrated for their learning? I will not mention *Isocrates*, and his two scholars, *Ephorus* and *Naucrates*; though they may claim the honour of giving the richest precepts of composition, and were themselves very eminent Orators. But who was possessed of a more ample fund of erudition?—who more subtle and acute?—or who furnished with quicker powers of invention, and a greater strength of understanding, than *Aristotle*? I may add, who made a warmer opposition to the rising fame of *Isocrates*? And yet *he*, though he forbids us to versify in prose, recommends the use of *numbers*. His hearer *Theodectes* (whom he often mentions as a polished writer, and an excellent artist) both approves and advises the same thing: and *Theophrastus* is still more copious and explicit. Who, then, can have patience with those dull and conceited humourists, who dare to oppose themselves to such venerable names as these? The only excuse that can be made for them is, that they have never perused their writings, and are therefore ignorant that they actually recommend the prosaic *metre* we are speaking of. If this is the case with them (and I cannot think otherwise) will they reject the evidence of their own sensations? Is there nothing which their ears will inform them is defective?—nothing which is harsh and unpolished?—nothing imperfect?—nothing lame and mutilated?—nothing redundant? In dramatic performances, a whole theatre will exclaim against a verse which has only a syllable either too short or too long: and yet the bulk of an audience are unacquainted with *feet* and *numbers*, and are totally ignorant what the fault is, and where it lies: but Nature herself has taught the ear to measure the quantity of sound, and determine the propriety of its various accents, whether grave, or acute.

Do you desire, then, my Brutus, that we should discuss the subject more fully than those writers who have already elucidated this, and the other parts of rhetoric? Or shall we content ourselves with the instructions which *they* have provided for us? But wherefore do I offer such a question, when your elegant letters have informed me, that this is the chief object of your request? We shall proceed, therefore, to give an account of the commencement, the origin, and the nature and use of *prosaic numbers*.

The admirers of Isocrates place the first invention of numbers among those other improvements which do honour to his memory. For observing, say they, that the Orators were heard with a kind of sullen attention, while the Poets were listened to with pleasure, he applied himself to introduce a species of metre into prose, which might have a pleasing effect upon the ear, and prevent that satiety which will always arise from a continued uniformity of sound. This, however, is partly true, and partly otherwise; for though it must be owned that no person was better skilled in the subject than *Isocrates*; yet the first honour of the invention belongs to *Thrasymachus*, whose style (in all his writings which are extant) is *numerous* even to a fault. But *Gorgias*, as I have already remarked, was the original inventor of those measured forms of expression which have a kind of spontaneous harmony,—such as a regular succession of words with the same termination, and the comparing similar, or contracting opposite circumstances: though it is also notoriously true that he used them to excess. This, however, is one of the three branches of composition above-mentioned. But each of these authors was prior to *Isocrates*: so that the preference can be due to *him* only for his *moderate use*, and not for the *invention* of the art: for as he is certainly much easier in the turn of his metaphors, and the choice of his words, so his numbers are more composed and sedate. But *Gorgias*, he observed, was too eager, and indulged himself in this measured play of words to a ridiculous excess. He, therefore, endeavoured to moderate and correct it; but not till he had first studied in his youth under the same *Gorgias*, who was then in Thessaly, and in the last decline of life. Nay, as he advanced in years (for he lived almost a hundred) he corrected *himself*, and gradually relaxed the over-strict regularity of his numbers; as he particularly informs us in the treatise which he dedicated to Philip of Macedon, in the latter part of his life; for he there says, that he had thrown off that servile attention to his numbers, to which he was before accustomed:—so that he discovered and corrected his *own* faults, as well as those of his predecessors.

Having thus specified the several authors and inventors, and the first commencement of prosaic harmony, we must next enquire what was the natural source and origin of it. But this lies so open to observation, that I am astonished the ancients did not notice it: especially as they often, by mere accident, threw out harmonious and measured sentences, which, when they had struck the ears and the passions with so much force, as to make it obvious that there was something particularly agreeable in what chance alone had uttered, one would imagine that such a singular species of ornament would have been immediately attended to, and that they would have taken the pains to imitate what they found so pleasing in themselves. For the ear, or at least the mind by the intervention of the ear, has a natural capacity to measure the harmony of language: and we accordingly feel that it instantly determines what is either too short or too long, and always expects to be gratified with that which is complete and well- proportioned. Some expressions it perceives to be imperfect, and mutilated; and at these it is immediately offended, as if it was defrauded of it's natural due. In others it discovers an immoderate length, and a tedious superfluity of words; and with these it is still more disgusted than with the former; for in this, as in most other cases, an excess is always more offensive than a proportional defect. As versification, therefore, and poetic competition was invented by the regulation of the ear, and the successive observations of men of taste and judgment; so in prose (though indeed long afterwards, but still, however, by the guidance of nature) it was discovered that the career and compass of our language should be adjusted and circumscribed within proper limits.

So much for the source, or natural origin of prosaic harmony. We must next proceed (for that was the third thing proposed) to enquire into the nature of it, and determine it's essential principles;—a subject which exceeds the limits of the present essay, and would be more properly discussed in a professed and accurate system of the art. For we might here inquire what is meant by prosaic *number*, wherein it consists, and from whence it arises; as likewise whether it is simple and uniform, or admits of any variety, and in what manner it is formed, for what purpose, and when and where it should be employed, and how it contributes to gratify the ear. But as in other subjects, so in this, there are two methods of disquisition;—the one more copious and diffusive, and the other more concise, and, I might also add, more easy and comprehensible. In the former, the first question which would occur is, whether there is any such thing as *prosaic number*: some are of opinion there is not; because no fixed and certain rules have been yet assigned for it, as there long have been for poetic numbers; and because the very persons, who contend for it's existence, have hitherto been unable to determine it. Granting, however, that prose is susceptible of numbers, it will next be enquired of what kind they are;—whether they are to be selected from those of the poets, or from a different species;—and, if from the former, which of them may claim the preference; for some authors admit only one or two, and some more, while others object to none. We might then proceed to enquire (be the number of them to be admitted, more or less) whether they are equally common to every kind of style; for the narrative, the persuasive, and the didactic have each a manner peculiar to itself; or whether the different species of Oratory should be accommodated with their different numbers. If the same numbers are equally common to all subjects, we must next enquire what those numbers are; and if they are to be differently applied, we must examine wherein they differ, and for what reason they are not to be used so openly in prose as in verse. It might likewise be a matter of enquiry, whether a *numerous* style is formed entirely by the use of numbers, or not also in some measure by the harmonious juncture of our words, and the application of certain figurative forms of expression; —and, in the next place, whether each of these has not its peculiar province, so that number may regard the time or *quantity*, composition the *sound*, and figurative expression the *form* and *polish* of our language,—and yet, in fact, composition be the source and fountain of all the rest, and give rise both to the varieties of *number*, and to those figurative and luminous dashes of expression, which by the Greeks, as I have before observed, are called ([Greek: *schaemaia*],) *attitudes* or *figures*. But to me there appears to be a real distinction between what is agreeable in *sound*, exact in *measure*, and ornamental in the mode of *expression*; though the latter, it must be owned, is very closely connected with *number*, as being for the most part sufficiently numerous without any labour to make it so: but composition is apparently different from both, as attending entirely either to the *majestic* or *agreeable* sound of our words. Such then are the enquiries which relate to the *nature* of prosaic harmony.

From what has been said it is easy to infer that prose is susceptible of *number*. Our sensations tell us so: and it would be excessively unfair to reject their evidence, because we cannot account for the fact. Even poetic metre was not discovered by any effort of reason, but by mere natural taste and sensation, which reason afterwards correcting, improved and methodized what had been noticed by accident; and thus an attention to nature, and an accurate observation of her various feelings and sensations gave birth to art. But in verse the use of *number* is more obvious; though some particular species of it, without the assistance of music, have the air of harmonious prose, and especially the lyric poetry, and that even the best of the kind, which, if divested of the aid of music, would be almost as plain and naked as common language. We have several specimens of this nature in our own poets [Footnote: It must here be remarked, that the Romans had no lyric poet before *Horace*, who did not flourish till after the times of *Cicero*.]; such as the following line in the tragedy of *Thyestes*,

"*Quemnam te esse dicam? qui in tardâ senectute*;

"Whom shall I call thee? who in tardy age," &c.;

which, unless when accompanied by the lyre, might easily be mistaken for prose. But the iambic verses of the comic poets, to maintain a resemblance to the style of conversation, are often so low and simple that you can scarcely discover in them either number or metre; from whence it is evident that it is more difficult to adapt numbers to prose than to verse.

There are two things, however, which give a relish to our language,—well- chosen words, and harmonious *numbers*. Words may be considered as the *materials* of language, and it is the business of *number* to smooth and polish them. But as in other cases, what was invented to serve our necessities was always prior to that which was invented for pleasure; so, in the present, a rude and simple style which was merely adapted to express our thoughts, was discovered many centuries before the invention of *numbers*, which are designed to please the ear. Accordingly *Herodotus*, and both his and the preceding age had not the least idea of prosaic *number*, nor produced any thing of the kind, unless at random, and by mere accident:—and even the ancient masters of rhetoric (I mean those of the earliest date) have not so much as mentioned it, though they have left us a multitude of precepts upon the conduct and management of our style. For what is easiest, and most necessary to be known, is, for that reason, always first discovered. Metaphors, therefore, and new-made and compounded words, were easily invented, because they were borrowed from custom and conversation: but *number* was not selected from our domestic treasures, nor had the least intimacy or connection with common language; and, of consequence, not being noticed and understood till every other improvement had been made, it gave the finishing grace, and the last touches to the style of Eloquence.

As it may be remarked that one sort of language is interrupted by frequent breaks and intermissions, while another is flowing and diffusive; it is evident that the difference cannot result from the natural sounds of different letters, but from the various combinations of long and short syllables, with which our language, being differently blended and intermingled, will be either dull and motionless, or lively and fluent; so that every circumstance of this nature must be regulated by *number*. For by the assistance of *numbers*, the *period*, which I have so often mentioned before, pursues it's course with greater strength and freedom till it comes to a natural pause. It is therefore plain that the style of an Orator should be measured and harmonized by *numbers*, though entirely free from verse; but whether these numbers should be the same as those of the poets, or of a different species, is the next thing to be considered. In my opinion there can be no sort of numbers but those of the poets; because they have already specified all their different kinds with the utmost precision; for every number may be comprized in the three following varieties:—*viz*. a *foot* (which is the measure we apply to numbers) must be so divided, that one part of it will be either equal to the other, or twice as long, or equal to three halves of it. Thus, in a *dactyl* (breve-macron-macron) (long-short-short) the first syllable, which is the former part of the foot, is equal to the two others, in the *iambic* (macron-breve)(short-long) the last is double the first, and in the *paeon* (macron-macron-macron-breve, or breve-macron-macron-macron)(short- short-short-long, or long-short-short-short) one of its parts, which is the long syllable, is equal to two-thirds of the other. These are feet which are unavoidably incident to language; and a proper arrangement of them will produce a *numerous* style.

But it will here be enquired, What numbers should have the preference? To which I answer, They must all occur promiscuously; as is evident from our sometimes speaking verse without knowing it, which in prose is reckoned a capital fault; but in the hurry of discourse we cannot always watch and criticise ourselves. As to *senarian* and *hipponactic* [Footnote: Verses chiefly composed of iambics] verses, it is scarcely possible to avoid them; for a considerable part, even of our common language, is composed of *iambics*. To these, however, the hearer is easily reconciled; because custom has made them familiar to his ear. But through inattention we are often betrayed into verses which are not so familiar;—a fault which may easily be avoided by a course of habitual circumspection. *Hieronymus*, an eminent Peripatetic, has collected out of the numerous writings of Isocrates about thirty verses, most of them senarian, and some of them anapest, which in prose have a more disagreeable effect than any others. But he quotes them with a malicious partiality: for he cuts off the first syllable of the first word in a sentence, and annexes to the last word the first syllable of the following sentence; and thus he forms what is called an *Aristophanean* anapest, which it is neither possible nor necessary to avoid entirely. But, this redoubtable critic, as I discovered upon a closer inspection, has himself been betrayed into a senarian or iambic verse in the very paragraph in which he censures the composition of *Isocrates*.

Upon the whole, it is sufficiently plain that prose is susceptible of *numbers*, and that the numbers of an Orator must be the same as those of a Poet. The next thing to be considered is, what are the numbers which are most suitable to his character, and, for that reason, should occur more frequently than the rest? Some prefer the *Iambic* (macron-breve)(short-long) as approaching the nearest to common language; for which reason, they say, it is generally made use of in fables and comedies, on account of it's resemblance to conversation; and because the dactyl, which is the favourite number of hexameters, is more adapted to a pompous style. *Ephorus*, on the other hand, declares for the paeon and the dactyl; and rejects the spondee and the trochee (long short). For as the paeon has three short syllables, and the dactyl two, he thinks their shortness and celerity give a brisk and lively flow to our language; and that a different effect would be produced by the trochee and the spondee, the one consisting of short syllables, and the other of long ones;—so that by using the former, the current of our words would become too rapid, and too heavy by employing the latter, losing, in either case, that easy moderation which best satisfies the ear. But both parties seem to be equally mistaken: for those who exclude the paeon, are not aware that they reject the sweetest and fullest number we have. Aristotle was far from thinking as they do: he was of opinion that heroic numbers are too sonorous for prose; and that, on the other hand, the iambic has too much the resemblance of vulgar talk:—and, accordingly, he recommends the style which is neither too low and common, nor too lofty and extravagant, but retains such a just proportion of dignity, as to win the attention, and excite the admiration of the hearer. He, therefore, calls the *trochee* (which has precisely the same quantity as the *choree*) *the rhetorical jigg* [Footnote: *Cordacem appellat*. The *cordax* was a lascivious dance very full of agitation.]; because the shortness and rapidity of it's syllables are incompatible with the majesty of Eloquence. For this reason he recommends the *paeon*, and says that every person makes use of it, even without being sensible when he does so. He likewise observes that it is a proper medium between the different feet above-mentioned:—the proportion between the long and short syllables, in every foot, being either sesquiplicate, duple, or equal.

The authors, therefore, whom I mentioned before attended merely to the easy flow of our language, without any regard to it's dignity. For the iambic and the dactyl are chiefly used in poetry; so that to avoid versifying in prose, we must shun, as much as possible, a continued repetition of either; because the language of prose is of a different cast, and absolutely incompatible with verse. As the paeon, therefore, is of all other feet the most improper for poetry, it may, for that reason be more readily admitted into prose. But as to *Ephorus*, he did not reflect that even the *spondee*, which he rejects, is equal in time to his favourite dactyl; because he supposed that feet were to be measured not by the quantity, but the number of their syllables;—a mistake of which he is equally guilty when he excludes the *trochee*, which, in time and quantity, is precisely equal to the iambic; though it is undoubtedly faulty at the end of a period, which always terminates more agreeably in a long syllable than a short one. As to what Aristotle has said of the *paeon,* the same has likewise been said by *Theophrastus* and *Theodectes.*

But, for my part, I am rather of opinion that our language should be intermingled and diversified with all the varieties of number; for should we confine ourselves to any particular feet, it would be impossible to escape the censure of the hearer; because our style should neither be so exactly measured as that of the poets, nor entirely destitute of number, like that of the common people. The former, as being too regular and uniform, betrays an appearance of art; and the other, which is as much too loose and undetermined, has the air of ordinary talk; so that we receive no pleasure from the one, and are absolutely disgusted with the other. Our style, therefore, as I have just observed, should be so blended and diversified with different numbers, as to be neither too vague and unrestrained, nor too openly numerous, but abound most in the paeon (so much recommended by the excellent author above-mentioned) though still in conjunction with many other feet which he entirely omits.

But we must now consider what number like so many dashes of purple, should tincture and enrich the rest, and to what species of style they are each of them best adapted. The iambic, then, should be the leading number in those subjects which require a plain and simple style;—the paeon in such as require more compass and elevation; and the dactyl is equally applicable to both. So that in a discourse of any length and variety, it will be occasionally necessary to blend and intermingle them all. By this means, our endeavours to modulate our periods, and captivate the ear, will be most effectually concealed; especially, if we maintain a suitable dignity both of language and sentiment. For the hearer will naturally attend to these (I mean our words and sentiments) and to them alone attribute the pleasure he receives; so that while he listens to these with admiration, the harmony of our numbers will escape his notice: though it must indeed be acknowledged that the former would have their charms without the assistance of the latter. But the flow of our numbers is not to be so exact (I mean in prose, for in poetry the case is different) as that nothing may exceed the bounds of regularity; for this would be to compose a poem. On the contrary, if our language neither limps nor fluctuates, but keeps an even and a steady pace, it is sufficiently *numerous*; and it accordingly derives the title, not from its consisting entirely of numbers, but from its near approach to a numerous form. This is the reason why it is more difficult to make elegant prose, than to make verses; because there are fixed and invariable rules for the latter; whereas nothing is determined in the former, but that the current of our language should be neither immoderate nor defective, nor loose and unconfined. It cannot be supposed, therefore, to admit of regular beats and divisions, like a piece of music; but it is only necessary that the general compass and arrangement of our words should be properly restrained and limited,—a circumstance which must be left entirely to the decision of the ear.

Another question which occurs before us, is—whether an attention to our numbers should be extended to every part of a sentence, or only to the beginning and the end. Most authors are of opinion that it is only necessary that our periods should end well, and have a numerous cadence. It is true, indeed, that this ought to be principally attended to, but not solely: for the whole compass of our periods ought likewise to be regulated, and not totally neglected. As the ear, therefore, always directs it's view to the close of a sentence, and there fixes it's attention, it is by no means proper that this should be destitute of *number*: but it must also be observed that a period, from it's first commencement, should run freely on, so as to correspond to the conclusion; and the whole advance from the beginning with such an easy flow, as to make a natural, and a kind of voluntary pause. To those who have been we'll practised in the art, and who have both written much; and often attempted to discourse *extempore* with the same accuracy which they observe in their writings, this will be far less difficult than is imagined. For every sentence is previously formed and circumscribed in the mind of the Speaker, and is then immediately attended by the proper words to express it, which the same mental faculty (than which there is nothing more lively and expeditious) instantly dismisses, and sends off each to its proper post: but, in different sentences, their particular order and arrangement will be differently terminated; though, in every sentence, the words both in the beginning and the middle of it, should have a constant reference to the end. Our language, for instance, must sometimes advance with rapidity, and at other times it's pace must be moderate and easy; so that it will be necessary at the very beginning of a sentence, to resolve upon the manner in which you would have it terminate; but we must avoid the least appearance of poetry, both in our numbers, and in the other ornaments of language; though it is true, indeed, that the labours of the Orator must be conducted on the same principles as those of the Poet. For in each we have the same materials to work upon, and a similar art of managing them; the materials being words, and the art of managing them relating, in both cases, to the manner in which they ought to be disposed. The words also in each may be divided into three classes,—the __metaphorical_,—the new-coined,—and the antique;—for at present we have no concern with words *proper*:—and three parts may also be distinguished in the art of disposing them; which, I have already observed, are *juncture*, *concinnity*, and *number*. The poets make use both of one and the other more frequently, and with greater liberty than we do; for they employ the *tropes* not only much oftener, but more boldly and openly; and they introduce *antique* words with a higher taste, and new ones with less reserve. The same may be said in their numbers, in the use of which they are subjected to invariable rules, which they are scarcely ever allowed to transgress. The two arts, therefore, are to be considered neither as wholly distinct, nor perfectly conjoined. This is the reason why our numbers are not to be so conspicuous in prose as in verse; and that in prose, what is called a *numerous* style, does not always become so by the use of numbers, but sometimes either by the concinnity of our language, or the smooth juncture of our words.

To conclude this head; If it should be enquired, "What are the numbers to be used in prose?" I answer, "*All*; though some are certainly better, and more adapted to it's character than others."—If "*Where* is their proper seat?"—"In the different quantity of our syllables:"—If "From whence their *origin*?"—"From the sole pleasure of the ear:"—If "What the method of blending and intermingling them?"—"This shall be explained in the sequel, because it properly relates to the manner of using them, which was the fourth and last article in my division of the subject." If it be farther enquired, "For what purpose they are employed?" I answer,—"To gratify the ear:"—If "*When*?" I reply, "At all times:"—If "In what part of a sentence?" "Through the whole length of it:"—and if "What is the circumstance which gives them a pleasing effect?" "The same as in poetical compositions, whose metre is regulated by art, though the ear alone, without the assistance of art, can determine it's limits by the natural powers of sensation." Enough, therefore, has been said concerning the nature and properties of *number*. The next article to be considered is the manner in which our numbers should be employed,—a circumstance which requires to be accurately discussed.

Here it is usual to enquire, whether it is necessary to attend to our numbers through the whole compass of a period, [Footnote: Our author here informs us, that what the Greeks called [Greek: periodos], a *period*, was distinguished among the Romans by the words *ambitus*, *circuitus*, *comprehensio*, *continuatio*, and *circumscriptio*. As I thought this remark would appear much better in the form of a note, than in the body of the work, I have introduced it accordingly.] or only at the beginning or end of it, or equally in both. In the next place, as *exact number* seems to be one thing, and that which is merely *numerous* another, it might be enquired wherein lies the difference. We might likewise consider whether the members of a sentence should all indifferently be of the same length, whatever be the numbers they are composed of;—or whether, on this account, they should not be sometimes longer, and sometimes shorter;—and when, and for what reasons, they should be made so, and of what numbers they should be composed;—whether of several sorts, or only of one; and whether of equal or unequal numbers;—and upon what occasions either the one or the other of these are to be used;-and what numbers accord best together, and in what order; or whether, in this respect, there is no difference between them;—and (which has still a more immediate reference to our subject) by what means our style may be rendered *numerous*. It will likewise be necessary to specify the rise and origin of a *periodical* form of language, and what degree of compass should be allowed to it. After this, we may consider the members or divisions of a period, and enquire of how many kinds, and of what different lengths they are; and, if they vary in these respects, *where* and *when* each particular sort is to be employed: and, in the last place, the *use* and application of the whole is to be fully explained;—a very extensive subject, and which is capable of being accommodated not only to one, but to many different occasions. But without adverting to particulars, we may discuss the subject at large in such a manner as to furnish a satisfactory answer in all subordinate cases.

Omitting, therefore, every other species of composition, we shall attend to that which is peculiar to forensic causes. For in those performances which are of a different kind, such as history, panegyric, and all discourses which are merely ornamental, every sentence should be constructed after the exact manner of *Isocrates* and *Theopompus*; and with that regular compass, and measured flow of language, that our words may constantly run within the limits prescribed by art, and pursue a uniform course, till the period is completed. We may, therefore, observe that after the invention of this, *periodical* form, no writer of any account has made a discourse which was intended as a mere display of ornament, and not for the service of the Forum, without *squaring* his language, (if I may so express myself) and confining every sentence of it to the strictest laws of *number*. For as, in this case, the hearer has no motive to alarm his suspicions against the artifice of the speaker, he will rather think himself obliged to him than otherwise, for the pains he takes to amuse and gratify his ear. But, in forensic causes, this accurate species of composition is neither to be wholly adopted, nor entirely rejected. For if we pursue it too closely, it will create a satiety, and our attention to it will be discovered by the most illiterate observer. We may add, it will check the pathos and force of action, restrain the sensibility of the Speaker, and destroy all appearance of truth and open dealing. But as it will sometimes be necessary to adopt it, we must consider *when*, and *how long*, this ought to be done, and how many ways it may be changed and varied.

A *numerous* style, then, may be properly employed, either when any thing is to be commended in a free and ornamental manner, (as in my second Invective against *Verres*, where I spoke in praise of *Sicily*, and in my Speech before the Senate, in which I vindicated the honour of my consulship;)—or; in the next place, when a narrative is to be delivered which requires more dignity than pathos, (as in my fourth Invective, where I described the Ceres of the Ennensians, the Diana of the Segestani, and the situation of Syracuse.) It is likewise often allowable to speak in a numerous and flowing style, when a material circumstance is to be amplified. If I myself have not succeeded in this so well as might be wished, I have at least attempted it very frequently; and it is still visible in many of my Perorations, that I have exerted all the talents I was master of for that purpose. But this will always have most efficacy, when the Speaker has previously possessed himself of the hearer's attention, and got the better of his judgment. For then he is no longer apprehensive of any artifice to mislead him; but hears every thing with a favourable ear, wishes the Orator to proceed, and, admiring the force of his Eloquence, has no inclination to censure it.

But this measured and numerous flow of language is never to be continued too long, I will not say in the peroration, (of which the hearer himself will always be a capable judge) but in any other part of a discourse: for, except in the cases above-mentioned, in which I have shewn it is allowable, our style must be wholly confined to those clauses or divisions which we erroneously call *incisa* and *membra*; but the Greeks, with more propriety, the *comma* and *colon* [Footnote: The ancients apply these terms to the sense, and not to any points of distinction. A very short member, whether simple or compound, with them is a *comma*; and a longer, a *colon*; for they have no such term as a *semicolon*. Besides, they call a very short sentence, whether simple or compound, a *comma*; and one of somewhat a greater length, a *colon*. And therefore, if a person expressed himself either of these ways, in any considerable number of sentences together, he was said to speak by *commas*, or *colons*. But a sentence containing more words than will consist with either of these terms, they call a simple *period*; the least compound period with them requiring the length of two colons.

Ward's Rhetoric, volume 1st, page 344.]. For it is impossible that the names of things should be rightly applied, when the things themselves are not sufficiently understood: and as we often make use of metaphorical terms, either for the sake of ornament, or to supply the place of proper ones, so in other arts, when we have occasion to mention any thing which (through our unacquaintance with it) has not yet received a name, we are obliged either to invent a new one, or to borrow it from something similar. We shall soon consider what it is to speak in *commas* and *colons*, and the proper method of doing it: but we must first attend to the various numbers by which the cadence of our periods should be diversified.

Our numbers will advance more rapidly by the use of short feet, and more coolly and sedately by the use of long ones. The former are best adapted to a warm and spirited style, and the latter to sober narratives and explanations. But there are several numbers for concluding a period, one of which (called the *dichoree*, or double *choree*, and consisting of a long and a short syllable repeated alternately) is much in vogue with the Asiatics; though among different people the same feet are distinguished by different names. The *dichoree*, indeed, is not essentially bad for the close of a sentence: but in prosaic numbers nothing can be more faulty than a continued or frequent repetition of the same cadence: as the *dichoree*, therefore, is a very sonorous number, we should be the more sparing in the use of it, to prevent a satiety. *C. Carbo*, the son of *Caius*, and a Tribune of the people, once said in a public trial in which I was personally engaged, —"*O Marce Druse, Patrem appello*;" where you may observe two *commas*, each consisting of two feet. He then made use of the two following *colons*, each consisting of three feet,—"_Tu dicere solebas, sacram esse Rempublicam:"—and afterwards of the period,— "*Quicunque eam violavissent, ab omnibus esse ei poenas persolutas*" which ends with a *dichoree*; for it is immaterial whether the last syllable is long or short. He added, "*Patris dictum sapiens, temeritas filii comprobavit*" concluding here also with a *dichoree*; which was received with such a general burst of applause, as perfectly astonished me. But was not this the effect of *number*? —Only change the order of the words, and say,—"*Comprobavit filii temeritas*" and the spirit of them will be lost, though the word *temeritas* consists of three short syllables and a long one, which is the favourite number of Aristotle, from whom, however, I here beg leave to dissent. The words and sentiments are indeed the fame in both cases; and yet, in the latter, though the understanding is satisfied, the ear is not. But these harmonious cadences are not to be repeated too often: for, in the first place, our *numbers* will be soon discovered,—in the next, they will excite the hearer's disgust,—and, at last, be heartily despised on account of the apparent facility with which they are formed.

But there are several other cadences which will have a numerous and pleasing effect: for even the *cretic*, which consists of a long, a short, and a long syllable, and it's companion the *paeon*, which is equal to it in quantity, though it exceeds it in the number of syllables, is reckoned a proper and a very useful ingredient in harmonious prose: especially as the latter admits of two varieties, as consisting either of one long and three short syllables, which will be lively enough at the beginning of a sentence, but extremely flat at the end;—or of three short syllables and a long one, which was highly approved of by the ancients at the *close* of a sentence, and which I would not wholly reject, though I give the preference to others. Even the sober *spondee* is not to be entirely discarded; for though it consists of two long syllables, and for that reason may seem rather dull and heavy, it has yet a firm and steady step, which gives it an air of dignity, and especially in the *comma* and the *colon*; so that it sufficiently compensates for the slowness of it's motion, by it's peculiar weight and solemnity. When I speak of feet at the close of a period, I do not mean precisely the last. I would be understood, at least, to include the foot which immediately precedes it; and, in many cases, even the foot before *that*. The *iambic*, therefore, which consists of a long syllable and a short one, and is equal in time, though not in the number of it's syllables, to a *choree*, which has three short ones; or even the *dactyl*, which consists of one long and two short syllables, will unite agreeably enough with the last foot of a sentence, when that foot is either a *choree* or a *spondee*; for it is immaterial which of them is employed. But the three feet I am mentioning, are neither of them very proper for closing a period, (that is, to form the last foot of it) unless when a *dactyl* is substituted for a *cretic*, for you may use either of them at pleasure;

because, even in verse, it is of no consequence whether the last syllable is long or short. He, therefore, who recommended the *paeon*, as having the long syllable last, was certainly guilty of an oversight; because the quantity of the last syllable is never regarded. The *paeon*, however, as consisting of four syllables, is reckoned by some to be only a *number*, and not a *foot*. But call it which you please, it is in general, what all the ancients have represented it, (such as *Aristotle, Theophrastus, Theodectes*, and *Euphorus*) the fittest of all others both for the beginning and the middle of a period. They are likewise of opinion, that it is equally proper at the end; where, in my opinion, the *cretic* deserves the preference. The *dochimus*, which consists of five syllables, (i.e. a short and two long ones, and a short, and a long one, as in *amicos tenes*) may be used indifferently in any part of a sentence, provided it occurs but once: for if it is continued or repeated, our attention to our numbers will be discovered, and alarm the suspicion of the hearer. On the other hand, if we properly blend and intermingle the several varieties above-mentioned, our design will not be so readily noticed; and we shall also prevent that satiety which would arise from an elaborate uniformity of cadence.

But the harmony of language does not result entirely from the use of *numbers*, but from the *juncture* and *composition* of our words; and from that neatness and *concinnity* of expression which I have already mentioned. By *composition*, I here mean when our words are so judiciously connected as to produce an agreeable sound (independent of *numbers*) which rather appears to be the effect of nature than of art; as in the following passage from Crassus, *Nam ubi lubido dominatur, innocentiae leve praesidium est* [Footnote: In the sentence which is here quoted from Crassus, every word which ends with a consonant is immediately succeeded by another which begins with a vowel; and, *vice versa*, if the preceding word ends with a vowel, the next begins with a consonant.]: for here the mere order in which the words are connected, produces a harmony of sound, without any visible attention of the Speaker. When the ancients, therefore, (I mean *Herodotus*, and *Thucydides*, and all who flourished in the same age) composed a numerous and a musical period, it must rather be attributed to the casual order of their words, than to the labour and artifice of the writer.

But there are likewise certain forms of expression, which have such a natural concinnity, as will necessarily have a similar effect to that of regular numbers. For when parallel circumstances are compared, or opposite ones contrasted, or words of the same termination are placed in a regular succesion, they seldom fail to produce a numerous cadence. But I have already treated of these, and subjoined a few examples; so that we are hereby furnished with an additional and a copious variety of means to avoid the uniformity of cadence above-mentioned; especially as these measured forms of expression may be occasionally relaxed and dilated. There is, however, a material difference between a style which is merely *numerous*, (or, in other words, which has a moderate resemblance to *metre*) and that which is entirely composed of *numbers*: the latter is an insufferable fault; but our language, without the former, would be absolutely vague, unpolished, and dissipated.

But as a numerous style (strictly so called) is not frequently, and indeed but seldom admissible in forensic causes,—it seems necessary to enquire, in the next place, what are those *commas* and *colons* before-mentioned, and which, in real causes, should occupy the major part of an Oration. The *period*, or complete sentence, is usually composed of four divisions, which are called *members*, (or *colons*) that it may properly fill the ear, and be neither longer nor shorter than is requisite for that purpose. But it sometimes, or rather frequently happens, that a sentence either falls short of, or exceeds the limits of a regular period, to prevent it from fatiguing the ear on the one hand, or disappointing it on the other. What I mean is to recommend an agreeable mediocrity: for we are not treating of verse, but of rhetorical prose, which is confessedly more free and unconfined. A full period, then, is generally composed of four parts, which may be compared to as many hexameter verses, each of which have their proper points, or particles of continuation, by which they are connected so as to form a perfect period. But when we speak by *colons*, we interupt their union, and, as often as occasion requires (which indeed will frequently be the case) break off with ease from this laboured and suspicious flow of language; but yet nothing should be so numerous in reality as that which appears to be least so, and yet has a forcible effect. Such is the following passage in Crassus:—"*Missos faciant patronos; ipsi prodeant*." "Let them dismiss their patrons: let them answer for themselves." Unless "*ipsi prodeant*" was pronounced after a pause, the hearer must have discovered a complete iambic verse. It would have had a better cadence in prose if he had said "*prodeant ipsi*." But I am only to consider the species, and not the cadence of the sentence. He goes on, "*Cur clandestinis consiliis nos oppugnant? cur de perfugis nostris copias comparant contra nos*?" "Why do they attack us by clandestine measures? why do they collect forces against us from our own deserters?" In the former passage there are two *commas*: in the latter he first makes use of the *colon*, and afterwards of the *period*: but the period is not a long one, as only consisting of two *colons*, and the whole terminates in *spondees*. In this manner Crassus generally expressed himself; and I much approve his method. But when we speak either in *commas*, or *colons*, we should be very attentive to the harmony of their cadence: as in the following instance.—"*Domus tibi deerat? at habebas. Pecunia superabat? at egebas*." "Was you without a habitation? You had a house of your own. Was your pocket well provided? You was not master of a farthing." These are four *commas*; but the two following members are both *colons*; —"*Incurristi omens in columnas, in alienos insanus insanisti*."

"You rushed like a madman upon your best supporters; you vented your fury on your enemies withput mercy." The whole is afterwards supported by a full period, as by a solid basis;—"Depressam, caecam, jacentem domum, pluris quam te, et fortunas tuas aestimâsti." "You have shewn more regard to an unprosperous, an obscure, and a fallen family, than to your own safety and reputation." This sentence ends with a *dichoree,* but the preceeding one in a *double spondee.* For in those sentences which are to be used like daggers for close-fighting, their very shortness makes our numbers less exceptionable. They frequently consist of a single number;— generally of *two*, with the addition perhaps of half a foot to each: and very seldom of more than three. To speak in *commas* or *colons* has a very good effect in real causes; and especially in those parts of an Oration where it is your business either to prove or refute: as in my second defence of Cornelius, where I exclaimed, "O callidos homines! O rem excogitatam! O ingenia metuenda!" "What admirable schemers! what a curious contrivance! what formidable talents!" Thus far I spoke in *colons*; and afterwards by *commas*; and then returned to the colon, in "*Testes dare volumus,*" "We are willing to produce our witnesses." This was succeeded by the following *period,* consisting of two *colons*, which is the shortest that can be formed,—"*Quem, quaeso, nostrûm sesellit ita vos esse facturos?*" "Which of us, think you, had not the sense to foresee that you would proceed in this manner?"

There is no method of expressing ourselves which, if properly timed, is more agreeable or forcible, than these rapid turns, which are completed in two or three words, and sometimes in a single one; especially, when they are properly diversified, and intermingled here and there with a *numerous* period; which *Egesias* avoids with such a ridiculous nicety, that while he affects to imitate *Lysias* (who was almost a second *Demosthenes*) he seems to be continually cutting capers, and clipping sentence after sentence. He is as frivolous in his sentiments as in his language: so that no person who is acquainted with his writings, need to seek any farther for a coxcomb. But I have selected several examples from Crassus, and a few of my own, that any person, who is so inclined, may have an opportunity of judging with his own ears, what is really *numerous*, as well in the shortest as in any other kind of sentences.

Having, therefore, treated of a *numerous* style more copiously than any author before me, I shall now proceed to say something of it's *utility*. For to speak handsomely, and like an Orator (as no one, my Brutus, knows better than yourself) is nothing more than to express the choicest sentiments in the finest language. The noblest thoughts will be of little service to an orator, unless he is able to communicate them in a correct and agreeable style: nor will the splendor of our expressions appear to a proper advantage, unless they are carefully and judiciously ranged. Permit me to add, that the beauty of both will be considerably heightened by the harmony of our numbers:—such numbers (for I cannot repeat it too often) as are not only not cemented together, like those of the poets, but which avoid all appearance of metre, and have as little resemblance to it as possible; though it is certainly true that the numbers themselves are the same, not only of the Poets and Orators, but of all in general who exercise the faculty of speech, and, indeed, of every instrument which produces a sound whose time can be measured by the ear. It is owing entirely to the different arrangement of our feet that a sentence assumes either the easy air of prose, or the uniformity of verse. Call it, therefore, by what name you please (*Composition, Perfection*, or *Number*) it is a necessary restraint upon our language; not only (as *Aristotle* and *Theophrastus* have observed) to prevent our sentences (which should be limited neither by the breath of the speaker, nor the pointing of a transcriber, but by the sole restraint of *number*) from running on without intermission like a babbling current of water; but chiefly, because our language, when properly measured, has a much greater effect than when it is loose and unconfined. For as Wrestlers and Gladiators, whether they parry or make an assault, have a certain grace in their motions, so that every effort which contributes to the defence or the victory of the combatants, presents an agreeable attitude to the eye: so the powers of language can neither give nor evade an important blow, unless they are gracefully exerted. That style, therefore, which is not regulated by *numbers*, is to me as unbecoming as the motions of a Gladiator who has not been properly trained and exercised: and so far is our language from being *enervated* by a skilful arrangement of our words (as is pretended by those who, for want either of proper instructors, capacity, or diligence, have not been able to attain it) that, on the contrary, without this, it is impossible it should have any force or efficacy.

But it requires a long and attentive course of practice to avoid the blemishes of those who were unacquainted with this numerous species of composition, so as not to transpose our words too openly to assist the cadence and harmony of our periods; which *L. Caelius Antipater*, in the Introduction to his Punic War, declares he would never attempt, unless when compelled by necessity. "*O virum simplicem*," (says he, speaking of himself) "*qui nos nihil celat; sapientem, qui serviendum necessitati putet.*" "O simple man, who has not the skill his art to conceal; and yet to the rigid laws of necessity he has the wisdom to submit." But he was totally unskilled in composition. By us, however, both in writing and speaking, necessity is never admitted as a valid plea; for, in fact, there is no such thing as an absolute constraint upon the order and arrangement of our words; and, if there was, it is certainly unnecessary to own it. But *Antipater*, though he requests the indulgence of Laelius, to whom he dedicates his work, and attempts to excuse himself, frequently transposes his words without contributing in the least either to the harmony, or agreeable cadence of his periods.

There are others, and particularly the *Asiatics*, who are such slaves to *number*, as to insert words which have no use nor meaning to fill up the vacuities in a sentence. There are likewise some who, in imitation of *Hegesias* (a notorious trifler as well in this as in every other respect) curtail and mince their numbers, and are thus betrayed into the low and paltry style of the Sicilians. Another fault in composition is that which occurs in the speeches of *Hierocles* and *Menecles,* two brothers, who may be considered as the princes of Asiatic Eloquence, and, in my opinion, are by no means contemptible: for though they deviate from the style of nature, and the strict laws of Atticism, yet they abundantly compensate the defect by the richness and fertility of their language. But they have no variety of cadence, and their sentences are almost always terminated in the same manner. He therefore, who carefully avoids these blemishes, and who neither transposes his words too openly,—nor inserts any thing superfluous or unmeaning to fill up the chasms of a period,—nor curtails and clips his language, so as to interrupt and enervate the force of it,— nor confines himself to a dull uniformity of cadence,—*he* may justly be said to avoid the principal and most striking defects of prosaic harmony. As to its positive graces, these we have already specified; and from thence the particular blemishes which are opposite to each, will readily occur to the attentive reader.

Of what consequence it is to regulate the structure of our language, may be easily tried by selecting a well-wrought period from some Orator of reputation, and changing the arrangement of the words; [Footnote: Professor *Ward* has commented upon an example of this kind from the preface to the Vth volume of the Spectator:—"*You have acted in so much consistency with yourself, and promoted the interests of your country in so uniform a manner; that even those, who would misrepresent your generous designs for the public good, cannot but approve the steadiness and intredipity, with which you pursue them.*" I think, says the Doctor, this may be justly esteemed an handsome period. It begins with ease, rises gradually till the voice is inflected, then sinks again, and ends with a just cadency, And perhaps there is not a word in it, whole situation would be altered to an advantage. Let us now but shift the place of one word in the last member, and we shall spoil the beauty of the whole sentence. For if, instead of saying, as it now stands, *cannot but approve the steadiness and intrepidity, with which you pursue them*; we put it thus, *cannot but approve the steadiness and intrepidity which you pursue them with*; the cadency will be flat and languid, and the harmony of the period entirely lost. Let us try it again by altering the place of the two last members, which at present stand in this order, *that even those who would misrepresent your generous designs for the public good, cannot but approve the steadiness and intrepidity, with which you pursue them.* Now if the former member be thrown last, they will run thus, *that even those cannot but approve the steadiness and intrepidity, with which you pursue them, who would misrepresent your generous designs for the public good.* Here the sense is much obscured by the inversion of the relative *them*, which ought to refer to something that went before, and not to the words *generous designs*, which in this situation of the members are placed after it. WARD'S Rhetoric. Vol. 1, p. 338, 339.] the beauty of it would then be mangled and destroyed. Suppose, for instance, we take the following passage from my Defence of *Cornelius,—"Neque me divitae movent, quibus omnes Africanos et Laelios, multi venalitii mercatoresque superarunt.*" "Nor am I dazzled by the splendor of wealth, in which many retailers, and private tradesmen have outvied all the *Africani* and the *Lelii*" Only invert the order a little, and say,—"*Multi superârunt mercatores, venatitiique,*" and the harmony of the period will be loft. Try the experiment on the next sentence;—"*Neque vestes, aut celatum aurum, & argentum, quo nostros veteres Marcellos, Maximosque multi eunuchi e Syriâ Egyptoque vicerunt*:" Nor do. I pay the least regard to costly habits, or magnificent services of plate, in which many eunuchs, imported from Syria and Egypt, have far surpassed the illustrious *Marcelli*, and the *Maximi*. Alter the disposition of the words into, "*vicerunt eunuchi e Syria, Egyptoque,*" and the whole beauty of the sentence will be destroyed. Take a third passage from the same paragraph;—"_Neque vero ornamenta ista villarum, quibus Paulum & L. Mummium, qui rebus his urbem, Italiamque omnem reserserunt, ab aliquo video perfacile Deliaco aut Syro potuisse superari:"—"Nor the splendid ornaments of a rural villa, in which I daily behold every paltry Delian and Syrian outvying the dignity of Paulus and Lucius Mummius, who, by their victories, supplied the whole city, and indeed every part of Italy, with a super- fluity of these glittering trifles!" Only change the latter part of the sentence into,— "*potuisse superari ab aliquo Syro aut Deliaco,*" and you will see, though the meaning and the words are still the same, that, by making this slight alteration in the order, and breaking the form of the period, the whole force and spirit of it will be lost.

On the other hand, take one of the broken sentences of a writer unskilled in composition, and make the smallest alteration in the arrangement of the words,—and that which before was loose and disordered, will assume a just and a regular form. Let us, for instance, take the following passage from the speech of Gracchus to the Censors;—"*Abesse non potest, quin ejusdem hominis fit, probos improbare, qui improbos probet*;" "There is no possibility of doubting that the same person who is an enemy to virtue, must be a friend to vice." How much better would the period have terminated if he had said,—"*quin ejusdem hominis fit, qui improbos probet, probos improbare*!"—"that the same person who is a friend to vice, must be an enemy to virtue!" There is no one who would object to the last:—nay, it is impossible that any one who was able to speak thus, should have been willing to express himself otherwise. But those who have pretended to speak in a different manner, had not skill enough to speak as they ought; and for that reason, truly, we must applaud them for their *Attic* taste;—as if the great DEMOSTHENES could speak like an *Asiatic* [Footnote: Quasi vero Trallianus fuerit Demosthenes.] *Trallianus* signifies an inhabitant of *Tralles*, a city in the lesser Asia, between *Caria* and *Lydia*. The Asiatics, in the estimation of Cicero, were not distinguished by the delicacy of their taste.,—that Demosthenes, whose thunder would have lost half it's force, if it's flight had not been accelerated by the rapidity of his numbers.

But if any are better pleased with a broken and dissipated style, let them follow their humour, provided they condescend to counterbalance it by the weight, and dignity of their sentiments: in the same manner, as if a person should dash to pieces the celebrated shield of *Phidias*, though he would destroy the symmetry of the whole, the fragments would still retain their separate beauty;—or, as in the history of Thucydides, though we discover no harmony in the structure of his periods, there are yet many beauties which excite our admiration. But these triflers, when they present us with one of their rugged and broken sentences, in which there is neither a thought, nor word, but what is low and puerile, appear to me (if I may venture on a comparison which is not indeed very elevated, but is strictly applicable to the case in hand) to have untied a besom, that we may contemplate the scattered twigs. If, however, they wish to convince us that they really despise the species of composition which I have now recommended, let them favour us with a few lines in the taste of Isocrates, or such as we find in the orations of *Aeschines* and *Demosthenes*. I will then believe they decline the use of it, not from a consciousness of their inability to put it in practice, but from a real conviction of it's futility; or, at least, I will engage to find a person, who, on the same condition, will undertake either to speak or write, in any language they may please to fix upon, in the very manner they propose. For it is much easier to disorder a good period, than to harmonize a bad one.

But, to speak my whole meaning at once, to be scrupulously attentive to the measure and harmony of our periods, without a proper regard to our sentiments, is absolute madness:—and, on the other hand, to speak sensibly and judiciously, without attending to the arrangement of our words, and the regularity of our periods, is (at the best) to speak very awkwardly; but it is such a kind of awkwardness that those who are guilty of it, may not only escape the title of blockheads, but pass for men of good-sense and understanding;—a character which those speakers who are contented with it, are heartily welcome to enjoy! But an Orator who is expected not only to merit the approbation, but to excite the wonder, the acclamations, and the plaudits of those who hear him, must excel in every part of Eloquence, and be so thoroughly accomplished, that it would be a disgrace to him that any thing should be either seen or heard with greater pleasure than himself.

* * * * *

Thus, my Brutus, I have given you my opinion of a complete Orator; which you are at liberty either to adopt or reject, as your better judgment shall incline you. If you see reason to think differently, I shall have no objection to it; nor so far indulge my vanity as to presume that my sentiments, which I have so freely communicated in the present Essay, are more just and accurate than yours. For it is very possible not only that you and I may have different notions, but that what appears true even to myself at one time, may appear otherwise at another. Nor only in the present case, which be determined by the taste of the multitude, and the capricious pleasure of the ear (which are, perhaps, the most uncertain judges we can fix upon)—but in the most important branches of science, have I yet been able to discover a surer rule to direct my judgment, than to embrace that which has the greatest appearance of probability: for *Truth* is covered with too thick a veil to be distinguished to a certainty. I request, therefore, if what I have advanced should not have the happiness to merit your approbation, that you will be so much my friend as to conclude, either that the talk I have attempted is impracticable, or that my unwillingness to disoblige you has betrayed me into the rash presumption of undertaking a subject to which my abilities are unequal.

www.ingramcontent.com/pod-product-compliance
Lightning Source LLC
Chambersburg PA
CBHW080907190726
48294CB00008B/2000

* 9 7 8 1 8 0 5 4 7 6 0 0 9 *